The Fighting Admirals

The Fighting Admirals

British Admirals of the Second World War

MARTIN STEPHEN

LEO COOPER   LONDON

First published in Great Britain in 1991 by
LEO COOPER
190 Shaftesbury Avenue, London WC2H 8JL
an imprint of Pen & Sword Books Ltd
47 Church Street, Barnsley, South Yorkshire

Copyright © 1991 Dr Martin Stephen

A CIP catalogue record for this book
is available from the British Library
ISBN 0 85052 7287

Printed and bound in Great Britain
by St Edmundsbury Press,
Bury St Edmunds, Suffolk

This book is dedicated to the memory of
Admiral Sir Bertram Home Ramsay.

Contents

Contents

Acknowledgements

I am very grateful to the Archivist and staff of the Churchill College Archives, University of Cambridge; the Cambridge University Library; the British Library; the Public Records Office; the Imperial War Museum, Mr Suddaby, and Mr Willis; the National Maritime Museum; and all those other librarians who have responded with such kind efficiency to a multitude of queries.

My warmest thanks go to Leo Cooper, Tom Hartman and Beryl Hill. In the compilation of this present work I am grateful for the assistance of Toby Buchan; Professor Eric Grove; Commander John Somerville; Commander Tom Phillips; Captain J.G. Stanning, CBE; Captain G.H. Stanning, DSO; G.L.B. Pit, OBE; Lieutenant F.P. Ladd; Robert Butler Esq; Vice Admiral Sir Kaye Edden, KBE, CB; Robert Shopland of *Ships Monthly*; Martin Edmonds; Lawrence James; Captain W.H.R. Lapper; Mr and Mrs G. Fisher; Charles Drury; and to Jenny, Neill, Simon, and Henry, who have lived with this book far too long.

A book such as this rests on the labours of those who were alive nearer the time of the events it describes, and who were able to collect and collate the reminiscences of those fortunate enough to know and work with the Admirals discussed in these pages. My particular thanks to Rear Admiral W.S. Chalmers, CBE, DSC, and to Captain Donald Macintyre, DSO, DSC, authors of three outstanding biographies.

The author and publisher have made extensive efforts to contact all those whose work or letters have been quoted from in this book, and would be delighted to hear from copyright holders we have been unable to trace. The author and the publisher are most grateful to the following for their permission to reproduce copyright material:

Lady Macdonald of Spinners Ash for the papers of Admiral Sir Algernon Willis; Major-General C. A. Ramsay, C.B., O.B.E., for the papers of Admiral Sir Bertram Home Ramsay; Oliver Warner and John Murray (Publishers) for extracts from *Cunningham of Hyndhope*; HMSO for extracts from Roskill, *The War at Sea*; Collins (Publishers) for extracts from Roskill, *Churchill and the Admirals* and Hough, *The Hunting of Force Z*; Commander J. Somerville, for extracts from the papers of Admiral Sir James Somerville; Commander T. Phillips, for extracts from the papers of Admiral Sir Tom Phillips; The Master, Fellows and Scholars of Churchill College in the University of Cambridge for extracts from the Ramsay papers, the Willis papers, the papers of Admiral Sir Dudley Pound, the papers of Viscount Cunningham of Hyndhope, the papers of Admiral Sir James Somerville, and the McLachlan Beesley collection; Thorsons Publishing Group Ltd for extracts from Woodward, *Ramsay at War*; Hutchinson (Publishers) for extracts from Vian, *Action This Day*; the Trustees of the Imperial War Museum for extracts from the papers of Admiral Sir William Wentworth; the Trustees of the British Library for extracts from the papers of Viscount Cunningham of Hyndhope; Ian Allan (Publishers) for extracts from Bennett, *The Loss of Prince of Wales and Repulse*; Batsford (Publishers) for extracts from Pack, *Cunningham the Commander*; Unwin-Hyman Ltd for extracts from Macintyre, *Fighting Admiral*; Routledge & Kegan Paul, for extracts from Humble, *Fraser of North Cape*; the Public Record Office for extracts from various ADM files; Oxford University Press for extracts from Grenfell, *Main Fleet to Singapore*; Marder, *From the Dardanelles to Oran* and *Old Friends, New Enemies*; Andre Deutsch Ltd for extracts from Thomas, *Crete 1941: The Battle at Sea*; Weidenfeld & Nicolson Ltd. for extracts from Hough, *The Rise and Fall of the Royal Navy*, *The Longest Battle* and *Former Naval Person*; A. M. Heath & Company Ltd., and the estate of Captain Jack Broome for extracts from *Make a Signal!*; Ewan Macnaughton Associates for extracts from *The Sunday Telegraph*; A. P. Watt Ltd for permission to quote from Middlebrook and Mahoney, *Battleship*, and Cunningham, *A Sailor's Odyssey*.

All the photographs are reproduced by kind permission of the Imperial War Museum.

1 The Making of an Admiral

At the height of the battle to evacuate Crete in May, 1941, Admiral A.B. Cunningham signalled to his forces:

> It takes the Navy three years to build a ship. It would take three hundred years to build a new reputation. The evacuation will continue.[1]

Somewhere in between these two figures lies the time it takes to make an Admiral.

Considerable work has been done on the development of naval policy in the inter-war years, on ship and weapons design, and on what might be described as the corridors-of-power political relationships between such figures as Churchill and Admiral Dudley Pound. Yet in the final count all the planning, design and strategic decisions in the world lead at some stage or other to the moment when a commanding officer has to take decisions that exert a decisive effect on the outcome of a naval engagement or campaign. Rather less work has been done on these men, the fighting admirals of this book's title. Many of the most famous – Cunningham, Fraser, Somerville, Ramsay, Vian – either published their own memoirs or were the subject of books in the post-war period. Many of the autobiographical books show an understandable desire on the part of the writers to interpret events from a selfish viewpoint, whilst some non-autobiographical books were so dependent on the active support of their subject that objectivity suffered. The first flush of victory has long faded, new information on various actions has come to light; the aim of this work is therefore to examine the British Admirals of the Second World War who were engaged in actual combat and to assess them as combat commanders. This is therefore a book about the more human side of naval conflict, the effect of tension, stress and responsibility on commanders, and an attempt to examine what goes into the making of a successful fighting admiral. In writing it I have taken to heart the stricture a reviewer placed on one of my earlier books, commenting that what it lacked was 'any indication that modern sea warfare is a cruel, savage business that allows no mercy for the crews of doomed ships'[2]. I am also very aware of the dreadful warning contained in some of Admiral Cunningham's papers:

> I get so tired of these young writers who in World War II were either not born or in their cradles writing that how easily the war would have been won if the General or Admiral hadn't been such an ass etc etc.[3]

The British Admirals of the Second World War were often *the* crucial figures in British naval actions throughout the war, and clearly they did not spring up overnight. The majority of them were born in the 1880s, a time when society and the Royal Navy were struggling to come to terms with the effects of the Industrial Revolution, and went on to *Britannia* at Dartmouth to be trained as officers. All were old enough to see service in the First World War. It is therefore necessary to examine briefly the national and naval culture that helped to form the officers who were to reach flag rank in the Second World War.

The Victorian Naval World

The late Victorian period combined certainty and confusion to a remarkable extent. There was little uncertainty about the role of the Royal Navy, which existed to repeat Trafalgar in the event of a European war, and to guard an Empire on which the country's economic prosperity was heavily dependent. There was much more uncertainty about the *matériel* that would be used to reach these ends, and not enough uncertainty about the tactics that would control the machinery and the men.

According to a leading authority the Royal Navy between 1850 and 1890 'completed a transformation of almost unimaginable scope'[4]. If the time is taken up to 1906, the year in which HMS *Dreadnought* was launched, the scale of the transformation becomes even more apparent – yet this transformation was at the same time a remarkably limited one, and almost exclusively technical. From wooden-walled fighting ships the Royal Navy, in this period, was required to come to terms with steam propulsion, ironclad hulls and armour plating, armour-piercing and exploding shells, torpedoes, oil-fired turbines and radio. The frantic attempts made by all navies to come to terms with these advances produced a bewildering succession of battleship designs, each reported capable of smashing its immediate predecessor to pieces, and a bewildering increase in cost – in the case of Britain from £10,492,935 on the Naval Estimates in 1880 to £38,327,838 in 1904[5]. The result of technological advance and vast expenditure was a capital ship that could steam faster, survive longer and hit harder than anything seen before on the world's seas. That much was obvious. What was less obvious was that for the first time that same capital ship could be placed at risk by a much smaller vessel such as a torpedo boat or, later, submarine, using the torpedo; that this same torpedo, varieties of mines and advances in air warfare meant that the doctrine of the close blockade was increasingly redundant. On land in the First World War commanders failed to realize that the bolt-action rifle, machine-gun, barbed wire, artillery and aerial reconnaissance hugely increased the defensive and stopping power of an army without a corresponding increase in offensive power. Similarly at sea technological advances rendered such time-hallowed tactics as the line-of-battle, capital ships and blockade increasingly redundant and unworkable, but did not provide an easy answer to what was to replace them.

Admirals who were to fight the Second World War passed out of the training institutions *Britannia*, Osborne and Dartmouth a few years either side of 1900 and were midshipmen at a time of maximum change in warship design. Most of them were sub-lieutenants when Admiral Sir John Fisher scrapped scores of obsolete warships 'which could neither fight nor run away'. He then redeployed the remaining British warships with a view to creating a large Home Fleet to contain Germany. Fisher was not afraid to use the Press in his search to gain support for the Royal Navy, nor was he afraid to break out from conventional attitudes to ship types. He pushed through the concept of the battlecruiser, a lightly armoured but heavily gunned and fast capital ship. This concept received a bad press after three ships of the type blew up at Jutland, and HMS *Hood* blew up in action against *Bismarck*, though it is possible that these losses were the result of failure to use the battlecruisers correctly, rather than a failure of the design concept itself.

Only the most extreme dullard of a young officer could have failed to absorb some of the excitement of those days. Old values were being overturned, new ones introduced. Men who were blooded as officers in this time of change may have found it easier than their predecessors to overturn the rule book when occasion demanded. Fisher's reforms and his enthusiasm for change may also have helped condition officers such as Somerville and Fraser to adapt readily to air warfare and radar, both in their own way as revolutionary as the advances contained in *Dreadnought*. Their earliest years as officers had been spent in an era when technological innovation and new ideas were as familiar as the rum ration to ratings. Fisher brought an immense frustration with the way things were to the job of running the Royal Navy. One suspects that such a feeling, when found elsewhere, is simply part of being a young officer trying to set the world to rights, but the combination of new technology and new leadership may have boosted this natural response in the case of such officers as 'Bertie' Ramsay, later to be in charge of the Dunkirk evacuation and much of the planning for D-Day. In 1914 he was writing:

> It's high time war came for the good of the Navy. So many officers of the higher branches are so warped by old sailing-ship days that they *would not think* of war or bringing themselves up to date. If the things which I hear and know were published there would be general consternation.[6]

It is interesting to note that two traditional but highly effective commanders in the Second World War, Cunningham and Tovey, were both violently opposed to the Royal Navy bringing back sail-training in the inter-war years, seeing this as a wholly retrograde step; traditionalists though many of the senior commanders in the Second World War were, they were neither mindless nor unthinkingly committed to the past, and this is perhaps a tribute to Fisher. So also may be the frustration with higher authority that was to lead Ramsay into conflict with his commanding Admiral, and into early retirement, before war service called him back to the Navy. Such frustration was not an entirely healthy emotion, or a safe one. Its presence in a young officer is hardly surprising given the Fisher years, and reading through the papers of various Admirals one suspects that very few changed dramatically from the days of their youth. Fisher brought change to the Royal Navy, perhaps more so than any other Admiral in history. Spiritually at least he was therefore the natural ally of the young officer bursting to change the world overnight; he made change respectable to at least some of them and left his mark on them when they in turn achieved high office.

Another essential factor in the make-up of future commanders was the experience of serving as a junior officer in a nation that ruled an empire. Cunningham fought in the Boer War. Ramsay took part in the Battle of Illig on 21 April, 1904, as part of the Naval Brigade serving from HMS *Hyacinth* alongside the 1st Battalion of the Hampshire Regiment. The men who were to become Admirals served for months and even years on end in cruisers and destroyers on foreign stations, where the Captain of the vessel was almost as much lord of all he surveyed as Captain Bligh had been in an earlier age. Such experience bred independence and a degree of dash and daring only possible to those out from under the Fleet commander's eye. It is referred to by Cunningham in his memoirs, when he was a midshipman on the cruiser *Fox* on the Cape Station in 1898:

> It was before the days of wireless . . . our captain . . . was monarch of all he surveyed. Gunnery and torpedo exercises hardly disturbed our routine . . . Once a quarter . . . a few rounds were fired by all the guns at a flag on a cask at a range of not more than 2,000 yards. Nobody cared very much whether the shots fell near or wide of the target.[7]

Such carelessness over target practise was something that Fisher's reforms would change, but, ironically, the Fisher reforms may have permanently dented the independence noted above. Fisher redistributed the Fleet in 1904–5:

> The famous Australia, China and East Indies stations were therefore to be amalgamated into the Eastern Fleet, based on Singapore, in time of war, whilst the South Atlantic, North America and West Africa stations were taken over

forthwith by a much expanded Cape Station; the Pacific Station was simply abandoned, and the number of vessels based upon the two new centres of concentration was greatly reduced. More important still, Fisher radically switched the weight of Britain's battleship fleets from the overseas stations into home waters.[8].

This renowned 'calling home of the legions' produced problems abroad, reducing 'Imperial policing' and the opportunity to send ships and men to sites of natural disaster[9]. Less well noted has been the fact that it reduced the opportunities for isolated and independent service for officers, and that the generation who became Admirals in the Second World War were almost the last to have had the opportunity of leading 'cutting out' parties on the China Station, or sailing in cruisers for months on end without sight or sound of higher authority. Perhaps in some ways that generation never grew up; certainly as a breed they had an independence and sometimes even an eccentricity that seemed absent from the generations which followed them. Something of that spirit is reflected in a description of a distinguished Vice-Admiral who passed out from *Britannia* near the turn of the century:

> Within a few months of passing out as a midshipman he took part with the Naval Brigade in the fighting south of Ladysmith in 1899 and 1900. Later in 1900 he was at the fighting at Tientsin and at the relief of Peking: all before the age of seventeen and a half.[10]

Cunningham gave some idea of the value he placed on the experience gained by a young man serving in the Navy of a fighting empire:

> From the purely Service point of view I doubt very much if the Boer War did me much good . . . It taught one responsibility and self-reliance; living, so to speak, on one's wits, and making do on improvisation. It also brought one into close contact with the Army, which was most useful in the years that were to come. Above all, it caused one to realise the cheerfulness and endurance, and

the many other sterling qualities, of that versatile and adaptable person, the British sailor.[11]

It is significant that two of the books cited in this chapter, both written after the Second World War, contain the words 'Rise and Fall' when applied to the Royal Navy. Commentators have seen in Fisher's actions, valid though the majority of them were, the beginning of the end of British naval supremacy. We may now perceive that. Fisher's midshipmen and sub-lieutenants certainly did not. For them the Royal Navy ruled supreme (a feeling that persisted well into the Second World War and after, summed up by the supposed reply to an American warship which signalled to a British vessel, 'How does it feel to be in the second largest navy in the world?', to which the reply was, 'How does it feel to be in the second best?')

A vital part of the Royal Navy, and a vital element in maintaining its *esprit de corps*, was *Britannia*, the training ship for officers, moored at Dartmouth. One of Fisher's great reforms was to do away with the ancient three-decker which for over thirty years had produced the mass of the Royal Navy's officers, but, as the nursery for the Admirals dealt with in this work, it provides essential insight into their background and pedigree.

HMS Britannia

Prior to 1857 boys entering the Royal Navy as officers had to obtain a nomination, pass a simple medical test and entrance examination, and were then allowed to proceed to sea at the age of twelve and a half or thirteen as 'volunteers of the first class'. In 1857 it was decided to send 'Cadets' to a stationary training ship at Portsmouth for a nine-month training course, and in 1859 an old three-decker, the *Britannia*, was taken over as the training ship. Portsmouth had a desperate reputation for insobriety and immorality at the time and, as it was deemed an 'unsuitable location' for the training of young people, *Britannia* was moved to Portland. The anchorage was not a good one. There were few playing fields or other relaxation areas of a 'suitable' nature available ashore, so *Britannia* moved in 1863 to Dartmouth. The vessel was starting to show her age, however, and in 1869 a steam-line-of-battle-ship (a wooden three-decker sailing ship with steam propulsion), the *Prince of Wales*, was converted for use as a stationary training ship and renamed *Britannia*. In 1864 the old *Britannia* had been joined by an old Indian teak two-decker, *Hindustan*, the latter being moored so that a covered gangway connected the bow of *Britannia* to the stern of *Hindustan*, and it was these two vessels that were to be known as *Britannia* and act as the training school for naval officers for over thirty years, until the establishment of shore-based facilities at Dartmouth in what is still know as the Britannia Royal Naval College, Dartmouth. By the time that the Admirals referred to in this work attended *Britannia* there was a competitive entrance examination in which for some 'terms' (the name given to what we would now call a class or year group) only a third of those sitting the examinations would pass.

Britannia was not open to all. It was a fee-paying establishment and one requiring each cadet to be nominated. The social background of its entry was predictable. Cunningham's father was Professor of Anatomy at Edinburgh University. Fraser's father was a General, Ramsay's a Brigadier. Somerville was the son of a New Zealand sheep farmer who became a country squire in Somerset. Perhaps the only surprising thing about the origins of the top commanders in the Second World War was the general absence of a specifically *naval* pedigree; less surprising is the extent to which the entry to *Britannia* was from primarily upper-middle-class families, the same class which provided the mainstay of the entry to the public schools. It has been suggested that in 1900 the fees at *Britannia* restricted the entry for naval officers to some 300,000 families and, at most, 750,000 sons, these being the numbers deemed capable of earning the £700 a year that would allow a son to attend *Britannia*[12].

It was common knowledge by the end of 1902 that a new scheme for the training of naval officers was soon to be introduced, and a second naval training establishment instituted at Osborne. This change was the result of joint action and thought by Admiral Sir John Fisher and Lord Selborne, who became First Lord of the Admiralty in 1900. What became known as the Selborne scheme proposed a four-year course of training, effectively a four-year naval public school education with entry at thirteen. A major feature of the new scheme was the reduction of the hitherto fierce distinction between the engineering branch and other officers.

Those are the facts; the truth about *Britannia* lies somewhat deeper and is infinitely harder to trace. A significant number of those who passed through the *Britannia* system remembered it with great affection. So did a significant number of those who passed through the public school system at the same time: all-male residential institutions provoke strong tribal feelings of support among their inmates, and in terms of historical sources there is an inbuilt tendency for the victors of the system, and those it favoured, to set the tone and to write the memoirs. *Britannia* produced a large number of extremely successful commanders and inevitably a fair number of ne'er-do-wells. Those who had something to be ashamed of in their time in *Britannia* and those who never rose above mediocrity in the Royal Navy were less inclined to write about either area than those who were a success. There is therefore an inevitable bias towards sources in favour of those who won by the system that *Britannia* had to offer.

Throughout its existence *Britannia* was subject to criticisms, most concering either cruelty and bullying amongst cadets, or the narrowness of the curriculum. Both of these complaints are part of a larger national concern, seen at its strongest in the complaints being raised from 1860 onwards against Britain's great and not-so-great public schools. Many of these had been founded by charitable bequests as free schools in Elizabethan times or even earlier. The growing wealth of the British middle classes as a result of the Industrial Revolution led to an increased demand for education and a growing awareness of its absence in the country as a whole. In the nineteenth century great headmasters such as Arnold at Rugby and Thring at Uppingham turned small local grammar schools into nationally and internationally famous institutions. Yet these schools – even the greatest of them – taught a syllabus consisting largely of the classics (fifty percent of the Staff at Eton in 1905 were classicists, and promotion went to classicists before all other academic disciplines[13]). It has been said that the English middle classes sent their children away to school in order to show that they would never need to work for a living, and could afford an unrestricted diet of classical learning.

A knowledge of Greek and Latin had become the mark of a cultured man. By this time schools such as Eton and Harrow had become enclaves for the upper and wealthier middle classes for whom the Classics served no other purpose than that of a status symbol[14].

It was fashionable to be disparaging about the curriculum at Dartmouth:

Our education in the years round about the turn of the century was very circumscribed—naval history (no ordinary history), navigation, seamanship, steam and heat, a little French, mathematics, and some rudimentary science; and that was about all.[15]

Instruction in drawing – and dancing – were also provided. Stodgy fare that this might seem, it was at least more modern than a diet of almost undiluted Greek and Latin. The examination for entry to *Britannia* was also very testing, and large numbers of Cadets attended special crammers in order to gain their place. Competition was fierce: at the end of the nineteenth century a typical year saw 240 Cadets nominated, sixty failing the medical examination, 180 sitting the entrance examination, and sixty-three being successful[16]. In order to be successful candidates had to be knowledgeable to a remarkably high level in Mathematics (Arithmetic, Geometry, and Algebra); English (language rather than literature); and two subjects out of Latin, French or German. In addition there were papers in English History, Geography, and the option of extra papers including Drawing and Natural Science[17]. Many a thirteen-year-old sitting for Eton or Harrow would have been hoplessly at sea with this range of subjects and the standards demanded – hence the creation of the naval 'crammers'. It is also a myth that the standard of teaching and teachers was high at the public schools. Certainly there were inspirational teachers at these schools; it is also true that there was much dross, and vast swathes of 'teaching' that in reality consisted of little more than rote-learning, and mindless repetition of translations taken from 'cribs'. It is true that many public schools had by 1900 a Modern or an Army side, but the resources, interest and commitment simply were not there to make these a success – hardly surprising when at Eton masters who did not teach Classics were considered socially inferior and for a long time were not permitted to become Housemasters[18]. By these standards the curriculum at Dartmouth appears remarkably modern and functional, particularly when the instructors could draw forth comments such as:

> These instructors [at Dartmouth] kept control and imparted knowledge in a manner I have never known excelled.[19]

The above comment has an element of the it-was-tough-but-it-did-me-no-harm-at-all spirit to it, but there are too many comments of this type for one to doubt that at times instruction could be very good. Certainly a general education was not available at Dartmouth;, nor was it anywhere else in the country. The difference was that the curriculum at Dartmouth could at least claim to be useful and relevant to a chosen career.

As regards bullying and general cruelty, it is again very unlikely that *Britannia* exceeded the general conditions prevailing in the public schools. As in any school, bullying ebbed and flowed depending to an extent on the staff and Captain of *Britannia*. A Cadet there could be flogged in public, but would not receive more than twelve cuts of the cane or birch; the nearest thing the public schools have to a saint, Thomas Arnold, once lost his temper and gave eighteen cuts to a sickly boy with a hernia, who happened to be innocent of the crime of which he was accused. Arnold afterwards apologized in public for the mistake he had made. Naval discipline simply would not have permitted this at Dartmouth. *Britannia* could be tough; there is no evidence with which I am familiar to suggest that it was any tougher than the majority of public schools. Certainly cadets at *Britannia* challenged each other to fights held out of the eye of authority in a local quarry on Sundays, but this was no different from what was taking place in the public schools. There is no evidence that conditions or attitudes at *Britannia* were any worse than those prevailing at most public schools: they may even have been better. There has been no research into homosexuality at *Britannia*, but there is no reason to suspect its prevalence was any more marked than at a public school, and some reason for suggesting it was far less prevalent. A Cadet in *Britannia* had rather less free time than his counterpart in a public school, and far fewer older boys in the environment, free time and elders being major factors in allowing homosexual liaisons in public schools. *Britannia* offered ample opportunity for sport, and in addition offered sailing for those who did not excel at team games; this was a life-saver for the Cadet who was later to become Lord Cunningham of Hyndhope. In any all-male school at the tail-end of the Victorian period a boy's capacity to excel at sport would help make or break him in terms of popularity, but the existence on non-team sports at *Britannia*, such as sailing, allowed more room for the individual character to impress his term. In many public schools academic success was a joke. Young Brooke in *Tom Brown's Schooldays* makes it clear to his house that winning the School House match matters more to him than winning a scholarship to Oxford:

> I know I'd sooner win two School-house matches running
> than get the Balliol scholarship any day   (frantic cheers).[20]

Yet at Dartmouth fierce examinations ranked a cadet in comparison with his term, and influenced his seniority as a midshipman. Thus one's performance in the academic syllabus at *Britannia* really did matter, in many cases far more so than at a comparable public school.

The food at the majority of public schools was awful and occasionally led to riots: on board *Britannia* it seems to have been remarkable good. Health was a cause for concern, though no more than might have been expected from a duet of draughty wooden-hulled sailing ships with lavatories discharging into a river whose water found its way back in several guises into the ship. Epidemics of childish illnesses did take place, but again a comparison with the public schools is interesting: many of them built huge sanatoriums as almost their first major capital expenditure once boarding has been established, these to act as isolation hospitals for contagious diseases. *Britannia* had its hospital on shore, but again the figures suggest that *Britannia* was no more a breeding-ground for illness than any other comparable institution. It is true that water from the 'heads' or lavatories discharged over the bow, from where water was also taken for washing purposes, and this may have had something to do with the outbreaks of 'pinkeye' that affected Cunningham among others. Again, this type of unhygienic practice was not unusual for the day, and a tidal river at least ensured a degree of movement in the water supply. Uppingham School had to leave the town of Uppingham for a year to force the town authorities to instal a water supply that did not link directly to local cesspits.

What *Britannia* did above all other things was to generate an *esprit de corps* and, in some of their most formative years, give naval officers two marked features, first a certainty and a pride in their vocation that combined with a glorious history to produce an intense loyalty to and faith in the Royal Navy, and secondly an intimate knowledge of fifty or sixty other naval officers launched into service at the same time as themselves. The extent to which officers in the Royal Navy were members of an elite band who often knew their contemporaries extraordinarily well is an intangible factor in assessing the effectiveness of these men as commanders. Cunningham and Somerville were class-mates and remained close friends throughout their lives, as did Cunningham and Tovey. It was Somerville who sent Cunningham the classic signal when he received his second knighthood, 'What? Twice a Knight at your age?'[21]. Close friendships and knowledge of fellow officers run like a thread through the history of the Second World War, sometimes the result of shared time at *Britannia*, sometimes the result of the comradeship that comes when men have undergone a common experience, the tie that draws so many people who never knew each other at school back to reunions. Admiral Somerville came down to relieve Ramsay at the height of the Dunkirk evacuation and give him some sleep, on the basis of friendship more than any official routine. 'Bertie Ramsay had been my friend for years,'[22] Cunningham was able to write of Ramsay when the two were working together on the naval planning of the invasion of Europe. This mutual knowledge did not always work out to the benefit either of the individuals or the Navy. There was clearly conflict between Cunningham and Fraser, and between Mountbatten and most of the Admirals covered in this book.

Britannia was tough, wholly single-minded about the Royal Navy, and limited by modern standards in the training it gave. It could be brutal and insensitive, and probably did nothing to reduce the great and ludicrous divide between the engineering branch and the other officers in the Royal Navy. By and large it did nothing to stop future officers in the Royal Navy being drawn from 'a certain class' of society, but in 1900 it would have served no useful purpose in so doing: as with any educational institution it was more a reflection of the society that spawned it, and a function of it, than a formative influence on that society, and in 1900 that was the way society was. The Fisher-Selborne reforms were necessary, but, as with so much that Fisher did, something ahead of their time. One of the most telling comments on *Britannia* is one of the shortest: 'At the *Britannia* the good boys came out on top,'[23]

The First World War

If *Britannia* exerted a major influence on future commanders, then so obviously and even more so did the combat experience of the First World War.

Two Admirals dominated the First World War, Jellicoe and Beatty. The claim that the former was the only man who could have lost the war in a day seems of very doubtful validity, and it seems increasingly clear that at Jutland the Royal Navy lost the battle but won the war. Jellicoe and Beatty summed up two styles of command in the Royal Navy, two styles that were to be seen time and time again in the Second World War. On the one hand there was Jellicoe, almost borne under by worries, an immaculate Staff planner and thinker, taking all the right decisions, yet seeing victory snatched from him by factors largely out of his control. On the other hand there was Beatty, throwing caution to the winds, frequently taking decisions of questionable validity, but somehow always emerging as the hero of the day with his vast and overwhelming desire to get at the enemy. The offensive spirit, the 'up-and-at-'em' philosophy, was a sure crowd-puller for the Royal Navy. Beatty had it in plenty, and because he had it he was forgiven much. The public forgave Cunningham the slaughter of Crete because he had been shown to have the offensive spirit. Churchill, who made it his god, got himself in continual hot water by threatening to court-martial officers who in his opinion did not have it, and a tired-out war horse such as Admiral Keyes was hauled back out of retirement because he had it, even though by that time he had little else and much of what he had was past its best. Admiral

Vian did not appear in almost every offensive action taken by the Royal Navy during the war by accident: after his early exploits and displays of aggression he was put there by Churchill, virtually becoming Churchill's naval mascot. Officers capable of long and serious thought were often seen not to have the offensive spirit, and at various times Somerville, Fraser and Phillips suffered as a result, usually very unfairly.

A Naval War Staff was not introduced in the Royal Navy until 1912. There was a distinction in the Royal Navy between those who fought by the seat of their pants and those of a more intellectual bent. Some of the most successful commanders of the war, most notably Cunningham, Somerville and Vian, abhorred paperwork of any type. Given a good Staff behind them this did not matter, but with a bad Staff severe problems could be created, both at the time and for successors. Two of the Admirals who have received the worst press in recent years were excellent Staff officers, and renowned for the time they took with paperwork – Pound and Phillips. The Royal Navy accepted a need for Staff officers; it did not have to like them.

Jutland itself taught many lessons, but few of them were to have a decisive impact on the men who were to command in a later war, except perhaps in the area of night-fighting. The German fleet was able to slip past the British fleet at night, and that lesson at least was taken to heart in the 1920s and 1930s, with Cunningham reaping the benefit at the Battle of Matapan. As Cunningham himself wrote:

At Jutland . . . night action had deliberately been avoided. From now on . . . it became an accepted principle that a highly-trained and well-handled fleet had nothing to lose and much to gain by fighting at night.[24]

Cunningham omits the fact that his fleet had allowed training for night action to lapse under the pressure of war, thus making the engagement at Matapan even more of a risk.

Bad signalling was a further reason why the German fleet at Jutland escaped, and it is just possible that Admiral Fraser was influenced by this in his pursuit and sinking of the German Battleship *Scharnhorst* in 1943, where if anything he erred on the side of too much signals traffic. It is certainly true that other officers, notably Phillips and Tovey, were almost obsessional about radio silence. Many of the failures at Jutland were technical. British armour-piercing shells did not pierce armour, British cordite was unstable, and basic flash-protection procedures may have been ignored. Despite Beatty's famous cry of 'There's something wrong with our bloody ships today!', these failures do not seem to have undermined confidence in British warship design among serving officers to any great extent. There are also remarkably few traces of criticism from the ordinary sailors, though they did make up for this in the inter-war period, christening the two new Washington Treaty battleships *Rodney* and *Nelson* 'Rodnol' and 'Nelsol' because of their apparent resemblance to fleet oilers, and describing *Repulse* and *Renown* as 'Refit' and 'Repair' because of their continual problems of hull strength.

The facts and figures of the war tell one story. A more significant one lies in the combat experience gained by the young officers who were to become the top commanders in the Second World War. For those who survived, the First World War came at a very convenient time, just when in their late 20's or early 30's they could expect a small command, and be in a position to benefit most from combat experience. Cunningham, Tovey and Ramsay commanded destroyers in the First World War (indeed, destroyer service was perhaps the greatest common denominator among top commanders in Hitler's war); Fraser was able to mount a field-gun on a capstan on board the light cruiser *Minerva* and use it as an anti-aircraft gun. The result, for all the future Admirals, was that they had for the most part had combat experience, whereas a far greater number of their German contemporaries had only experienced being locked up with the battle fleet in Kiel. Jutland left an immense feeling of frustration, but the end of the war gave the victory clearly to the Royal Navy. The sheer confidence, audacity and optimism of many of the engagements of the Second World War can be traced back to the existence of those feelings, in large measure, at the end of the First World War.

The Inter-War Period

The 1920s and the 1930s were a crucial time in the development of the Royal Navy. It is remarkable to note how much was done with so little.

In the inter-war period the Royal Navy tried to hang on to the concept of the battle fleet dominated by the battleship. For the most part all that was available was ageing First World War designs. In a reversal of the craze for speed which had produced the battlecruiser designs of the First World War, Britain's battle fleet came to consist of ships which placed defensive capability over speed and offensive capacity. Much of this had to do with the Washington Treaty limitations, which in the inter-war period sought to limit the number of vessels in the navies of the major world powers, and the size of any new vessels built. The British honoured the Treaty terms, and their designers were forced to produce battleships of relatively modest size and tonnage. Wrestling with the three priorities of battleship design – speed, protection, and armament – and knowing that the ideal provision for all three could not be provided within the limited size permitted, the Royal Navy opted for a heavy main battery, excellent armour protection, and a very low top speed. The first new battleships built by the Royal Navy after the First World War, *Rodney* and *Nelson*, emerged with the heaviest main battery of any British battleships (nine 16″ guns in three triple turrets), excellent armour protection, and a top speed of twenty-three knots. This was very slow indeed when compared with the later German, Italian and American battleships, all capable of over 30 knots. Virtual reconstruction of some of the 'Queen Elizabeth' First World War battleships again produced excellent main armament (eight 15″ guns in four double turrets), good armour protection and a top speed only a knot or so faster than *Rodney* and *Nelson*. Something had to go if Britain was to comply with Washington Treaty limitations, and high top speed was what was chosen. The loss of three fast but under-armoured British capital ships at Jutland was a contributory factor in this choice: experience had shown the British designers that the carthorse might be less glamorous than the racehorse, but the former at least lived to fight another day.

The remainder of Britain's older capital ships fell into two distinct categories. The 'R' class battleships were never reconstructed, and for most of the war were a liability. Somerville was given four of them in the Far Eastern Fleet in 1942, and it was their presence that prompted him to compare his fleet to the ill-fated Russian fleet at the Battle of Tsushima.[25] The 'R' class were pushed to reach even eighteen knots, had very low endurance and range, no air-conditioning, wholly inadequate water-purification facilities and weak armour protection against air attack. Other than the 'R' class, the Royal Navy had three battlecruisers, though one of the these, the *Hood*, had sufficient armour to qualify as a fast battleship. The other two, *Renown* and *Repulse*, were lightly-armoured, fast, but with a small main battery of only six 15" guns. These were the only three British vessels capable of catching and outgunning a German commerce raider such as *Graf Spee*. *Hood* was to blow up under the fire of the German *Bismarck*, *Repulse* to be sunk by Japanese aircraft, and in one sense their fate justified the British insistence on adequate armour at the expense of speed.

The first of the 'King George V' class battleships were completed in 1940. Designed to comply with the 1936 London Naval Treaty, and 10,000 tons or so heavier than *Rodney* or *Nelson*, they were the best-protected vessels of their size in the world. This time weight of armour had been provided not so much at the expense of speed (28 knots), more at the expense of armament. The main battery consisted of relatively lightweight 14" guns (15" to 18" was the norm in other countries), though admittedly there were ten of them. As an exercise in design these vessels were near-masterpieces, producing from treaty limitations a very workable compromise. There were two weaknesses in the design. Firstly, even the best compromise cannot satisfy all demands, and one price the British paid was in range and endurance. The 'KGV's' at twenty knots had half the fuel endurance of their American counterparts, and their actions throughout the war were dogged by fuel shortage. Secondly, whilst the design may have been excellent in theory, in practice there was much that was wrong. The quadruple 14" turrets were a disaster and plagued by continual breakdown. The secondary armament of the class was an innovatory dual-purpose (anti-surface *and* anti-aircraft capacity) 5.25" weapon, but weaknesses in the fire control system and perhaps even the central concept of so heavy a dual-purpose weapon raised many doubts about its effectiveness. In addition the vessels were very wet forward, and their engines and electrical generators inadequately cushioned against the shock from torpedo hits. The 'King George V' class were not a bad design, but in many respects the technology of the day was not able to supply what the designers had envisaged and hoped for. Churchill railed against the fact that two 'King

George V' battleships were needed to match one German modern battleship such as *Bismarck* or *Tirpitz*: in doing so he failed to acknowledge that the Germans had largely ignored the treaty limitations that had so cramped the British design. The displacement of *King George V* at full load was 42,237 tons; that of *Bismarck* 49,136: the difference in tonnage between the two vessels is very nearly the equivalent of the standard displacement of the British 6″ gun cruiser, or the full load displacement of three First World War destroyers.

What happened with the battleships was to an extent mirrored in other designs. The British were too honourable to cheat on treaty restrictions, and on paper at least their designs for 8″ gun cruisers lagged a long way behind those produced for the German, Japanese and American navies, all of which exceeded the nominal Treaty limitations. Far too few escort vessels were built in the inter-war period, though there were compelling reasons for this, the overwhelming one being that growing financial restrictions meant hard sacrifices having to be made in terms of ship procurement. Until the mid-to late-1930s no European power seemed able to threaten Britain's trade by means of a submarine arm.

Weaknesses were evident also on the human side. Shortly after the war Sir Eric Campbell Geddes wielded the 'Geddes Axe', doing away with 1,200 unwanted lieutenants and lieutenant-commanders. Just as Dr Johnson believed that when a man knew he was to be hanged it concentrated the mind wonderfully, so the Geddes Axe may have done much good; it is probable also that, like the Beeching axe many years later, the distastefulness of the act was equalled only by its inevitability. However, that was not a view shared by all, and Cunningham believed that:

> The 'Geddes Axe' was one of the greatest injustices, and incidentally the worst advertisement, the Royal Navy ever suffered.[26]

It is probable that some babies were thrown out with the bathwater. More serious was the Invergordon Mutiny of 1931, though this cloud had a silver lining in that it provided a shock for many officers and acted as a warning against complacency for many years to come.

The achievements of the Royal Navy in the inter-war years were certainly as remarkable as its failures. It recognized the threat from the submarine, as indeed it would have been hard not to. Merchant shipping losses had been staggering in the First World War, and the battlefleet's actions towards the end of the war were severely restricted by the submarine threat. It was clear that a technological rather than a tactical answer was called for. The result was the development of sonar, or asdic as it was first known. Rather more surprisingly, as it had posed precious little of a threat in the war, the Royal Navy was also active in spotting the threat from aircraft, and found its answer in the multi-barrelled pom-pom, or 'Chicago piano'. With hindsight we can see clearly that asdic and pom-poms were never on their own going to be a solution for either the submarine or the aircraft threat. That view was not accepted in the inter-war period. Sir Samuel Hoare, ex-First Lord of the Admiralty, was only expressing a general view in November 1937 when he wrote: 'The submarine is no longer a danger to the British Empire.'[27]

Early asdic was limited in its operational capacity by being fixed-direction only and giving no real clue as to the depth of the target. Without radar it also prompted the U-boat or submarine to attack on the surface, where its speed of eighteen knots and very low surface profile made it a potent threat and one with which asdic could not cope. The pom-pom was only a part answer, with aircraft being the only really effective weapon against other aircraft. Nevertheless, the Royal Navy had perceived a problem and taken steps to counter it.

Another major achievement was the development of aircraft carriers. Again, this was by no means an undiluted success story. In *Ark Royal* the British developed an excellent carrier design, but the Royal Navy did not gain control over its own air arm until 1938. By this time it had lost vital time in the development of naval aircraft, which were designed to very undemanding specifications. Cunningham complained:

It is quite dreadful to think of the straits the Fleet Air Arm domination by the R.A.F. in matters of design has brought us to. We are like two men in open country, one armed with a rifle and the other with a shot-gun.[28]

The absence of effective aircraft and the absence of the money to fill the ships' hangars anyway, even if the aircraft had been there, imposed design limitations on later carriers and were to prove a handicap to British air operations throughout the war. The fact remains that the Royal Navy won two major victories, at Taranto and against the *Bismarck*, because of its willingness to take on board some of the implications of air power. Two other major victories – Matapan and North Cape – and a host of minor ones were won by radar as a major influencing factor, and in the development of this the Royal Navy was again well to the fore.

The real weakness of the Royal Navy in 1939 was that it was not sufficiently a force designed round commerce protection, except where that involved protection against surface raiders. There was a chronic shortage of escort vessels, no effective provision for air cover of convoys and a serious weakness in the provision of small craft, both in numbers and design, for areas such as the Channel. Its weaknesses were certainly not in its potential commanders. Most of these had been through a system which produced intense loyalty to the service, and which gave those with gifts of personality or intellect the opportunity to shine. They entered a service which almost immediately went through major and much-needed reforms, had ample opportunity to be blooded in action, and between the wars were members of a service which had to make painful choices, but which did so in a manner that was to give potential commanders the technical and scientific back-up that allowed them to meet their opponents on an equal or superior footing. If they did not have enough ships, or the experience to fight what was often a new type of warfare as it should have been fought, most of them showed that they could learn quickly and adapt.

In the final count it is difficult to spot what contribution was made to the Admirals of the Second World War by *Britannia*, and what contribution was made by the wider social, military and cultural background, and by their own personalities. It is still possible to discern certain distinguishing features about the top British commanders in the war. They were men of the strongest views, but at the same time showed a remarkable ability to work with each other and with their often troublesome allies. British officers had a loyalty to the Royal Navy that could make them devils to work with as far as the other armed services were concerned, but which at the same time could allow them to override personal prejudice and even ambititon to a remarkable extent. One major example is that of Fraser refusing the offer of becoming First Sea Lord in favour of Cunningham, because Fraser believed that Cunningham was the man the Navy wanted and the man it needed. In dealing with allies, Cunningham disarmed the French fleet literally and figuratively at Alexandria in June, 1940; Somerville charmed his way past that most truculent of allies, Admiral Ernest King of the United States Navy. The Admirals of the Second World War were capable of being ruthless or even callous about losses, were never frightened of taking decisions, and would always tend to err on the side of the offensive rather than adopt a defensive role. They were remarkably willing to take full responsibility for their actions, were generous in word and deed to their enemies, and intensely loyal to their service. One feature of this was a remarkable absence of bitchery in the post-war memoirs that were published, and veils of silence drawn over relationships with 'colourful' figures such as Mounbatten, and over the inevitable personal feuds. Though one or two had genuine technological awareness (perhaps most notably Fraser, Somerville and Horton), the majority were salt-water sailors who would cheerfully use whatever weapons came their way to hurl at the enemy. It was not any great respect for the aircraft carrier that brought about the first aerial attack on an enemy fleet in the case of Taranto, rather more a desire to hurl whatever was available at the enemy regardless of its origins or modernity. Perhaps more than the top commanders of any other navy they showed a sense of humour in their dealings with each other and with the Admiralty. That sense of humour was frequently of a very childish type, though elements of wit were often present in it. Cunningham, renowned for his sharp eyesight, once sent a signal: 'The left ear of the bowman of your motor boat needs attention.' The reply came back: 'Reference to your earlier signal, this rating has been examined both by his Flotilla Medical Officer and a specialist, and nothing can be found wrong with the ear in question.' The reply from Cunningham was 'It had a fag end on top.'[29]

As types these Admirals divide neatly into two sections. The planners and the thinkers were headed by figures such as

1 'Supply and other administrative problems bedevilled him and made him appear a lesser man than he was.' Harwood (holding mast) at Benghazi.

2 The attack on the *Graf Spee*.

3 'To Admiral Lyster and myself the project seemed to involve no unusual danger.' *Illustrious*, in a dangerous state, gives the lie to Cunningham shortly after Taranto.

4 Taranto after the raid.

Ramsay, Phillips and perhaps Fraser: Dudley Pound was another such from a slightly earlier generation. Then there were the doers, the hard fighters who appeared to sail by the seat of their pants, whose language was often as vivid as their actions, and who were not above staging what would now be seen as deliberate public relations exercises to boost their image and standing. Cunningham, Mountbatten and Somerville were the acknowledged masters of this game, an essential one where so often morale needed to be at its highest when resources were at their lowest. It is one of the greatest tributes to Ramsay in particular that he managed to bridge the gap between the two styles of leadership more effectively than any other commander. There is some evidence of bad blood between Cunningham and Fraser, and between Fraser and Somerville. Mountbatten appears to have struck a number of other commanders on the raw. Phillips was not loved by some of his contemporaries, although as a much maligned figure he also commanded immense respect from a number of very shrewd judges. Vian and Horton were far from easy figures to get on with and aroused considerable hostility. All this is inevitable, but Ramsay's ability to do the job regardless and be loved for it stands out above all others. The reason may be a very simple one; Ramsay was renowned for his lack of tact, and as a result of falling out with Sir Roger Backhouse he resigned and spent four years ashore with time on his hands. That experience may have taught him more than his contemporaries ever learnt about getting on with people; it certainly allowed Ramsay a freedom no other naval officer ever acquired, that of actually teasing Montgomery and remaining a close personal friend at the same time.

History had played into the hands of the British by deciding that war would break out in 1939. Poised to take over the top jobs at that time were officers who had been through major reforms, and whose weaker brethren had been weeded out by war and by administrative and executive purges. Lack of money had led to glaring holes in the provision of ships for the Royal Navy, and there was simply not the experience of intensive submarine and aircraft warfare on which to base effective tactics, but just as the RAF had the benefit of wise technological investment behind it for its great battle, in the shape of radar, the Spitfire and the Hurricane, so the Royal Navy had the capacity, if not the time or the money, by 1939, to give the commanders what they needed to fight the war. Perhaps most of all the Royal Navy and its Admirals in 1939 had confidence in their ability to win. It was to be justified.

2 The Battle of the River Plate and Dudley Pound

Chronology of Events

1939

3 August. Supply and support vessel *Altmark* sets sail from Germany.

21 August. German commerce raider *Graf Spee* sets sail from Germany.

24 August. German commerce raider *Deutschland* with supply vessel *Westerwald* sets sail from Germany.

3 September. Great Britain declares war on Germany. Winston Churchill made First Lord of the Admiralty.

3/4 September. Liner *Athenia* (13,000 tons) torpedoed and sunk by *U30*.

5 September. *Bosnia* (small steamer) is torpedoed by *U47*, thus becoming first British freighter of the war to be sunk by U-boat.

14 September. Carrier *Ark Royal* narrowly survives torpedo attack by *U39*, which is sunk, the first U-boat to become a victim of the Royal Navy.

16 September. First convoy leaves Halifax for England.

17 September. Carrier *Courageous* sunk by *U29*: British Admiralty abandon idea of independent submarine-hunting groups with aircraft carrier forming part of the the force.

30 September. German U-boats had now sunk forty-eight merchant vessels amounting to 178,644 tons, for loss of two U-boats. *Graf Spee* sinks first victim, S.S. *Clement*.

6 October. Commerce raider *Deutschland* sinks British steamer *Stonegate*.

13 October. Admiral Dönitz authorizes first 'wolf pack' operation by U-boats against convoy H.G. 3.

14 October. *U47* penetrates defences of Scapa Flow and sinks battleship *Royal Oak*.

1 November. Commerce raider *Deutschland* ordered to return home after sinking two merchant vessels (7,000 tons).

21 November. German battleships *Scharnhorst* and *Gneisenau* put to sea for Atlantic foray.

23 November. German magnetic mine recovered intact from mud flats. Armed merchant cruiser *Rawalpindi* sunk by German battleships *Scharnhorst* and *Gneisenau*.

13 December. German commerce raider *Graf Spee* spotted by Allied cruisers *Exeter*, *Ajax* and *Achilles*.

17 December. *Graf Spee* scuttled by its crew off Montevideo harbour. *Graf Spee* accounts for 80 per cent of Allied vessels sunk by surface raiders in 1939; in the first four months of the war U-boats account for twelve times the number of ships and eight times the tonnage sunk by *Graf Spee*.

There may have been a 'phoney war' elsewhere in 1939, but for the Royal Navy the real war started immediately and raged until 1945. Indeed for some people it was as if the last war had not ended:

> It might have been the September of an earlier German war, and many older officers and ratings remarked on the already ominous similarity between the two wars. 'It was as if time had stood still,' remarked one captain who had been a young sub-lieutenant in 1916. 'A lot of the ships were even the same.'[1]

In some respects there were very depressing similarities. The lesson of protecting the anchorage of Scapa Flow had been learnt in the First World War and should have been remembered, though here again the villain of the piece was finance rather than wilful or unwitting negligence: a navy desperate for ships is not going to put base defences as a priority on the very reasonable basis that there is no point in having a base if there are no ships to go in it. *U47* made it into Scapa Flow because of expenditure restrictions, because the base was not yet alerted to the realities of the war, and because the commander of the U-boat was exceptionally skilful and courageous. Perhaps even more depressing was the loss of the *Rawalpindi*. In the First World War two German vessels named *Scharnhorst* and *Gneisenau* had annihilated Rear Admiral Sir Christopher Cradock's hopelessly inferior force at the Battle of Coronel. In 1939 their descendants were to wipe out an armed merchant cruiser, perhaps one of the most suicidal ideas ever invented by an Admiralty starved of ships. The armed merchant cruiser could not match any likely commerce raiding opponent in terms of weapons, speed, protection or fire control, yet its status and name made it a matter of honour that it should try and attack its enemy.

Few naval commentators have even attempted to excuse the Royal Navy's early inclination to form submarine hunting groups based round an aircraft carrier, these groups having considerable independence of action. The aircraft carrier *Ark Royal* was a member of such a group in 1939, and only the inadequate performance of German torpedoes saved her from being sunk then, almost before her war had started. The carrier *Courageous* was not so lucky, succumbing to three torpedo hits. Yet this condemnation of the strategy is very surprising in some respects, and a perfect example of hindsight. In theory the principle of the hunting groups was very sound. The First World War had shown that aircraft were a potent force in hunting submarines, and later events were to prove that air cover was a major factor in defeating U-boats. Aircraft could force the submarine to submerge; a submerged submarine could only proceed very slowly for a few hours – and as a submerged vessel was open to detection by asdic and bombing by depth charge. *Courageous* had an escort of five destroyers, and the fact that the escort for *Ark Royal* succeeded in finding and sinking one of only two German U-boats sunk in 1939 is perverse proof of the theory behind the hunting groups. They failed, as we now know, because no aircraft carrier at that time could keep a 24-hour patrol airborne, radar was needed to spot the submarine before it was able to threaten the carrier, and asdic was too short-ranged and too inaccurate to guarantee keeping the attacker at stand-off range. Nevertheless, as an idea based on the hoped-for performance of aircraft and asdic, it was perfectly reasonable and worthy of rather less scorn than it has received.

Despite the battle being waged against the U-boats, it was a classic surface encounter that took the battle honours and the public attention in 1939. In many respects the Battle of the River Plate was a strange business, drawn from an earlier and simpler age, influenced only minimally by radar and aircraft. It was a battle fought by very brave and very honourable men on both sides, but its historical and strategic significance was always far less than its emotional appeal. It provided the first instance in the war of a battlefield promotion, but its recipient, Henry Harwood, was to sink almost without trace in the Navy's career structure once the battle was over.

The Germans had launched the first of their *Panzerschiffe* (armoured ships) in 1931, naming it *Deutschland*. Their designers had laboured under the burden of a 10,000 ton displacement limit, and even with their cavalier attitude to such limits (*Graf Spee* was 12,000 tons standard displacement, 16,200 tons at full load) they faced serious problems. What they came up with, under the circumstances, was a masterpiece. The tag 'pocket battleship' given to the three vessels by the British Press was misleading. The three *Panzerschiffe* were specifically designed for commerce raiding. They carried six 11″ guns in two triple turrets, diesel engines designed to give a top speed of twenty-six knots but which achieved twenty-eight and a half on trial, and over three inches of armour. The 11″ guns meant that in theory they could smash any cruiser, and at the time they were built only the British had battlecruisers that could outrun and outgun them. Their armour was in theory proof against 8″ shellfire (though the theory was disproved at the Battle of the River Plate), and their diesels gave them a quick-start capacity, minimal smoke output and excellent endurance. *Graf Spee* also had 'Seetakt' FuMo22 radar, primitive by later standards but highly effective for the time. The vessel had weaknesses, it was true. As well as the armour proving vulnerable to 8″ gunfire when put to the test, the Captain of the vessel needed an armoured conning position for combat, and *Graf Spee* was supplied with only one aircraft, and that (the Arado Ar196) of an unreliable design. Even with these weaknesses, all three vessels that were finally built were superbly designed for their given task.

When battle came, the British were able to bring something of a mixed bag against *Graf Spee*. Only 8″ guns stood any chance of inflicting serious damage on the German ship, and of the three cruisers which engaged her only one was so armed, *Exeter*. Among numerous other stipulations, the 1922 Washington Naval Treaty limited cruisers to a maximum of 10,000 tons, with guns not over eight inches. The British built thirteen 'County' class cruisers, but found them too expensive and so moved down the scale to the smaller 'B' type. Only two were built, half-sisters, *York* and *Exeter*, and neither was to survive the war. *Exeter* carried only six 8" guns, this number being deemed the minimum for accurate spotting of fall of shot, whereas the larger 'County' class carried two more. Though given 3" armour in parts, *Exeter* was a relative lightweight, and no match at all for *Graf Spee*. In *Ajax* and *Achilles* the British had arguably the best light cruiser designs of the war, the 'Leander' class, chosen when the 8" designs became too expensive. Excellent though they were, they were again individually no match for the *Panzerschiffe*.

It is not the concern of this book to describe the build-up to the Battle of the River Plate, which has been done in depth in other books. Suffice it to say that Captain Langsdorff set sail from Germany in August and mounted a very successful raiding cruise half way round the world, deciding to take a final stab at the merchant shipping round the River Plate before returning to Germany. He sank only nine vessels, but in the process tied up a force of four battleships, four battlecruisers, six aircraft carriers and over twenty cruisers.

The victor of the Battle of the River Plate, Commodore (later Admiral Sir) Henry Harwood, achieved his victory through one inspired piece of guesswork. One of *Graf Spee's* victims, the *Doric Star*, was able to radio a position before being sunk. The position placed the raider 3,000 miles away from the River Plate. Harwood was convinced the ship would be tempted by the rich pickings available in the South Atlantic – but possible areas of operation stretched half way down the coast of South America, from Rio de Janeiro, past the River Plate, to the Falkland Islands. With impeccable timing and insight Harwood ordered the 8" gun cruiser *Exeter* (Falkland Islands) and the 6" *Achilles* (off Rio de Janeiro) to rendezvous with him in the 6" *Ajax* off the River Plate. Twenty-four hours after the vessels joined forces, 150 miles off the Plate estuary, *Graf Spee* was spotted coming over the horizon. Thus ended one of the shrewdest guesses in naval history. Or was it?

Captain Stephen Roskill's judgement of Harwood was harsh, and it is clear that he saw Harwood as a limited man brought to undue and possibly undeserved prominence by one action[2]. In this area at least Roskill's judgement seems to be confirmed by others who knew Harwood. He was seen as a kindly, very robust man, capable of impetuosity, but with generally sound if unexciting judgement. In comparison with many of those who achieved flag rank in the war he was not a great leader, nor a great brain. He reached his peak as the captain of a ship, and did that job very well. His promotion to flag rank after the Battle of the River Plate may have placed him higher than his abilities merited: he had been passed over prior to the battle. His career after his promotion was lacklustre, though when he took over command in the Mediterranean after Cunningham it was clear that supply and other administrative problems bedevilled him, and may have made him appear a lesser man than he was. Nevertheless the track record of this fine but uninspired sailor makes the decision to rendezvous off the River Plate all the more remarkable – unless one suggests that instead of 'brilliant timing'[3] all that Harwood did was to gather his three vessels bang in the middle of the area in which *Graf Spee* might decide to operate. His central position obviously put him the shortest steaming distance away from wherever the German might choose to go, be it Rio to the north or the Falklands to the south. Harwood's grouping may have been inspired guesswork; it is just as likely to have been a sensible compromise, given that the only certainty was the destruction of anything less than three cruisers to meet the threat of *Graf Spee's* 11″ guns and armour. Indeed, it would have been folly for Harwood to concentrate his forces anywhere *else*.

Attacking an enemy commerce raider was certainly something the Royal Navy had rehearsed in the inter-war years. Harwood's plan of battle was simple. His force would split into two, *Exeter* forming one division, *Ajax* and *Achilles* the other. The aim was to split the enemy fire, capitalizing on what was seen as a weakness of the enemy vessel in its inability to engage multiple targets. *Exeter* would flank mark for the other two cruisers while they fired as one group, passing range and elevation details over the radio. This latter idea worked for only twenty minutes before battle damage rendered it impractical.

The battle itself was also quite straightforward. When the

British force was sighted Langsdorff made for it and swung his ship round so that both 11″ turrets could bear on *Exeter*. Secondary armament (eight 5.9″ guns) was brought to bear on the other two cruisers. *Graf Spee's* third salvo straddled *Exeter*. Shortly afterwards an 11″ shell put 'B' turret out of action, swept the bridge with splinters and killed all on the bridge except Captain Bell and two others. *Exeter* was then hit twice more, though she retained her full speed capacity. Twelve minutes after opening fire, Langsdorff had gone a long way towards disabling the only British cruiser whose armament had a hope of piercing his armour, but with *Exeter* very close to destruction Langsdorff diverted his main armament fire away from her and on to the other two cruisers. Seven minutes later *Graf Spee* made a sharp turn to port and started to make smoke, beginning her run into Montevideo. At the same time Langsdorff returned the fire of his main armament to *Exeter*, and in a very short space of time had reduced her to one turret firing under local control. Thereafter the battle became a chase. *Exeter* was forced to drop out altogether, savagely wounded and no longer capable of fighting. Both *Ajax's* after turrets were put out of action, reducing the total broadside of the British force to twelve 6″ guns: regarding the effect of 6″ fire of *Graf Spee*, Harwood commented: 'We might just as well be bombarding her with a lot of bloody snowballs'.[4] Believing (wrongly as it turned out) that *Ajax* had only twenty percent of ammunition remaining, Harwood broke off the action, determined to shadow the German vessel and close in again at nightfall. In the event *Graf Spee* headed straight for Montevideo harbour, shadowed by the two British cruisers. *Graf Spee* had forty percent of her ammunition remaining. Thirty-six of her crew were dead, six seriously wounded and fifty-three others wounded. She had been hit by three 8″ and seventeen 6″ shells. A hole had been knocked in her bow; her water purification plant, bakery, galley and plant for purifying fuel oil had been wrecked. *Graf Spee* was still in good fighting trim, though not in an ideal position for making a long sea journey.

British historians have frequently taken an appallingly jingoistic view of Captain Langsdorff:

> The British squadron had fought gallantly against odds, and
> had manoeuvred so cleverly and worried at the *Graf Spee*

so effectively that she was glad to leave the ring, the loser
on points. It was a craven act after an incompetently
handled fight.[5]

Langsdorff's act was far from craven, his handling of the fight
far from incompetent. He knocked out of the ring and nearly
killed the one opponent who could do him serious damage, and
seriously mauled another. It is just as likely that by turning to
Montevideo he took one of the bravest decisions of any commander in the Second World War. The two British cruisers had
a speed advantage over him and it was unlikely that he could
shake them off, or that his six-gun salvoes could finish off even
one cruiser jinking at long range. They would certainly have
signalled his position far and wide, and he must have known of
the sheer number of ships out searching for him. Even if he
escaped the cruisers, the absence of pure water and engine oil
made a journey home problematic (*Graf Spee's* engines were
due for service before she set sail, and had given smoke problems
throught her cruise), particularly with limited ammunition. In
all probability Langsdorff realized that his ship's number was
up. He could stand, fight and be destroyed, if not off the River
Plate then on his way home – or he could run for cover and save
the lives of his crew who had served him so well. British naval
tradition would have praised him for fighting and dying; the
relatives of those who died on *Rawalpindi* or at the Battle or
Coronel might have more sympathy for Langsdorff's view.
Needless to say, to an honourable man the saving of his crew
meant that he had to sacrifice his own life, in order to show
that he personally was no coward. Langsdorff's suicide duly
took place: his own life was forfeit, but in sinking nine vessels
he had managed not to lose a single enemy life. Shortly before-
hand he had ordered the scuttling of his vessel, having gained
Hitler and Dönitz's consent to this act.

No one can deny that Harwood had fought gallantly against
odds. The tactical brilliance of the action was less marked: the
British cruisers clung on grimly and by good manoeuvering did
what they could to avoid being hit. Like so many good ideas,
the oft-rehearsed concentration firing planned by *Ajax* and
Achilles did not work out in practice, exposed radio antennae
being almost the first to go in close surface combat. British
gunnery was by and large very good under the circumstances,

though British 6" fire had only a shrapnel effect and did no serious damage to *Graf Spee's* structure.

It is possible to quibble with the tactics adopted by the British on the day, though most comments would tend to represent the worst aspects of armchair history. One might question the wisdom of putting *Exeter* on her own. As Harwood's most potent weapon it was in his interest to preserve her for as long as possible, and putting her in with one of the 6" cruisers may have delayed slightly her receiving *Graf Spee's* concentrated fire, though equally it could have ensured the destruction of one of the light cruisers. The cruisers might also conceivably have used their speed to try and station themselves fore-and-aft of *Graf Spee*, thus forcing her to divide her main armament to some extent. Perhaps the only other option available to Harwood was to use his two light cruisers as destroyers and, by heavy use of smoke, launch a torpedo attack on *Graf Spee*, the torpedo being his only real chance of sinking the ship. Torpedoes were launched by *Exeter* in desperation when she had been severely hit, and it was this attack in part which forced Langsdorff to turn away. *Graf Spee's* fire was accurate (as in the First World War, the German long-base range finders gave accuracy very early on in the engagement) from the main armament at least. This suggests that the cruisers would have been blown out of the water had they come close enough to launch a realistic torpedo attack, and also that Langsdorff would have been too wily to let them do it. It is, however, the only other tactic that might seriously have been adopted, for all its risk, and torpedoes were the only weapons the British had that could have sunk the *Graf Spee*. One wonders which option a commander such as Vian might have taken.

The difference between Harwood and Langsdorff was that Harwood had very few decisions to take. He had a pre-existing plan, and stuck to it; ironically the only decision he did take was to break off the action, so making exactly the same decision as his enemy. Harwood fought bravely and tenaciously, but the River Plate was no Nelsonian triumph, and Harwood was no Nelson, merely an excellent ship's captain with all the sterling virtues of tenacity and courage that were to see the Royal Navy through the war.

One footnote to the Battle of the River Plate leads on to a far wider issue, the nature and influence of Admiral Sir Dudley

Pound, Admiral of the Fleet and First Sea Lord for the first part of the Second World War. One authority believes that Pound was instrumental in stopping Winston Churchill from sending operational orders to Harwood in the course of the battle[6]; the attempt and the rebuttal would have been typical of both men. Pound was not a 'fighting' admiral in the strict sense of the word, in that he was not directly in command of any specific action, but as First Sea Lord his influence pervades all actions up to his death in 1943 from a brain tumour, and no study of this nature would be complete without at least a glance at Pound. He has been the subject of acrimonious debate between the two leading naval historians of this century, Stephen Roskill and Arthur Marder. Roskill argues that 'even after Churchill became Prime Minister, he continued to act as though he were still First Lord'[7], while Marder argues that Pound was 'a tough officer to whom no one could dictate, least of all Churchill'.[8]

The First Lord of the Admiralty (effectively the Navy Minister) was A.V. Alexander. Marder tends to see Alexander as a stooge, compliant to Churchill, while Roskill is more circumspect about his influence. Alexander's papers in the Churchill College archives reveal little about the man and have all the blandness of political expertise.

Churchill's role in the war has been well documented. Some would argue that it has been played to death. He was obsessed with the offensive spirit, frequently annoyed commanders on the spot by interfering or sending prodding signals, and was capable of taking rash decisions on promotions, though he occasionally struck gold. Churchill did not suffer fools gladly, worked totally to his own timetable and was infuriating, exasperating and uplifting to work with. His association with the Royal Navy in the First World War had been one of love and hate, and it seems clear that he distrusted and perhaps feared Admirals and parts of the Naval hierarchy; whatever the truth, whoever had to work with Churchill in wartime as First Sea Lord had an unenviable task.

Sadly for a nearly great man, Pound has come to be associated with the disaster of Convoy PQ17, ordered to disperse and slaughtered piecemeal by the Germans when it was feared that *Tirpitz* was on its way to massacre the merchant ships and their escort. There is no doubt that the decision was Pound's and that it was a mistake, but there is far more to Pound than PQ17. He has attracted a surprisingly varied press. He was what now would be described as a workaholic, driving himself through the night and frequently appearing tired; accusations that he tended to fall asleep in meetings may, though, have more to do with his brain illness than his overwork. He hated changes to his Staff and was loyal to a fault in trying to keep the same men around him. He was a great admirer of Tom Phillips, had him appointed VCNS (Vice Chief Naval Staff), and personally selected him as the commander of the ill-fated Force Z. This was the fleet consisting of the battleship *Prince of Wales* and the battlecruiser *Repulse* which was sent to the Far East in a belated attempt to deter Japan from war, and which was then promptly sunk by Japanese aircraft. The very close relationship between Pound and Phillips sometimes helped neither of them. They were seen in certain quarters as a cabal, and a malign influence on the development of the Navy.

It was POUND and PHILLIPS, with their storekeeper
minds, who quenched all the spark in the fleet. Everything
was scheduled, even a snipe shoot in a Greek swamp went
into a book because ships were told to report full details of
all sport when cruising independently.[9]

Pound was certainly bad at decentralizing, but he was far from unique in this; it had been the root cause of the problem between Sir Roger Backhouse and Admiral Ramsay. There were other complaints against him:

[Pound] was a disaster. Not only should he have gone
much sooner: he should never have been there at all. He
was a member — fortunately the last member — of a sort
of private clique who turned over the senior jobs to each
other progressively from about 1930 to 1940. (Len Holland
in *Hood* was another). Fortunately this came to an end
when Bruce Fraser took over – a magnificent man with an
absolutely first class brain and an inspiring leader.[10]

Pound also manifested worrying psychological features to some people, though these were not always widely noted:

His silences and remoteness were real handicaps and he was liable to have obsessions. One of these was that naval ratings ashore deliberately omitted to salute him. The complete absence of books in Pound's cabin was noticeable.[11]

Pound's tactics with Churchill seem to have been to avoid head-on confrontation:

> I have the greatest admiration for W.C., and his good qualities are such and his desire to hit the enemy so overwhelming, that I feel one must hesitate in turning down any of his proposals.[12]

Pound's technique was to let ideas from Churchill that were non-starters die quietly, or be overtaken by another flood of ideas the next week. By and large he managed to defuse some of Churchill's more bizarre proposals. He failed over Crete and Greece, which will be dealt with later, and some of his bad press has come about as a result of the errors of judgement that he did let Churchill make, often in the form of signals to commanders. For example, a ludicrous signal was made in the *Bismarck* chase suggesting that British capital ships, running low on fuel, could be towed back to harbour after having disposed of *Bismarck*. Cunningham summed up the resentment felt against Churchill at times, and inevitably some of this resentment rubbed off on Pound for not protecting his commanders more:

> It was in the sort of 'prodding' message received by me on June 5th that Mr Churchill was often so ungracious and hasty. We realized, of course, the terrible mental and physical strain under which he was labouring; but so were we. Such messages to those who were doing their utmost with straitened resources were not an encouragement, merely an annoyance. Moreover, as they implied that something was lacking in the direction and leadership, they did positive harm.[13]

While all this is true, it took traditional sailors such as Cunningham some while to realize that the days of the truly independent command were dead and gone. Radio and improved communciations in general, together with a world-wide war in which actions unknown to a commander could have serious implications for his own operations, meant that a greater degreee of centralized command for those at sea was inevitable. The enhanced intelligence available to the Admiralty through the breaking of German codes (ULTRA) also meant more 'interference'. The Admiralty did not always get it right – PQ17 was the most tragic example – but Pound died before he could defend himself, and his actions represent not merely personal failing, but also a command structure coming to terms with totally new factors.

Pound was also at times seen as unduly pessimistic. Throughout his own highly successful career, Admiral Cunningham tended to specialize in back-handed or double-edged compliments. Cunningham's first major victory came in the Mediterranean when Swordfish aircraft under his command sank or disabled three Italian battleships in Taranto harbour. Pound had been Commander-in-Chief in the Mediterranean, and so knew something about local conditions there, and the plan for an air attack on the Italian fleet's main base had been drawn up before the war. Cunningham wrote that the attack on Taranto

had, of course, already been mentioned in my correspondence with Sir Dudley Pound, though to him the operation always appeared as the last dying kick of the Mediterranean carrier before being sent to the bottom. To Admiral Lyster and myself the project seemed to involve no unusual danger.[14]

This comment is often taken as evidence of Pound's pessimisim; the fact that Pound was correct is less often reported. The carrier Cunningham used at Taranto, *Illustrious*, drew unwelcome attention to herself by her exploits, and two months later the vessel was reduced to a near-wreck by German Stuka dive-bombers. Only superb damage control saved her from sinking, and repairs took many months. Taranto *was* the last dying kick of the Mediterranean fleet's carrier. If Cunningham really did believe that the operation against Taranto seemed to involve no unusual danger, then he was a blinkered fool.

On 27 June, 1940, Pound signalled Cunningham that it might be a good idea to abandon the Eastern Mediterranean, though the idea was squashed by Cunningham and Churchill.[15] This suggestion could be seen as defeatism. It could also be seen as a wise redistribution of forces for a country whose survival was increasingly going to depend on mercantile traffic across the Atlantic, rather than on the outcome of sea battles off Alexandria. The importance of the whole Mediterranean campaign can be overstated, just as was the Battle of the River Plate. The latter joined with Cunningham's Mediterranean campaign in that both provided much-needed victories and proof that we were fighting back. The value for morale of such victories was immense, their strategic significance much less than that of the outcome of the U-boat war. Pound had many weaknesses, but being a fool was not one of them. His concern about the drain on scarce resources caused by a campaign in the Eastern Mediterranean was a serious one from a serious man.

Cunningham summed up a great deal about Pound when he wrote:

> Winston wore Pound down. He was so tired of fighting the Prime Minister that he made up his mind to fight only for the essential factors. But apparently he did not regard support of his Flag-Officers at sea as always an essential factor, and I think he always favoured getting a scapegoat.[16]

This seems a fair and shrewd comment. Churchill placed Pound under immense pressure, forcing him to defend his rear when he and the Navy were being attacked from front and side anyway. Here perhaps the great Royal Navy virtues of loyalty and hard work did not operate as they should, keeping Pound at the treadmill when it might have been better for a stronger man to come in, one who could stand up to Churchill. One has to say 'perhaps' because Churchill's tolerance of those who did not agree with him was not high. He looked for the offensive spirit in those around him, but he also appeared to seek a degree of subservience at the same time. This was not a happy combination of features. Churchill's admiration of the offensive spirit was narcissistic. He liked to see in his subordinates a reflection of his own ideas and aggression. When these subordinates quite naturally came out with ideas of their own, some of which might conflict with the Churchillian scheme of things, then they were likely to be given short shrift. Keyes, Phillips and

Tovey all lost Churchill's approbation when they disagreed with him.

Where Churchill, Pound and perhaps Phillips did appear to unite was in the search for scapegoats. Dudley North and the Dakar affair may have been one such instance. Certainly there was a move from the Admiralty to have the captain of *Prince of Wales* court-martialled after the *Bismarck* episode, and this may only have been stopped when Admiral Tovey, Commander-in-Chief of the Home Fleet, threatened to resign and act as prisoner's friend. When Admiral Somerville drove off a superior Italian force at Spartivento, but remained with the convoy instead of chasing off after the Italians, an immediate Board of Enquiry was set up, with Churchill as the leading light behind the move. It cleared Somerville, but left a bad taste, and inevitably some of the flavour was Pound's, even if Churchill was the main ingredient. It did not help that Somerville disliked and was disliked by Tom Phillips, Pound's right-hand man. Pound's apparent willingness to seek a scapegoat may have been linked to his brooding melancholy. Churchill's willingness was probably nothing more than impatience and a desire for instant solutions.

However, all was not gloom during Pound's tenure of office. Cunningham again wrote:

> I was distressed to see that attacks were being made on Sir Dudley Pound in the Press and in Parliament. To one like myself who had a fair idea of his difficulties and vast responsibilities and the stout-hearted manner in which he was facing up to them, this malicious gossip seemed cruelly and unwarrantably unjust.[17]

Pound's problem was that he was not only having to fight a war, but muzzle a bulldog in his back yard at the same time. He clearly annoyed Cunningham at times, but Cunningham's loyalty to him never wavered. Admiral Sir Philip Vian was never the easiest of men to please, and his comment on Pound is instructive: 'a stoic: a slow, but profound, thinker, immune from ordinary emotion.'[18] Pound's stoicism, his capacity to endure stress, cannot be underestimated as a major requirement for a successful First Sea Lord in the first three years of a war for which much had been left unprepared. Cunningham was responsible for only one theatre of war, the Mediterranean, until called home, and even he came near to chucking in the towel after the appalling losses suffered by his command in Greece and Crete. Admiral Somerville reached a state of almost terminal despair with the Royal Navy on three occasions, once when he was unfairly invalided out, a second time when he was responsible for opening fire on the French fleet at Mers-el-Kebir, and thirdly when given command of the Eastern Fleet on 15 December, 1941: 'This damned appointment gives me no kick at all, and I keep asking myself why the hell am I here at my age.'[19] Ramsay put himself on the beach for four years because he could not work with a senior officer. Tovey fell out with Churchill, being seen as stubborn and obstinate, and probably put paid to his chances of becoming First Sea Lord in so doing. Phillips also fell out with Churchill because he made very reasoned and reasonable objections to policies held holy by the Prime Minister. The list of naval casualties caused by sheer strain or by a strained relationship with Winston Churchill is extremely long – and Sir Dudley Pound had more of both than any other serving officer in the war. For that reason he should be remembered with honour. The strain may even have helped to kill him, and if that is so he died fighting for a cause no less valuable to the Royal Navy than those who died in actual combat. He could not stop all the excesses of Churchill, or avoid making major errors. In maintaining his loyalty to Churchill he possibly put too much weight on Tom Phillips, but there were many worse choices he could have made. In maintaining his loyalty, he also avoided a personality clash that could have had appalling consequences for the naval side of the war, harnessed the aggression of Churchill while reducing some of its more harmful side-effects, and managed to ensure that those given top positions were, with the exception perhaps of Keyes and Harwood, the right men for the job. Pound and Ramsay were the least dramatic of men. For that reason their contribution to the the war has sometimes been underestimated. It is not a mistake that should continue.

3 Narvik, Dunkirk, and Ramsay

Chronology of Events

1940

16 February. Crew of British destroyer *Cossack* (Captain Vian) board German tanker *Altmark* and release prisoners taken by *Graf Spee*.

18 February. *Scharnhorst*, *Gneisenau* and *Hipper* sail to attack convoys.

11 March. German auxiliary cruiser (commerce raider) *Atlantis* sets sail, the first of several such vessels to be sent out in 1940.

3 April. First German vessels set sail for invasion of Norway.

6/7 March. German warships set sail for Norway.

7 April. British Home fleet leaves Scapa Flow in response to reports of German heavy warship movements; British fleet consists of two battleships, one battlecruiser, two cruisers, ten destroyers.

8 April. British destroyer *Glowworm* rams German cruiser *Hipper*, after becoming detached from main fleet.

9 April. British battlecruiser *Renown* lands hits on *Scharnhorst* and *Gneisenau* off Vestfjord; German vessels retire behind smokescreen. German heavy cruiser *Blücher* destroyed by Norwegian gun and torpedo shore batteries. German mountain troops take Narvik. Heavy air attacks on British ships off Bergen, with destroyer *Gurkha* sunk. German cruiser *Karlsrühe* sunk by British submarine *Truant*.

10 April. First phase of Battle of Narvik. British destroyers under Captain Warburton-Lee force passage to Narvik. Two German destroyers sunk; several merchant ships and four German destroyers damaged; British lose Warburton-Lee and two destroyers; two more seriously damaged. Fleet Air Arm Skua dive-bombers spot and sink the damaged German light cruiser *Königsberg*.

11 April. German *Panzerschiffe Lutzow* (ex-*Deutschland*) torpedoed by British submarine *Spearfish* and put out of action for a year.

13 April. Second battle of Narvik. Battleship *Warspite* and nine destroyers make sortie into Narvik and sink remaining eight German destroyers. Two British destroyers severely damaged.

17 April. Germans consider evacuating Narvik.

2/3 May. Allies evacuate Namsos. French destroyer *Bison* and British destroyer *Afridi* sunk by air attack.

5 May. British submarine *Shark* captured by two German floatplanes.

10 May. Winston Churchill becomes Prime Minister, A.V. Alexander First Lord of the Admiralty.

19 May. Admiral Ramsay given responsibility for Operation Dynamo, the evacuation of British Expeditionary Force from beaches of Dunkirk.

27 May. Operation Dynamo starts.

3 June. Germans occupy Dunkirk; Operation Dynamo ends.

4 June. *Scharnhorst*, *Gneisenau* and *Admiral Hipper* set sail to attack Allied evacuation of Norway.

8 June. German vessels above sink British carrier *Glorious*, and two destroyers *Ardent* and *Acasta*. *Scharnhorst* hit by torpedo.

10 June. Italy declares war on France and Britain. Norway capitulates.

12 June. Italian submarine sinks British cruiser *Calypso*, first success achieved by Italian navy.

22 June. France signs armistice with Germany.

The Narvik campaign was both a victory and a crushing defeat, as was the evacuation from Dunkirk which followed it. In a tragic echo of an earlier war (and perhaps all wars), failures in the higher command were to some extent redeemed by the bravery and tenacity of those lower down the naval hierarchy. Narvik showed that the British ability to mount a combined operation was abysmal; that high level bombing was ineffective against surface ships; and that fighter cover was essential to protect a fleet against dive bombers. It also brought the first serious examples of confusion of responsibility between the Admiralty in London and the commanders of the squadrons at sea. Attempts to control operations from London in most instances resulted in massive confusion, and considerable resentment on the part of those at sea who felt the main weight of Admiralty interference.

Hitler had decided to risk virtually the whole of the small German surface fleet to carry out his invasion of Norway, the country being essential to Germany for its iron-ore trade. It was an obvious target, and equally obvious to Germany's enemies. Churchill, who throughout the war tended to combine grasping the right idea with the wrong way of carrying it out, proposed a hare-brained scheme for invading Norway which in the confusion of the time was dropped in favour of a plan to mine the approaches to various strategic Norwegian ports. Had this mining operation taken place on 5 April, 1940, as originally planned it might have had a serious effect on the German invasion. As it was its postponement until 8 April was crucial – the first part of the German invasion force had set sail on 3 April. The result was that when the invasion took place the British had no good intelligence of German plans or actions, no mines laid and no effective pre-existing plan for a combined operation to support Norway. It was a recipe for chaos, and chaos came along.

The first phase of the battle was shadow boxing between two fleets, albeit shadow boxing which landed some very painful hits. In response to rumours and vague intelligence the British fleet set sail for Norway and brushed against the enemy without ever intercepting its main units in force. The destroyer *Glowworm* rammed the German heavy cruiser *Hipper* and was then herself sunk after she had become detached from the main British fleet and stumbled into a German force. Various German transports were sunk. The new German heavy cruiser *Blücher* was sunk by Norwegian shore defences, and the German light cruiser *Königsberg* was sunk by Fleet Air Arm Skua dive bombers, the first warship of the war to go down in an air attack and one of the first in history. The British submarine *Truant* torpedoed the German light cruiser *Karlsrühe*, damaging her so badly that she had to be sunk by her own side, while *Spearfish* torpedoed the pocket battleship *Lutzow*, came within a whisker of sinking her and put her out of action for a year. The venerable battlecruiser *Renown* had landed a long-range hit on the German battlecruiser *Gneisenau* and thus seen off this vessel and her near sister. All this was fine and well, with the balance of ships lost going very much in favour of the British, but the underlying fact was that the British had failed to intercept the major German units and failed to stop the Germans landing sufficient troops to take over Norway. The basic problem was that the British did not have accurate information as to what the Germans were doing, and even when it did emerge (when a German troopship was torpedoed and the surviving troops talked proudly of their impending invasion) the Admiralty was unable to sort the wheat from the chaff. Throughout the early phases of the operation, and even when it was quite clear that an invasion of Norway was in progress, the Admiralty was divided between sinking a German invasion force (demanding an inshore role for naval forces), or guarding against a breakout into the Atlantic by heavy German surface units (demanding an offshore role). Somewhat in the manner of a tragic ballet, the British moved their forces offshore when German forces were inshore, and moved them inshore when the birds had flown. The obsession with a breakout by large surface vessels was given its first airing in the Norwegian campaign, but was to come near to dominating Admiralty thinking almost to the end of the war. Admiral Sir Charles Forbes, Commander-in-Chief of the Home Fleet, was guilty of not backing his hunches. Convinced that a German invasion of Norway was taking place, he failed to dispose his ships accordingly. Admiral Whitworth was in command of the largest detachment of the Home Fleet at sea during the operation, but the Admiralty continually issued orders over his head and denied the wisdom of leaving tactical decisions to the judgement of the man on the spot.

The only hero of the early phase of the Norwegian campaign was Admiral Sir Max Horton, at the time the Vice Admiral commanding British submarines. Almost alone of British admirals, he was convinced that the Germans were invading Norway and took the risk of ordering no less than ten submarines to take up station off Norway to intercept German forces; the risk was implicit in the narrow waters in which these vessels would have to operate. All in all British submarines sank or severely damaged no less than sixteen German warships and merchant vessels, for the loss of two submarines. However, the Admiralty managed to steal some of Horton's fire as well, and considerably reduced the impact of his orders sending six more submarines to sea. On 7 April they ordered submarines to cover the approaches to Heligoland Bight in order to intecept German heavy forces, at the expense of a close watch on the Norwegian ports.

The British failure to impede the German invasion of Norway was redeemed to some extent by the actions of Captain Warburton-Lee. He was a part, in theory at least, of Admiral Whitworth's force, but, like all forces at the time, subject to direct Admiralty orders. The British campaign was redeemed also by the fact that ten German destroyers, short of fuel and ammunition, were penned up in the Norwegian fjords long enough to become sandwiched between the rocks on one side and British forces on the other.

The first battle of Narvik had a confused ancestry, as confused as any of the rest of this most confused of campaigns. Warburton-Lee was the senior officer of Admiral Whitworth's destroyers. Admiral Forbes had singalled: 'Send some destroyers up to Narvik to make certain that no enemy troops land,'[1] while the Admiralty signalled direct to Warburton-Lee:

Press reports state one German ship has arrived Narvik and landed a small force. Proceed Narvik and sink or capture enemy ship. It is at your discretion to land forces if you think you can recapture Narvik from number of enemy present.[2]

Luckily, Warburton-Lee was worried about inadequate information and stopped at the pilot station at Tranöy in Vestfjord, where he was told that six German warships and one submarine had gone up the fiord, possibly mining the entrance to Ofotfjord.

Warburton-Lee had been tipped for high office almost from the minute of his entering the Royal Navy. He showed why in three decisions. Firstly, he stopped to take information from the pilot station. Secondly, his response to the threat of mines was to propose an attack at high water, in which he hoped to float over moored mines. Thirdly, he ignored an Admiralty order to patrol the entry to Ofotfjord during the night to guard against an enemy breakout. Had he done so, German patrols would certainly have spotted him and lost him the advantage of surprise that he enjoyed on the day. Warburton-Lee should have lived to become one of the Royal Navy's most successful fighting admirals; one of the German victories of the Second World War was that they killed him before he could do so.

In the event Warburton-Lee dashed up the fjords and fought a magnificent engagement with the German destroyers which had failed to take their chance of escape after landing German troops. In the first Battle of Narvik the German destroyer on picket or patrol duty had left station. Warburton-Lee sank two German destroyers and severely damaged two others before he was sandwiched between three German destroyers which appeared from the north and two more which sprang up from the seaward side. The result was that *Hardy* was severely damaged and had to be beached, with Warburton-Lee mortally wounded; *Hunter* was set on fire, disabled, and eventually sank; *Hotspur* collided with *Hunter*, though both escaped, and only *Havock* and *Hostile* escaped damage. On the other side out of ten German destroyers, two were sunk, three rendered unseaworthy, one heavily damaged, one lightly damaged and three left undamaged. Captain Bey, later to become the Admiral who led *Scharnhorst* to her death, was in command of the destroyer flotilla. He tried to break out with two seaworthy destroyers, but turned back when he caught sight of the silhouette of British warships: later historians have suggested he was cowardly, and that his vessels could have slipped past their jailers. Later historians have, by and large, never been asked to back their judgement against the visible shape of a British cruiser and two destroyers.

On 12 April the Admiralty ordered Admiral Whitworth to mount an attack on the German vessels off Narvik with the 15" gun battleship *Warspite*, four 'Tribal' class destroyers and five smaller destroyers. *Warspite's* spotting aircraft not only signalled the presence of German destroyers lying in ambush, thus negating their power of surprise, but also sank *U64*, thus completing what must rank as the most succesful day of any naval aircraft in the Second World War, with the possible exception of the Swordfish which landed the crucial hit on *Bismarck*. For the British, *Cossack* was grounded, *Punjabi* damaged and *Eskimo* had her whole forepart blown off – but all ten German destroyers were sunk, a crippling loss to a fleet never well supplied with this class of vessel.

Narvik was a victory in line with the Curate's egg. It showed that, firstly, the Royal Navy had excellent resources of sea-going officers and ships to defend Norway, but had a command structure where the views of the man on the spot were all too likely to be overruled by the Admiralty, who were to attempt the exercise of direct command over many of the forces engaged. Secondly, the admirals commanding were the product of peace-time and lacked many of the features of successful wartime commanders. Thirdly, the British were unable to provide adequate air cover. Fourth, there was no tradition of combined operations and no effective command structure for a liaison between army, navy and air force (whereas German military success was based on such a union at least for its major land campaigns). Fifth, the British army were babes in the wood when it came to mounting at short notice armed landings on distant shores. Sixth, British intelligence was inadequate. Seventh, the Germans could decipher most British naval radio traffic rapidly and correctly.

Despite all the above, and the confusion and delay which typified the whole campaign, one crucial feature emerges from it, from the River Plate and from most of the engagements of the war. The Royal Navy had an overwhelming confidence in itself, and an overwhelming offensive spirit, both of which combined to allow it to send a flotilla of destroyers up a narrow fjord to face whatever it might find, and follow it up with nothing less than a 15″ gun battleship. Jellicoe was in command at Whitehall for all Churchill's influence: Beatty was still at sea, and able to drag a form of victory out of defeat.

The 'phoney war' was something which affected the Army and the RAF far more than it did the Royal Navy, but for all the action the Navy was involved in during the first year or so of conflict it took longer than this for peacetime appointments to work through or be dismissed, and for genuine war leaders to emerge. For all that they were decent men doing a very competent job, Harwood, Forbes and Whitworth were not going to set naval warfare alight. The only top commander who had manifested real dash and daring was Horton. His finest hour was yet to come, ironically as Commanding Officer of the Western

Approaches where he was to win his battle against the very weapon he had commanded so well throughout the Norwegian campaign, the submarine.

It took a defeat to focus public attention on one of the greatest fighting admirals of the war. Bertram Home Ramsay was born on 20 January, 1883, the son of a Brigadier who at one time had had Winston Churchill under his command. Ramsay's two brothers served in the Army, and his two sisters both married soldiers. He did have at least one naval ancestor, Rear Admiral Sir William Ramsay, KCB, but the choice of the Royal Navy for him probably hinged on *Britannia* being a cheap and honourable alternative to public school. Families with a military tradition of service were not always wealthy, and the large families that were common in Victorian and Edwardian times sometimes made placing all the children a serious problem for parents.

Ramsay attended Foster's Preparatory School at Stubbington, a school well known for specializing in cramming for the *Britannia* examination. He joined *Britannia* on 15 January, 1898, passing out from there to serve as a Midshipman for three years on a cruiser on the North American and West Indies station. By 1904 he was a Sub-Lieutenant, and on 21 April took part in the Battle of Illig as part of a naval brigade, gaining from this promotion, a mention in despatches and the award of the Africa General Service medal with 1904 bar. *Britannia*, service overseas, a colonial battle . . . with different names and places this was a typical progression for a naval officer of the time, and parallels Cunningham's early career, even down to their attending the same prep school. Even in this utterly conventional roll call, one or two clichés are shown to be false. For example, the idea that the peacetime Navy valued different virtues in its officers from those that held sway once war broke out, and that it took a shooting war to find the real command material, is demonstrably untrue in Ramsay's case, and in the case of three of the greatest commanders studied in this work – Cunningham, Somerville and Fraser. All four appear to have had stars against their names from the start, and if two, Ramsay and Somerville, were on the retired list when war broke out it was not because the Navy had failed to spot their virtues. In Ramsay's case he had fallen out with a senior officer and spent four years on the beach, but he got rid of the Navy rather than the Navy getting rid of him. Somerville was invalided out in a manner which said a great deal for the incompetence of the Naval medical service, but which did not reflect any failure on the part of the Navy to see him for what he was worth. Gunnery is also often cited as the Navy's favoured way to promotion and success, but, having achieved a plum job in 1906 as a gunnery officer in charge of one of the turrets on the brand-new *Dreadnought*, Ramsay decided to change to Signals – partly because he always was bloody-minded, partly because even then he was interested in the business of moving whole fleets, and partly because he did not like getting his hands dirty. There certainly were top commanders who were gunners in the Second World War: the majority were not.

The need for a Naval War Staff had been clear for many years to all except the senior commanders of the Navy, and finally the inevitable was introduced in 1912, although too late to have the impact it should have done on the conduct of the First World War. Ramsay was selected at the age of thirty to attend only the second course ever held for Naval staff officers, which helped give him an appointment to *Dreadnought* again when war broke out in 1914, this time as Flag Lieutenant, Signals Officer, and War Staff Officer. In 1915 he refused a post as Flag Lieutenant to Sir Robert Arbuthnot in the cruiser *Defence*, thus probably saving his life: *Defence* was blown up at Jutland. Instead, Ramsay commanded first a monitor, and then the destroyer *Broke*. His career then followed a standard path – executive officer of a battleship (*Benbow*), command of a cruiser, appointments as an Instructor at Greenwich and the Imperial Defence College. Command of a battleship (the *Royal Sovereign*) then followed, with promotion to Rear Admiral coming in May, 1935. Ramsay had served for twenty-nine years in the Royal Navy and commanded nearly every type of warship for thriteen of them, including a destroyer, three cruisers and a battleship. After this star-studded career, he then proceeded to shoot himself in somewhere rather more central than the foot. Admiral Sir Roger Backhouse was an old friend and had been Gunnery Officer in *Dreadnought* when Ramsay had served in the ship. When appointed Commander-in-Chief of the Home Fleet, Backhouse immediately asked Ramsay to be his Chief of Staff. It was a disastrous appointment. Backhouse was a workaholic and a one-man band, hopeless at delegating. Ramsay was highly able, often tactless and chafed horribly at the bit when

Backhouse centralized authority more and more on himself, cutting out his Staff. Ramsay accepted the post on 20 August, 1935. Four months later he asked to resign, describing himself as a 'mere cipher'[3]. Backhouse was to die later as a result of 'a serious brain affliction brought on by overwork[4]'. Ramsay killed his career by his resignation. He was offered the post of Senior Naval Officer on the Yangtze, but turned it down, and was placed on the retired list in October, 1938. If Backhouse was at fault in the split with Ramsay he did much to redeem his error by nominating him as Flag Officer in charge of Dover in the event of war, the appointment from which sprang Ramsay's command of the Dunkirk operation, and much more. Ironically, Cunningham became Deputy Chief of Naval Staff to Sir Roger Backhouse as First Sea Lord, on 17 October, 1938. Later on in the war the relationship between Cunningham and Ramsay was to be crucial in ensuring the success of the invasion of Europe, the culmination to two careers which seemed from the start to intertwine. This is the romantic view. A more prosaic one would argue that the Royal Navy was in reality so small that a degree of intermeshing was inevitable, and that it was in practise an enlarged family in which almost everyone knew everyone else. As one example, when Ramsay was Commander of *Benbow* one James E.F. Somerville was Flag Captain in the same ship to Admiral 'Joe' Kelly, the future Admiral Somerville of Force H. In fact Cunningham and Ramsay were quite different. Where Ramsay saw himself as a mere cipher, Cunningham had a different view:

> [Backhouse had] great personal charm, outstanding ability and was a prodigious worker . . . He really had little use for a staff and preferred to do everything, even to the smallest details, himself . . . a fine man with whom to work.[5]

Not everyone would have agreed. It was fine for Cunningham, who hated paperwork and may well have been thrilled to see so much of it done by his senior officer; less fine for Ramsay, who hated nothing that was essential to the success of the service he worshipped, and who would have taken on a battleship full of paper if his job demanded it.

The bare details of Ramsay's career and professional suicide say very little about the man himself, one of the most complex and intriguing figures of the war. Ramsay is unusual in that his private papers reveal an ability to express himself that is uncommon, or seemingly so, for officers of the time. His parents had gone to India when he was twelve, and when they returned five years later he was abroad as a Midshipman. It is always tempting to look back at family life in late Victorian times and advance theories for the behaviour pattern of children brought up then. It is tempting to see such things as being brought up by nannies, or being separated from parents, as crucial factors in forming the adult. Undoubtedly it was, provided it is remembered how normal separation, physical or emotional, from one's family was for an upper-middle-class child. In the early 1900's it was not done to say that one missed one's parents, but Ramsay's early letters sometimes display a pique that is perhaps as near as one could come at that time to admitting unhappiness:

> I have not heard from India for almost 6 weeks and it is too bad of you. Elsie happened to announce to me in an unceremonious way that Sue was engaged to a Captain Garstin. . . . Now I want to know why I have not been informed of it & all the facts. I consider it very bad form for all this to have been going on & myself having been ignorant of the facts.[6]

Another endearing feature of Ramsay's correspondence is his eye for the feminine form. It must be stressed that there is nothing unhealthy in the references in the letters, merely that they display a vigorous enthusiasm for appraising some of the more evident external features of the girls he meets:

> Violet Bullock is such a nice girl & she has grown quite pretty & has an awfully nice figure. She dances most beautifully. She is generally run after by naval officers.[7]

> Thank you very much for your letter which I received yesterday & also for Elsie's photo, which I think was excellent. She is not at all bad looking.[8]

> Tea with Mrs Hyde. Liked her. Very shapely & pretty.[9]

> Not bad show but ugly women.[10]

This type of comment is unusual for a Naval officer of the period. *Britannia*, the Royal Navy and society in general were aggressively masculine, and women tend not to appear at all in diaries, letters or private papers. If they do it is usually in a bawdy or smutty context, or as the enshrined emblem of 'mother' or 'sister'. Ramsay is unique in steering a course between the two. He seemed genuinely to enjoy the company of women, and his professionalism and aggression were underpinned by a deep sensitivity. There was a depth and a capacity for suffering in Ramsay that one suspects may have been shared by at least two of the other commanders covered here, Somerville and Horton, a sensitivity that may have surprised those who worked with them. In Ramsay's case it is best seen at a moment of major crisis. When on a world tour with Jellicoe in the battlecruiser *New Zealand* Ramsay met and fell in love with an Australian girl, Joan Russell. She died of influenza shortly after her engagement to Ramsay, prompting agonized diary entries:

> She was my all in all and my future was built round her. Now I am without an object in life & follow listlessly the path ahead.[11]

> Infinity is so awful.[12]

> I am a weak man, in that I am not strong enough to fight depression & to stand up to the world & life.[13]

Ramsay recovered, and six years later was able to write:

> What I want [for the New Year] is good health, a good wife & a good job.[14]

He was to have all three, marrying Helen Margaret Menzies in 1925.

As a personality, Ramsay was an enigma. In common with very many of his successful fellow officers, he was obsessive about physical exercise, being particularly keen on riding; he may even have suffered heart strain from driving himself too hard physically as a Midshipman. He was also something near to obsessional about dress and clothing, as was Cunningham, and about the appearance of ships. He had obtained a 'secret' formula for paint mix while on *Benbow* that made the vessel the envy of the fleet. He was sharp to the point of savagery when he felt officers or men were 'slack':

> If something isn't done soon the Navy will have sunk so
> deep in sloth that it will never recover except by
> revolutionary means.[15]

He referred to a dismissed steward as 'this mentally deficient idiot'[16], and to another officer, 'I think he is a useless bit of trash as an officer in general'.[17] The fighting admirals of the Second World War were ruthless in the face of incompetence: the joke about Cunningham when he was in command of the destroyer *Scorpion* in the Mediterranean concerned a fellow vessel which heard a bump from alongside where *Scorpion* was moored. 'Don't worry,' an officer said, 'it's only another First Lieutenant getting the chuck from *Scorpion*.' In other respects it would be easy to categorize Ramsay as an old-school martinet, concerned with outmoded concepts of appearance, discipline and tradition. In a War College document dating from 1928 he shows no real awareness of the submarine threat:

> So far as modern technical and tactical development have
> proceeded, no submarine or surface vessel can neutralize
> the action of stronger surface vessels, though the
> submarine can cause a great expenditure of effort.[18]

In this same paper Ramsay presumes that the main threat to trade will be enemy cruisers. It would also be easy to typecast him as the right-wing Admiral, as it would many of his fellows. Comments such as: 'Give an Oriental an inch and he considers you a fool,'[19] and: 'The pilot was an English subject but looked French & spoke indistinctly. He smelt strongly of cheap scent & he babbled incessantly. . . .The new pilot was a real Englishman & an excellent pilot,'[20] are from the same stable of thought as Somerville's continuing references to 'Wops', and his evident severe distaste when he was in command of the Far Eastern fleet that British nurses were 'compelled to carry out most menial tasks' nursing 'Asiatics', and that these same Asiatics were bragging of white women doing this[21]. Cunningham appeared singularly impressed by the right-wing methods of a

Venezuelan President, and anyone searching for left-wing or liberal tendencies among the fighting admiral of the war will be disappointed:

> We also met President Gomez, a fine-looking old man and a strict disciplinarian. Some students who had demonstrated against his régime were at that moment imprisoned at Puerto Cabello and working daily on making roads. This soon cured their discontent.[22]

In the parlance of the late twentieth century, at least one of the great naval commanders of the Second World War was sexist, and all three were racist, yet these labels are wholly misleading in coming to a judgement of these men. They were products of their time and their Empire, which tended, as any Empire has done, to patronize those it rules over: and further examination reveals just how complex Ramsay and his fellow officers were, far more complex than the convenient tag of a traditionalist martinet would suggest.

Firstly, Ramsay was tough and ruthless when the need arose, a feature which above all unites the successful British admirals of the war – Cunningham, Somerville, Vian and Horton – leaving out only Pound and perhaps Fraser. That ruthlessness did not always endear Ramsay to other officers:

> About a month ago I remarked at lunch that I supposed it was recognized that if a ship of the Fleet got hit by a submarine, she could expect no assistance from other ships. The Vice-Admiral said that I was too bloodthirsty and pessimistic for anything, and why should I always be thinking of the worst side of things?[23]

However, if ruthlessness were the only thing that Ramsay had he would not have been the man he was. He combined it with a capacity to relate to people, and with a sense of humour. There were few men who could write to Montgomery:

> On the other hand, I have observed, with some disapproval and not without amusement, that in your messages . . . you have been in the habit of issuing unilateral edicts on matters which require joint agreement,[24]

6 'Cunningham, throughout his career, showed considerable distrust of "gadgets" or anything "new-fangled"'. Cunningham about to sink a microphone.

5 Above: 'Very many successful officers were obsessive about physical exercise.' Tovey on the golf course, an addiction he shared with Horton and Ramsay in particular.

7 'A tough officer to whom no one could dictate' or 'a stooge, compliant to Churchill'? Pound, flanked by U.S. Admirals Stark and King, on board *Prince of Wales*.

8 'P. Vian has been on my mind for some time, owing to his peculiar behaviour. I think he is not quite normal at times.' Ramsay (centre) with Vian on the right.

9 'The capacity to work with others was crucial to both Ramsay's great victories . . .' Ramsay (third from right) with his Staff for the invasion of Europe.

and receive the reply:

> I have your letter of 7th April. . . . It is magnificent! I am
> having it framed!![25]

The capacity to work with others was crucial to both Ramsay's
great victories, at Dunkirk and with Overlord. Both were combined operations, though obviously very different in scale, and
one being almost the exact reverse of the other. Yet here was a
man who left the service because of an outwardly trivial dispute
with his Admiral, and who earlier on in his career had fallen
out very seriously with Admiral Keyes, so seriously that Keyes
was cited as the reason for Ramsay not gaining his DSO in
1918.[26] Written on the papers of this time in longhand is a
comment which appears to have been pencilled in by Ramsay's
widow:

> Reflection 1967. Maybe BHR was too intolerant and
> opinionated at times![27]

Perhaps the rift with Backhouse and the four years of enforced
reflection it brought about are the key to understanding how
Ramsay acquired his proven ability to command a team and
relate with maximum efficiency to those above and below him
in rank. Those four years were not an experience shared by
Admiral Somerville, who, despite a remarkable ability to relate
to all and sundry (and in particular the terror of Anglo-American
naval relations, Admiral 'Ernie' King), fell foul of Dudley Pound,
Churchill and Mountbatten in a way that did not help either his
career or his happiness.

Ramsay's capacity to work harmoniously with others was not
restricted to the top brass. There is a chemistry that operates
between men and their commanding officers, some of which is
explicable through logic, part of which is alchemy and magic.
Ramsay lacked the power of Cunningham and the dramatic
talents of Somerville, but he commanded a deep and abiding
respect from those who knew and worked with him. For many
sailors it is as simple as luck: some admirals were lucky, some
were not. Ramsay was tough, fair and successful. For many of
the seamen he commanded, that was enough:

> In my opinion it is through your sort that the war was
> fought to *win*, and you are a *little man* that I admire, and
> look upon as a fighter and born gentleman.[28]

Ramsay fought single-mindedly to win, but treated his own
men like human beings. He was also highly intelligent, again
something of a challenge to the salty-old-sea-dog image, and
again something that links him to others, most notably Somerville, Horton, Phillips and Fraser. Oddly, it was Cunningham
who seems to have had the least intellectual grip, and perhaps
even a 'sluggish brain'[29]. Scores at *Britannia* suggest that Cunningham was not stupid, but it seems he never refined his
ability, and throughout his life he retained an element of
intellectual indolence. Ramsay's intelligence was of a particular
type:

> Ramsay had one of those comparatively rare brains,
> capable of grasping and retaining an extraordinary
> knowledge and appreciation of detail without ever losing
> sight of the overall picture.[30]

His intelligence distanced him to an extent, a point made by a
junior officer who served with him:

> He was very charming and very able. He was not easy to
> get to know, and did not talk to anyone except his equals
> about operations. His brain was much too big for me.[31]

His ruthlessness was for much of the time a manifestation of an
inability to compromise on standards. It never stopped him
from seeing that the men who manned the Royal Navy were as
valuable as the ships. When in 1923 he commanded the old
cruiser *Weymouth* for the trooping trip to Hong Kong he
produced five recommendations for improved conditions
necessary if a Far Eastern Fleet were to become an effective
reality: ships designed to suit the climate (for an Empire fleet
the Royal Navy was far too long in realizing the need for air-
conditioning on board ships); altered routines (it was Ramsay
who set the pattern for the fleet to sling hammocks *after* the
evening meal instead of before it, a simple change that brought

considerable benefits in comfort and space); an end to over-crowding; a suitable tropical uniform, and barracks built in or on the hills so that men could recuperate. Ramsay may not have suffered fools, but at the same time was 'kind, considerate and appreciative'[32]. As for his being old-fashioned:

> He had a blend in service matters between a very modern technical and military outlook on the one hand, and the real old navy as regards smartness and internal organization on the other.[33]

His broad-mindedness is illustrated by one of his own diary entries: 'To stick to an opinion is the privilege of fools.'[34] But there were fools enough in the Navy:

> My faults are that I can't sit still & see things done in an antiquated and unprogressive manner & I must put my word in & it is very difficult to do this without being a little firm and perhaps unpleasant . . . the V.A. [Vice-Admiral] resents that I should have any ideas, especially modern ones, on any subject but signals.[35]

Ramsay showed considerable prescience when it came to the Washington Conference, arguing forcibly that Britain was spending too much time and money on the expensive 8" cruisers: 'It is numbers that count with cruisers.'[36] In the event the high-decked, three-funnel 'County' class cruisers, though strikingly beautiful, were outclassed by other designs, and the brunt of the war was borne by the more numerous and smaller cruisers such as the River Plate's *Ajax* and *Achilles*. Ramsay also took the air threat seriously and in 1933 was arguing strongly for what we would now call escort carriers to attend all convoys[37]. Later he argued for torpedoes to be banished from battleships and cruisers, and a reduction of the surface gun armament on destroyers, making them torpedo-carrying vehicles.

In 1925 he records a speaker putting his success down to 'the working of fear on imagination', and adds, 'I think that this indicates very clearly my own case'.[38] He was an outwardly confident, spruce and dynamic figure who was capable of intense depression. Sensitivity, depression and ruthless determination were three points on the triangle of Ramsay's personality. Acting together they produced a driving energy that provoked conflict with senior officers, and a tactlessness that offended a number of them. When war came the energy was poured into the fight against Germany and the edge taken off his relationships with senior officers. It is to the credit of the Royal Navy that Ramsay's sometimes tactless intensity did not stop him climbing the career ladder until he threw himself off it. A devotion to the Royal Navy and a concern for its traditional interest in appearance and ceremonial were coupled with a willingness to take on board any idea that did things better. A capacity to become infuriated with higher authority became in the war years coupled with an ability to work with all and sundry without even the luxury of final authority. Highly intelligent and reserved, at the same time he showed a great fondness for socializing and parties, one thing at least he did not share with Cunningham.

This mass of well-controlled contradictions was appointed Vice Admiral, Dover, in October, 1939. Germany invaded the Low Countries on 10 May, 1940, prompting a suggestion from Dudley Pound to Admiral Sir R.P. Ernle-Erle-Drax, Commander-in-Chief Nore, that Dover revert to the Nore command. Drax said he had full faith in Ramsay, and that anyway Chatham was too far away to exercise control in the Channel and the man on the spot needed the power to take decisions. It was fortunate he resisted Pound. The basic details of the evacuation of Dunkirk, Operation Dynamo, are well known. In confusion reminiscent of the Norway campaign, the Admiralty were still thinking of supporting troops on the Continent on 19 May, 1940, at the same time as considering the evacuation of 45,000 other troops. Ramsay appears to have been one of the few senior officers who could see what was coming and had an accurate idea of the likely scale of the evacuation. His destroyers evacuated Boulogne at the same time as the Admiralty ordered them to land troops at Calais. Ramsay brought home 4,368 men from Boulogne and 1,000 men from Calais, and, left to his own devices, would in all probability have rescued the greater part of the Calais garrison. He did all this at the same time as being faced with the massive task at Dunkirk.

The task was unprecedented. He was helped by the fact that

transport had been gathered for the prospect of a Dutch evacuation, but hampered by the fact that there was no effective Combined Operations staff or system and no experience of an instant mass evacuation. Ramsay succeeded for a variety of reasons. Firstly, he had the ability to select an excellent staff who showed both initiative and resourcefulness. He was especially fortunate in Captain W.G. Tennant, who was the senior naval officer at Dunkirk for the evacuation, and who later was captain of *Repulse* when it was sunk by the Japanese with *Prince of Wales*. Tennant revealed one of Ramsay's secrets: 'All of us with a job to do felt that we were trusted.'[39] Tennant sent signals to Ramsay telling him what he was going to do, not asking for permission to do it, and Ramsay showed himself a superb delegater. Furthermore, he had an ability which in an operation such as Dunkirk was crucial, that of being able to improvise and let his subordinates do likewise. Ramsay was willing to take a risk, another of the features which appear to have been essential for success in the Second World War. He admitted as much himself in his own description to the Admiralty of the evacuation:

> The initial problem called for a maximum effort over a limited period, regardless of the future; accordingly all resources in the way of small boats were thrown on the beaches before adequate provision had been made for their maintenance off the coast, relief of the personnel and the provision of large beach parties.[40]

The ruthlessness mentioned above is nowhere better illustrated than in the decision to use small boats for the evacuation. For all the glamour that has surrounded their use, to send them in without support against the most professional army and air force in Europe could – and perhaps should – have resulted in a true slaughter of the innocents. It was not a slaughter that would have impaired the war effort, whereas a slaughter of the professionals (the destroyers) would have done so, and the troops were essential. Ramsay took the risk and won. He had that most elusive quality of luck: something like two-thirds of the troops were evacuated by non-naval transport.

Ramsay also had another very traditional virtue: courage. It took courage to back his subordinates to give them a free hand;

courage to chance everything on one big throw before proper provision had been made; courage for a professional sailor to send in the small boats with their amateur crews, when the success of the operation and the commander's future in the Royal Navy hinged on them doing a professional job.

Dynamo also succeeded because it went on for so long, when a cautious commander might have ended it much earlier. The fact that the officers and personnel involved sustained their efforts beyond all reasonable levels is also down in part to Ramsay's leadership. He himself worked all hours unrelentingly and uncomplainingly, showing no sign of strain to those around him. The closed world of naval relationships covered in this book is shown by the fact that another Admiral on the retired list, James Somerville, volunteered to relieve Ramsay for the few hours in the day when he slept. Somerville's contribution to Operation Dynamo has possibly been underestimated. Without his help Ramsay's grip on events must have been threatened; Somerville managed that most difficult of things, taking over the running of an unplanned and frantic operation at odd hours without ever threatening the authority of the commander or allowing any break in the pattern and style of orders to be seen. It was a masterly performance. The early decision to move evacuation from the port to the beaches of Dunkirk, though obvious with hindsight, was less so at the time and required courage to take. As with the convoy system, concentrating the evacuation in the port concentrated the target for the enemy, but also concentrated the defences, and to spread a whole hotch-potch of vessels out along a coastline in full view of U-boat, aircraft, E-boat and even tank gun was a decision of no mean tenor.

Operation Dynamo ended officially at 2.23 pm on Tuesday, 4 June 1940. 338,226 troops had been rescued; the Admiralty initially had hoped to get out 45,000. Forty-one destroyers took part; six were sunk, fourteen damaged by bombs and twelve damaged by collision. They alone rescued 96,197 troops, though one does wonder how people had the time to be quite so precise in the official figures. It was a rare example of accident putting the right man in the right place at the right time. Ramsay had a mind capable of matching the broad sweep with the tiny detail, essential in someone planning so hasty and unconventional an operation. He was outwardly unflappable and capable of finding that extra gear to see himself through a time of intense stress. He trusted his subordinates and chose them well, even more vital than normal in an operation where subordinates were required to take twenty or thirty decisions an hour with no command back-up and no previous experience. He was determined enough to extend the operation beyond its initial target, flexible enough to let it develop in the light of changing circumstances. Finally, he was not thrown out or outwardly depressed by the news of losses and was capable of immense hard work and optimism. He actively enjoyed the responsibility, perhaps again a result of four years of domestic existence cut off from mainstream Navy life:

He seemed utterly tireless and completely unafraid of the responsibilities thrust on him.[40]

He was awarded the KCB and was cheered on cinema screens when his picture was shown, an irony for a man who never sought the limelight and had no interest in any acclaim other than that of his beloved service. Operation Dynamo was a victory in defeat, but the victory part of the equation was a victory for *ad hoc* planning, something Ramsay himself pointed out:

We can always count on glorious deeds, but less often on good direction and management. This may sound as self-praise, but you know that I count little for myself and think solely of the wider aspect of the job to be gained.[41]

4 Oran and Taranto

Chronology of Events

1940

3 July. British Force H under Admiral Somerville opens fire on and largely destroys French warships based at Mers el Kebir.

6 July. Air attack on Mers el Kebir destroys more French vessels.

7 July. Admiral Cunningham negotiates peaceful disarming of French vessels in Alexandria.

9 July. Battle of Calabria. Admiral Cunningham drives off superior Italian battlefleet, scoring hit on *Guilio Cesare*.

25 September. Attempt by General de Gaulle to occupy Dakar called off; British battleship *Resolution* torpedoed by French submarine *Beveziers* and severely damaged.

23 October. Panzerschiffe Admiral Scheer sets sail on commerce raiding cruise.

5 November. Admiral Scheer sinks armed merchant cruiser *Jervis Bay*, which nevertheless manages to save most of convoy by its action.

11/12 November. Admiral Cunningham attacks Italian naval base at Taranto by air: three battleships sunk at anchor (two later raised).

27 November. Force H under Admiral Somerville in action with Italian heavy units off Cape Spartivento.

7 December. German heavy cruiser *Admiral Hipper* sets sail on commerce raiding cruise.

25 December. Admiral Hipper opens fire on convoy in shipping lane to Sierra Leone; strong escort and engine room failure cause *Hipper* to break off action.

27 December. Admiral Hipper puts into Brest.

31 December. Largest gathering of German ships in southern
   hemisphere of whole war: *Admiral Scheer* (heavy cruiser);
   Thor (commerce raider); two tankers, two supply ships,
   and British refrigerated cargo prize vessel. Six German
   auxiliary cruisers sink 54 ships in 1940, totalling 376,000
   tons.

Narvik, Dunkirk and the bombardment of the French fleet at
Mers el Kebir (Oran) was a desperate trilogy for the Royal Navy,
with none of these engagements envisaged or planned for in the
inter-war years. In command of the attack on the French fleet
was Admiral James Somerville.

Somerville's father had made money sheep farming in New
Zealand and came back to rescue a Somerset estate from its
mortgages. James Somerville was born on 17 July, 1882, joining
HMS *Britannia* in January, 1987. One of his term mates was
Andrew Cunningham, and the two men maintained a close
friendship throughout their lives. As with so many of the figures
covered in this work, Somerville was a mass of contrasts.
Described when young as 'under-sized' and 'shy'[1], he was to
become one of the Navy's greatest extroverts, with a fine sense
of the dramatic and a flair for knowing what would be noticed.
The man whose biographer described him as 'shy and diffident
in unfamiliar company . . . displaying a rather solitary nature
. . .'[2] was also the same man who in a BBC broadcast in 1940
could announce in a loud aside: 'Good God! They've given me
water!'[3] He was also the author of an immense number of
signals that have gone down in history. One example was when
Force H received a signal from the Flag Officer Gibraltar:

   Small round object sighted 180 degrees 5 miles from
   Europa Point. Probably mine.

Somerville's reply was:

   Certainly not mine.[4]

Somerville was unusual in that he chose to specialize as a
torpedo officer, which at that time covered all matters electrical.
The result was that 'wireless telegraphy' and, later on, radar

came his way. This confirms the point made in an earlier chapter that gunnery was not the magic path to promotion it has sometimes been thought to be. Ramsay and his specialization in Signals was one example of a different path, and Fraser and Max Horton were both fascinated by the technical side of the Navy. The admirals discussed in this work suggest that a new breed was in evidence by 1939, a breed which welcomed the more technical side of service life, and saw no shame in being involved with it. Somerville in particular showed a huge excitement when faced with technological advance. His classmate and friend, Cunningham, was certainly not in this bracket and throughout his career showed considerable distrust of 'gadgets', or indeed anything 'new-fangled'.

In the First World War Somerville saw service in the Dardanelles as Fleet Wireless Telegraphy Officer, for which he won the DSO. He then moved with the same Admiral de Robeck to the Grand Fleet and was later appointed Experimental Commander of the Signal School at Portsmouth. He then faced, as Ramsay was about to do, the major hurdle – Executive Officer and Second-in-Command of a battleship (*Ajax*) in the Mediterranean Fleet. Around this time in his career the change to the extrovert appears to have happened. The major influence on this change was Admiral 'Joe' Kelly. Somerville had first met John Kelly when, as a Midshipman, he had joined the cruiser *Royal Arthur*, and Kelly, as the officer of the watch, had met Somerville and predicted, 'He won't last long!'[5] They met again on the cruiser *Sutlej* on the China Station in 1904, when Kelly was Executive Officer, and Kelly asked for Somerville as his Flag Officer in the battleship *Benbow* – the same ship in which Ramsay was making such a good name for himself as Executive Officer. The closed world of the Navy is again apparent, and the extent to which a form of patronage was still possible. Later on, in 1931, Kelly was appointed Commander-in-Chief, Home Fleet, in the aftermath of the Invergordon Mutiny. He immediately selected Somerville as one of the two senior captains responsible for visiting every ship in the Fleet to investigate the problems which had led to the mutiny and to listen to the men.

Kelly was a flamboyant commander and Somerville learnt from him: 'Many of the characteristics he showed to the world, the tricks of leadership, unorthodox behaviour and little eccentricities, were largely an act put on deliberately.'[6]

Somerville was not universally popular. Some of those around him saw a hypocrisy in his 'put-on' manner, others considered him a 'vulgar little man', or guilty of an 'ungentlemanly taste in humour'[7]. Certainly his humour, at least in its most public form, tended to centre round balls and bowels, as in the signal after the successful bombardment of Sabang:

We caught the Nips with their heads down and their kimonos up.[8]

Or in one of the many signals exchanged between Cunningham and Somerville; in this instance when *Nelson* had been torpedoed after a successful convoy operation. Cunningham signalled:

I hope that these my congratulations will compensate for a slap in the belly with a wet fish.

Somerville replied:

Thank you. At my age kicks below the belt have little significance.[9]

Yet here again this aspect of Somerville's personality, and his reputed use of foul language, have to be placed in context. Admiral Cunningham's favourite expression was 'It's too velvet-arsed and Rolls Royce for me!' and his language was explosive. The lavatory humour that was common among even senior officers is often described euphemistically in biographies from an earlier age of decorum as 'schoolboyish', and such humour was frequently a product of all-male institutions (and professions) at the time. Partly this humour and strong language was the result of:

A conscious urge to be the centre of the stage and to act the unorthodox Admiral who was talked about at all levels.[10]

It was also compounded of many other features. It was a product of a closed and often all-male service. It was a method of relieving tension, particularly so in the case of Cunningham and

Somerville. It was a way of relating to the lower-deck, whose standards in these matters were less than middle class, though if not carefully handled it could lose the respect of the men, who had their own ideas as to how officers should behave. In its cruder forms it was a testing agency, a rough and ready push in the chest to see if the victim would pick himself up and come out fighting. Many of the successful British Admirals of the war were initially antagonistic to those they met, accused of being bullies and willing to dismiss people who did not stand up to them (and sometimes to dismiss those who did). It has already been mentioned as a feature of Cunningham's commands, and it was certainly a feature associated with Horton, Vian, Somerville and Ramsay, though bad language was alien to the last-named. Somerville hated pomp and slowness in those he met. He was intolerant of anyone whose mind did not work as fast as his:

I'm so damned impatient and can't bear delays.[11]

Like his friend Ramsay, Somerville drove himself too hard physically. He nearly died from illness as a midshipman and was seriously ill again in 1924, when he came home from *Benbow* and served for two years as Director of the Admiralty Signal Division. Ramsay, Cunningham and Horton were golf fanatics; Somerville's most obvious physical indulgence – almost an obsession – was the small boat that he rowed round ships in his command, often in the early hours of the morning. He was not above boarding the ships in his command on these jaunts:

But he was an enormously human person. He had a dinghy, which he used to take out into Kilindini Harbour at a very early hour in the morning, dressed in nothing but a pair of shorts. He would come alongside an unsuspecting ship and come aboard, presumably to test security. It is said that, on one occasion, the Quartermaster asked who he was, and when James said 'the Commander-in-Chief', the QM replied 'And I'm f*****g Churchill!!'[12]

However, it was his lungs that were to see him invalided out of the Navy in bizarre circumstances. He was appointed Vice

Admiral in September, 1937, and to command of the East Indies Station in 1938. He became ill in the Spring of 1938, overdid it and got active TB. The illness had gone by the time he returned home and it is almost certain that the decision to invalid him out was a wholly mistaken, or at least unnecessary, one. He was given the Order of the Bath and placed on the retired list on 31 July, 1939. Opinions differ as to how much this decision hurt. There is no doubt that Ramsay deeply resented being on the retired list and saw his restoration to the active list as one of the greatest honours in his career. Somerville, on the other hand, appear to have been far less interested in his reinstatement, though fired with apoplexy over the medical service's diagnosis of his case:

> I did not wish to be restored [to the active list] if this
> would affect the promotion of other officers on the flag
> list.[13]

However, his family believe his reinstatement did matter to him greatly.

Somerville made a major contribution to the development of naval radar in the inter-war years and was also besotted with flying. He took every opportunity to go up in aircraft and was one of the very few Admirals in the Second World War who could claim to have flown and acted as a wireless operator in an Osprey aircraft whilst Rear Admiral of Destroyers in the Meditteranean, a post which he took over from Cunningham. Somerville shared many things with Cunningham – intense loyalty to the Navy, a burning desire to get at the enemy, a hatred of cant and humbug, use of colourful language and a dislike of paperwork. In his professional relationships he was also a figure of extremes. Somerville followed Cunningham yet again to Washington as British Liaison Officer, dealing with the often impossible Admiral 'Ernie' King:

> Although Somerville's staff sometimes found his peculiar
> brand of bawdy humour, and his repartee heavily laced
> with obscenities, tedious and overdone, he was the most
> successful of all British admirals in handling 'Ernie' King.[14]

Yet this was the same man who fell foul of both Churchill and, possibly, Admiral Tom Phillips, when the latter was Vice Chief of Naval Staff, and who had an even more serious clash of personalities with Mountbatten when the latter was appointed Supreme Commander of South-East Asia. One reason is not hard to see. It takes a very powerful personality to be a true fighting Admiral, and wherever there is power there is also the potential for disruption. It could be pointed out that Cunningham had many fewer such clashes in his most distinguished career, but Cunningham was in the right place at the right time and won two smashing victories in quick succession at Taranto and Matapan. Such victories gave Cunningham tremendous power: he was too much the famous victor to be removed from office with any degree of ease. This was a power that Somerville was denied through no fault of his own. From very early on in the war Cunningham made himself indispensable: Somerville was put in a position where he was very nearly dispensed with.

His public war started, as we have seen, when he helped out Admiral Ramsay in the Dunkirk operation. Roughly a month after being involved in that operation he was sent to command *Ark Royal, Hood, Valiant* and *Resolution* in the Mediterranean. This force, later to become known as Force H, was given from the outset a horrendous task:

> [To] secure the transfer, surrender, or destruction of the French warships at Oran and Mers el Kebir, so as to ensure that these ships should not fall into German or Italian hands.[15]

Somerville, who had taken up his sea-going command with huge enthusiasm, was appalled at the task, and rightly so. The French had until this moment been allies, fighting alongside the British in the Mediterranean. Cooped up in harbour, the French vessels were sitting ducks. Somerville, and Cunningham who was entrusted with the same mission at the other end of the Mediterranean, viewed the prospect of opening fire on their erstwhile allies with total repugnance.

The outcome is well known. Cunningham persuaded his portion of the French fleet at Alexandria to submit to him, but Somerville was forced to open fire in the face of the recalcitrant French Admiral Gensoul. To add insult to injury, Somerville failed to damage the battlecruiser *Strasbourg*, which escaped, with five destroyers, and a second air attack had to be launched against the rump of the French fleet a few days later. 1,147 Frenchmen died in the bombardment; one battleship (*Bretagne*) was sunk; one battleship heavily damaged (*Provence*); a battle-cruiser (*Dunkerque*) heavily damaged. A further 150 men lost their lives in the air attack on 6 July.

Why was Somerville forced to open fire, and why did he allow a vital French capital ship to escape? It is tempting to compare Somerville and Cunningham. The latter persuaded his portion of the French fleet to disarm without having to bombard them, largely by sending his men round the French ships and by word of mouth and placards displayed in boats appealing direct to the officers and men under the French Admiral's command. Somerville worked through an intermediary rather than visiting Admiral Gensoul himself, and he mined the harbour to prevent the escape of the French ships before negotiations were even started – in one sense a wise precaution, in another an inflammatory act. Certainly his friend Cunningham criticized him after the war:

> About Oran I always thought that James Somerville's great error was in sending Holland [Captain C. S. Holland of the carrier *Ark Royal*] alone. I have always held that had he gone himself with Holland as interpreter only he would have brought Gensoul to reason. It took a very wide-awake man to resist James's blandishments.[16]

However, the unpublished memoirs of Admiral (later Admiral of the Fleet) Sir Algernon Willis claim that the suggestion of undermining the French Admiral Godfroy through his captains came from Willis rather than from Cunningham.[17] Cunningham's autobiography says that 'we' decided on this ruse, though it does not specify who 'we' consisted of, and Cunningham has tended to be given the credit.

Criticism of Somerville's action is largely unfounded. Defences at Oran meant that he would have been an utter fool to bring his ships in closer, and an utter fool to trust himself to the dubious mercies of Oran and Admiral Gensoul when this meant leaving his ships without their commander opposite a strong naval base and force of ships, significantly superior to the

British force. For this same reason it was essential that Somerville mine the entrances to Oran in advance. It could not have helped his cause to suggest that the British did not mean business, and the mining was necessary to *protect* his own force, regardless of the need to pen in the French. Furthermore, Admiral Gensoul was twice the man in malice and treachery of the Admiral Godfroy whom Cunningham faced in Alexandria. It was a situation in which nobody could win. Somerville took the only course open to him. His failure did not lie in the fact that he had to open fire – with Gensoul at the helm of the French fleet an archangel would have been on a lost cause – but rather in the escape of the *Strasbourg*. This was a simple enough mistake: the vessel had been reported by aircraft as being on the move, but was ignored because there had been too many false warnings. Somerville's force had withdrawn to seaward because of increasingly accurate fire from French shore batteries, and so was unable to intercept the French battleship. This escape, Somerville's only real error, was in part explained by himself:

> We all feel thoroughly dirty and ashamed. . . . But I feel I
> shall be blamed for bungling the job and I think I did. But
> to you I don't mind confessing that I was half-hearted and
> you can't win an action that way.[18]

The initial attack had drained Somerville; he had little heart for the aftermath.

The attack on Oran was a distasteful episode and it sowed the seeds of later trouble for Somerville. Throughout the operation he had been pestered by bombastic signals from the Admiralty, who insisted after Oran in diverting resources against the French in a manner that Somerville considered diversionary and unwise. He objected to Admiralty policy and interference and was thus seen as troublesome and as lacking the necessary offensive spirit. He bitterly resented being ordered to open fire, and, as a contemporary commented:

> If only they had given Somerville more time he might have
> achieved a comparable result at Oran [to the peaceful
> disarming at Alexandria].[19]

The Admiralty cornered and pressurized Somerville in a way that reduced his room for manoeuvre and hampered his ability to conduct the operation his own way. Later events were to confirm the inaccurate impression of a lack of offensive spirit. Somerville was a stickler for training (something he shared with Horton and Ramsay). Force H was a hastily-gathered fleet, containing many ships over twenty years old. It is a recipe for disaster for any force to lack training. When it was clear that much of Force H's time would be spent shepherding random collections of naval and merchant shipping through the Mediterranean under continual threat of Italian air attack or a breakout of vastly superior Italian forces, it was clear that its need to act as a united force was more pressing than ever. Instead of this, a series of signals from the Admiralty pressed Somerville into offensive action before either he or his ships were ready, including suggestions that *Ark Royal's* aircraft should attack Taranto or engage in action against Naples. Somerville restricted himself to convoying activities and successful attacks against Cagliari airfield. The phrase 'restricted himself' should not be taken as a criticism of Force H: convoy escort was its major triumph and one of Somerville's greatest achievements. After Dunkirk (Somerville was on the last boat out of Calais), and as an aviator himself, he was well aware of the strength of air power, far more so than the Admiralty at that time or Cunningham at the far end of the Mediterranean, and he was simply not prepared to risk *Ark Royal* for a possible minor, morale-boosting victory. Vessels under his command rarely needed their morale boosted: morale elsewhere was not a sufficient reason for him to risk losing *Ark Royal*.

He made two other mistakes. He opposed the assault on Dakar, an operation which was a predictable failure and merely alienated the French even more, but he was then in the position of having been proved right at the wrong time, a failure compounded by his support of Admiral Sir Dudley North, who lost his post when French six warships were allowed to reach Dakar. The Dudley North affair gave rise to a controversy that lasted for many years and was eventually resolved in favour of North, but at the time Somerville was backing a losing horse. He even attempted to ride it. North had been flag officer commanding at Gibraltar. Somerville wrote formally to the Admiralty stating that it was his opinion that the Admiral commanding Force H was responsible for intercepting vessels trying to break out of the western Mediterranean, and that therefore he, not North, was responsible for any failure. He added insult to injury by pointing out that, while he had brought his flagship to full steam when news of the French vessels' approach was reported, he had not and would not have taken any further action because Admiralty signals had suggested they knew about the force and wanted it left alone.[20] This behaviour was honourable, and unwise: it may have been that Somerville only retained his position because he and Force H were familiar figures at home, too familiar for Somerville to be made a convenient scapegoat. He was aware of his enemies at the Admiralty, and in particular considered them to be Churchill and Rear Admiral Tom Phillips, Vice-Chief of Naval Staff.

This hostility came to a head with the Battle of Cape Spartivento. It was late November, 1940, and Force H was entrusted with the task of covering a convoy of three large merchant vessels from the Straits of Gibraltar to Malta, together with the cruisers *Manchester* and *Southampton* carrying between them 1,400 troops. When fully assembled, Somerville had under his command the battlecruiser *Renown*, the old battleship *Ramillies* (restricted to twenty knots), the aircraft carrier *Ark Royal*, and five 6" gun cruisers. Of these only one, *Sheffield*, was fighting fit. Two others, *Berwick* and *Newcastle*, had machinery problems, while the other two had problems of a different nature – 1,400 troops on board. Opposed to these was an Italian force of two battleships, *Vittorio Veneto* and *Giulio Cesare*, the former a new 15" gun vessel, the latter a fully-modernized vessel, and six 8" gun cruisers. In speed, weight of broadside and mechanical reliability the Italian force far outstripped the British. When the two forces met, the Italian cruisers fired with unusual accuracy against the British, and the British launched a Swordfish attack against the Italians, but after inconclusive skirmishing the Italian force turned away. Somerville refused to chase the Italians and rejoined his convoy which reached its destination successfully.

Force H returned to Gibraltar to find bands playing and cheering sailors welcoming its return and on the following day news came that a Board of Enquiry headed by Admiral of the Fleet the Earl of Cork and Orrery was on its way to Gibraltar to enquire into Somerville's conduct of the action, with only Somerville's signalled summary of events to go on. This was an almost unheard-of action, and with a lesser leader it could have had a disastrous effect on the morale of the whole force. It was clear that Churchill wanted Somerville replaced because of his 'cowardice'.[21] As it was the Court of Enquiry cleared Somerville completely, pointing out that he did exactly the job he was entrusted with, and that the safe arrival of the convoy had been made the major aim for Force H in Somerville's orders. Somerville did not pull his punches when reporting the episode to Cunningham:

I believe he [Cork] considered the whole thing [the Enquiry] a bloody disgrace.[22]

and summed up the operation himself quite accurately:

But the facts which emerged were that I had fought an action with a superior enemy force and driven him off to the very approaches of his defended base.[23]

Despite this, the Admiralty still stated that Somerville had been 'over-influenced by his anxiety for the security of the convoy'[24] and that he could have pursued the Italian force for longer. This was and is hogwash. There was every likelihood that the Italians could have been leading him into a trap, or away from another force waiting to intercept the convoy. His orders and his instinct made Somerville treat the convoy as the main priority, and while a glory-boy chase after the Italian fleet might have satisfied the Admiralty if it had been a success, it would also have given them Somerville's head on a plate had he set off after the Italians and delivered up the convoy to the enemy. Perhaps of more concern to Somerville was the loss of life that would have resulted. A further point not made even by his biographer concerns the nature of Somerville's fleet. *Renown* was a battle-cruiser, with hopelessly inadequate armour for a battle against capital ships. The Admiralty proved this point themselves when they ordered *Renown* not to engage *Bismarck* at a later date. The other capital ship, *Ramillies*, was a First World War design whose armour against aerial attack or plunging fire was almost as hopeless as *Renown's*, and considerably less strong even than that of *Hood*, which fell prey to 15" gunfire. Somerville showed immense courage in pressing on to meet the Italians in the first stages of Spartivento. Had he kept on after the Italians he would have been merely foolhardy.

Somerville won his battle with the Admiralty, but the price was increased bitterness on his part towards the Admiralty, and Churchill and Tom Phillips in particular. There is an irony in Somerville's distrust of Admiralty politicking. While he could write: 'I reckon it is time the old Navy was purged of politics & honest men left to ply their trade without interference,'[25] he and his friend Cunningham were seen in some quarters as a tight and exclusive coterie whose grip on the reins of power was not brought to an end until the promotion of Admiral Fraser. Cunningham, Tovey, Horton, Leach and Holland were certainly drawn from a blood-and-guts school of naval officering, very much in the Beatty tradition, but Somerville's technical knowledge distinguishes him from this group and makes him a crucial link between the old and the new Navy. The tragedy was, as the above comment suggests, that he was a relative innocent abroad when it came to political intrigue. Politics was an inevitable companion of high command, as the history of all navies makes very clear. There is an element of naivety in any man who thinks a leading Admiral in wartime can be left to ply his trade without interference. Yet in personal contact Somerville was irresistable, and his weakness, if indeed it was one, lay solely in his impatience with office politics. Without a great victory to back him up, it put him at a disadvantage with Churchill and Pound, and it was to lead to his dispute with Mountbatten.

In January, 1941, the Admiralty actually sent out Somerville's recall, probably in response to his continued criticism of their French policy, but then changed their minds. A signal was sent instructing that a letter addressed to Somerville be returned unopened. The letter, which was not actually addressed to Somerville, was returned unopened, after Somerville had allowed himself the luxury of a teasing signal.[26] Pound's account of this episode, in a letter to Cunningham, is revealing:

You will have seen that an enquiry is to be held into the conduct of the operation to the south of Sardinia. I felt like a pricked balloon when I read FOH [Flag Officer, Force H's] signal saying he had given up the chase and was going to the convoy. However, there may be some reason we do not know of. As a matter of fact we have not been very satisfied with James Somerville's outlook and a letter had actually been approved telling him that the force for the Oran business had to be collected in a hurry, and a Flag Officer of experience, who was immediately available in London, selected, even though he was on the Retired List, but that now that an Active Service Officer was available he was to be relived. When we got news that he was chasing the Italians we naturally had to hold the letter up.[27]

Pound's timing and Somerville's account do not quite tie up, but either way the attitude of the Admiralty to Somerville is clear, and the pressure (and hurt) this put on him cannot be underestimated.

On 9 February, 1941, he put himself back in favour with Churchill at least by bombarding Genoa, an extremely risky operation which at one time led to Force H passing a far superior Italian force, at night, a bare fifty miles apart. Churchill's signal had a sting in its tail:

I congratulate you on the success of the enterprise against Genoa which I was glad to see you proposed yourself.[28]

In return Somerville never lost his distrust of Churchill, and wrote to Cunningham in June, 1941:

Important decisions are not usually relegated to the middle watch amidst the aroma of very old brandy and expensive cigars. I speak with some acidity because I've seen it all happening.[29]

Whatever the Admiralty may have thought, Somerville's record while in charge of Force H was exemplary. He welded it into a coherent entity that showed above all a tremendous loyalty to its commander, even after it became known that his conduct was to be examined by an Admiralty Board of Enquiry. That same force performed its job of guardian of the Straits and shepherder of convoys with immaculate precision, taking on the enemy when occasion allowed and never losing sight of its main objectives. Force H could well have been a sacrificial lamb, destined for the same altar on which Admiral Dudley North was sacrificed, and which ironically would later see the death of Admiral Tom Phillips: the altar was Churchill's restless desire for offensive action at all and any cost. It is to Somerville's great credit that his lamb never went to the slaughter: instead, it killed the *Bismarck*.

It is interesting to compare Somerville with his classmate Cunningham. As has been seen, the two were contemporaries and close friends, but their careers followed different paths. A few days before Somerville's action of Cape Spartivento Cunningham had achieved lasting fame with his attack on the Italian naval base at Taranto. The two actions reflect the relative combat success of both commanders, but not their respective worth and merit. In many respects Somerville was the greater man of the two – and this is not to belittle the magnificence of Cunningham.

A. B. Cunningham was born on 7 January, 1883. Both grandparents were Scottish, and in 1904 Cunningham's father moved from Dublin, where Cunningham was born, to be Professor of Anatomy at Edinburgh University. Andrew started his education at Edinburgh Academy, but when it was decided he should join the Royal Navy he was sent to Stubbington House Preparatory School, the same school which Ramsay attended. At *Britannia* he passed out eleventh of sixty-five, and with a reputation as a fighter. He opted out of team games as far as possible 'because there were many others in my term so much better than myself'[30], but became an excellent and keen sailor. In common with so many of his contemporaries, he came under fire when young, this time as a member of the Naval Brigade in the South African War in 1900. One of the most important steps in his career came in January, 1911, when he was appointed to command *Scorpion*, a three-month-old coal-burning destroyer. He went through the Dardanelles campaign with *Scorpion*, and various features of his command style became apparent at that time. He was ruthless in disposing of First Lieutenants who did not come up to his standard and acquired a reputation as a very hard taskmaster. He showed a total lack of fear and a burning desire to get at the enemy. Something of his style can be gauged from the following exchange, reported by Cunningham when *Scorpion* had been hit and was on fire:

The stoker petty officer in charge of the fire party arrived on the bridge and informed me that the mess deck was on fire, to which I coldly replied, 'Then put it out'.[31]

Destroyer service, and the Mediterranean, were two loves that Cunningham never lost. Both were to prove the major testing ground for the Admirals of the Second World War. After *Scorpion* Cunningham stayed with destroyers, joined the Dover Patrol, and was chosen for the third attempt to block Ostend, an attempt which in the event was called off. He was made Captain on 1 January, 1920, an early promotion. After various postings, including one as Flag Officer on the America and West Indies station, he took command of the battleship *Rodney* on 21 December, 1929, leaving it in 1930 to become Commodore of the Royal Naval Barracks at Chatham in July, 1930. In between this and *Rodney* he went into hospital for the second time 'to have his insides sorted out'. He became a Rear Admiral in 1932, and Rear Admiral (Destroyers) in the Mediterranean Fleet in 1934. Admiral Vian was under his command as officer in command of the 19th Destroyer Flotilla, based at Malta, and James Somerville was to succeed him as Rear Admiral (D) for the Mediterranean. On 17 October, 1938, Cunningham succeeded where Ramsay had failed, and became Deputy Chief of Naval Staff to Sir Roger Backhouse, the First Sea Lord. Cunningham noted the weaknesses in Backhouse that drove Ramsay into desperation, but reacted to them differently, as the quotation from him on Backhouse given in Chapter 3 shows.

Cunningham received the command which made him famous when Dudley Pound was offered the post of First Sea Lord in succession to Backhouse, who was terminally ill. Pound's post of Commander-in-Chief Mediterranean went to Cunningham, while Cunningham's job as Deputy Chief of Naval Staff went to Tom Phillips. It was in this post that Cunningham won his two great victories, Taranto and Matapan. Before considering Taranto, it is perhaps worth looking at Cunningham as he appeared before the two battles that were to earn him undying fame. He was an almost 'overpowering personality':

One felt at once that he could be the master of every situation. He was someone one would obey instantly, and at first meeting one would stand in awe.[32]

His aggression did not decline when he left Dartmouth. He had a total commitment to meeting the enemy, preferably head on, and a total lack of visible fear. He despised cant and humbug, was wholly loyal and committed to his service and his country, and had immense drive and energy. He was beyond any shadow of doubt an outstanding commander and an outstanding individual – but as with all the commanders covered in this work he was also a mass of contradictions and by no means as straightforward as history has tended to paint him.

He was ruthless with those who did not come up to his standards. Mention has already been made of the succession of Sub-Lieutenants who were removed from *Scorpion* when he was in command. In common with Somerville, Horton and Vian, Cunningham could be seen as a bully:

> There were those who could not stand him, considering
> him a bully and careless of other people's opinions and
> feelings.[33]

Another commentator, Admiral J. H. Godfrey, talks of 'VSOV' – Very Senior Officer Veneration – and cites Cunningham as wanting this as his due. Godfrey may well be biased in that he believed active service in destroyers produces 'all little tin gods', but his comments on Cunningham are caustic: 'When he knew he was beaten . . . he started bellowing.'[34]

He was not always an easy man to work with. One commentator summed him up as: 'A wonderful man to serve, though at times rather difficult.'[35]

The same authority cites a rather alarming instance of Staff manipulation of a senior officer, one which, to my knowledge, has not been published before. As background, it is necessary to explain that Cunningham was remowned for his parsimony and objection to anything expensive:

> 'That's right – make the war expensive' was a frequent cry
> when ABC took exception to a particular measure . . . of
> course he was quite right to keep an eye on
> expenditure. . . . All the same, the questioning of
> administrative decisions taken by the Staff became very
> frustrating and wearing, leading sometimes to definite
> rows. So eventually I arranged with the Secretary, A. P.

Shaw, to issue administrative instructions to the Fleet by memorandum instead of by signal, which I signed 'For Admiral', and his Secretary undertook not to let the C-in-C see them. Very improper, but this seemed to be the only way to get necessary things done without the constant criticism.[36]

The impression given in the above extract is confirmed elsewhere:

One or two members of Cunningham's staff complain that ABC did not appreciate administrative or logistic problems . . . one, who prefers to be unnamed, writes: 'Broadly I would say that he was quite superb at sea, and unequalled during the Second World War. This not only applied to his tactics but also his friendliness especially when matters seemed to be going very badly indeed. In harbour it was a different matter altogether, and here I believe he did us a great deal of harm. He refused to spend money on harbour defences, or allow enough men to serve ashore. Philip Vian was quoted to me as saying after a Flag Officers' meeting in harbour, 'The C-in-C ought to be put in a refrigerator as soon as we get back to harbour and not allowed out until we go to sea again.'[37]

Comments by Admiral Vian need to be taken with a pinch of salt: at a later stage in the war when Vian was commanding some naval forces for the D-Day landings, Admiral Ramsay expressed serious doubts about Vian:

He [Vian] is d--d temperamental & at times a great annoyance . . . he is always apt to work against rather than with me.[38]

and:

P. Vian has been on my mind for some time owing to his peculiar behaviour. I think he is not quite normal at times.[39]

Even if the comment by Vian is the pot calling the kettle black, the kettle remains the same colour. Cunningham never really understood how to use a Staff:

> Two distinguished officers, both of whom knew Cunningham well, deplored the fact, from the point of view of his own development, that he paid so little attention to staff work, and that he could never entirely overcome his boredom with administration, which at times caused serious inconveniences to subordinates, and left difficulties for successors.[40]

Cunningham's hatred of anything he saw as luxurious or expensive was to have one very serious result. On 19 December, 1941, Italian midget submarines entered Alexandria harbour and sank the battleships *Queen Elizabeth* and *Valiant*, leaving them resting on the bottom. In the course of the attack two Italians were found clinging to the anchor chain of *Valiant*. Cunningham ordered the vessel's bottom to be swept, but did not attempt to move the ship. Rear Admiral Cresswell, in charge of security at Alexandria, had asked for an Extended Defence Officer for the boom penetrated by the Italians, but had been refused by Cunningham on the grounds of Cresswell's supposed 'insatiable' demands for officers.[41]

At times of crisis Cunningham could be the most humanitarian of men, showing a sympathy and capacity to go straight to the heart of the matter that were totally independent of his rank and uniform. At the end of the evacuation of Crete the exhausted Captain of the *Calcutta* blew his top when ordered out on the last night of the evacuation, and was brave or foolhardy enough to blow it in front of Cunningham. Instead of bellowing at him, Cunningham took him to one side, talked to him 'like a father', and after quarter of an hour sent out a Captain who thought, with many others: 'What a very great man'.[42] That very great man was also in tears when the ships' crew of *Calcutta* were landed shortly afterwards, their vessel having been sunk.

Another story is told of a Leading Telegraphist on *Warspite* who homed in a Swordfish on a reciprocal rather than a true bearing, meaning that the aircraft was being directed away from its home vessel rather than towards it. The aircraft and crew were lost. There was much anger and talk of retribution. Cunningham's response was, 'You'll do nothing with him. The b---y man has enough on his conscience already.'[43]

Cunningham's image of 'up-and-at-'em' vigour has been allowed to dominate history's perception of him. At heart he had native shrewdness, a feature that his Scottish ancestors would have seen as being 'canny'. It is shown in a letter he wrote to his mother in 1914:

The sinking of *Good Hope* and *Monmouth* was a bad show, wasn't it? I can't imagine what the Admiral was up to; he could not hope to fight the German squadron with success.[44]

The two cruisers, led by Admiral Cradock, who at one time had commanded *Britannia*, had undertaken a vain action against Admiral Von Spee's raiding cruisers *Scharnhorst* and *Gneisenau*. Here the great fighter reveals a truth about his actions that has not always been given due credit: Cunningham was a master of the calculated risk, and both his great victories, Taranto and Matapan, were a triumph for that doctrine. He had no belief in stupid sacrifice or vain glory, much as he might respect Cradock's courage.

For a man of strong views, language and feelings Cunningham's autobiography is surprisingly bland. It contains no direct reference to the rift between him and Admiral Fraser, springing from the fact that Fraser had been offered the post of First Sea Lord before Cunningham, and turned it down in favour of Cunningham. Fraser appears to have been universally adored, but not by Cunningham. Cunningham did not like the obligation Fraser's magnificent gesture placed him under. There was no love lost between Cunningham and Mountbatten either, but nothing disloyal or hostile appears in any of Cunningham's published work, nor indeed in his private correspondence. Cunningham's anger does appear in one aspect only, and is directed against Churchill:

It was in the sort of 'prodding' message received by me on June 5th that Mr Churchill was often so ungracious and hasty. We realized, of course, the terrible mental and physical strain under which he was labouring; but so were we. Such messages to those who were doing their utmost with straitened resources were not an encouragement, merely an annoyance. Moreover, as they implied that something was lacking the direction and leadership, they did positive harm.[45]

Cunningham was a firm traditionalist and a stickler for uniform in particular. He objected violently to the use of khaki by sailors, and even frowned on shorts as tropical rig. He has sometimes been accused of not having sympathy for the submarine service. The truth is probably that he could use submarines for all they were worth, but he was antagonized by the pirate image of many submariners, and in particular the relaxation of dress regulations that submarine service made essential. A more damaging conservatism arose when he initially refused to adopt American signalling practices when British forces joined the American Pacific fleet for the final assault on Japan. Though he had to bow to pressure, British signalling was reintroduced immediately the period of co-operation came to an end. If Cunningham was unwilling to acknowledge the future need of the Royal Navy to work with and sometimes under the largest navy in the world, he was also at times unwilling to acknowledge technology:

I have had to deal with many technical gadgets in my time and when one has gone wrong I have found there are two things I could do, either get a new technical gadget or a new technical officer, and I have invariably found that the more satisfactory alternative was to get a new technical officer.[46]

This semi-jocular remark has serious implications. Its tenor is that officers are a disposable commodity, and on closer examination it has all the weight of a joke in an after-dinner speech – good on first hearing and utter nonsense on closer examination. Did Cunningham really think that an endless succession of subordinates was a viable way of coming to terms with technological advance? One wonders what effect this attitude would have have had in the Battle of the Atlantic, where inexperienced and hardly-trained officers and men were trying to cope with radar, asdic and all the other technical paraphernalia that came to dominate the war against the submarine. One shudders to think of the result of applying Cunningham's philosophy to the cryptographers at Bletchley Park. They were quite capable of being anarchic in appearance and, sometimes, behaviour. The 'technical gadgets' they were dealing with to help decipher German codes were the forerunners of modern computers, and the essential silliness of Cunningham's statement is shown by the fact that his pompous and self-satisfied *dictat* would have had these indispensable men out on their ears the first time a machine failed. Cunningham's comment suggests that any decent chap can sort out a problem with a machine; it suggests also that in this area at least he was a dinosaur.

His character was as colourful as his language, and, as has already been noted, both he and Somerville favoured 'vivid' language. At the Battle of Matapan he was seen leaning over the bridge after the first Italian cruiser had been smothered by two broadsides: 'Good! Give the next bugger some of the same!'[47], a comment not noted in the *Times* report of the action. There was an insatiable aggression in Cunningham which did not make him good at considering the long-term answer to any problem. It made him chronically impatient, and while the Scottish puritanical streak in him led to parsimony, his aggression led to the opposite as regards men, a commodity he seemed to regard as being in endless supply. In time of war very large numbers of officers and men have to be grafted on to the small body of the professional navy. The ability to do this helped make the U-boat arm the potent force it was throughout the war, and was a major factor in allowing the United States to achieve air supremacy over the Japanese. In order for it to happen the assumption had to be made that even the rawest recruit was trainable. Cunningham expected perfection from those who served under him; his aggression and impatience stopped him from contributing to the forging of that perfection.

When he was introduced to the automobile, he rapidly became accident prone, largely as a result of his apparently only conceiving of two speeds in a car, full ahead and stop. In many respects this speaks for the man as a whole. One commentator said of him:

Like the giant panda he had endearing qualities, but he could bite you if he got too close.[48]

Cunningham cited 'recklessness and callousness' as the two most important qualities needed by a commander. Impatience and brutality are less honourable words, but possibly a little nearer to what Cunningham possessed. Of the successful commanders of the war, only Ramsay was neither reckless nor callous. Cunningham was frequently a risk-taker, but always when the odds were on his side, and was also quite ruthless. Somerville appeared reckless, was rarely callous and at all times showed an immense concern for his men. Above all, Cunningham's career shows the dash, daring and occasional bloody-mindedness of a destroyer captain.

A destroyer captain might seem considerably removed from the Admiral in charge of an air attack against a well-defended enemy base, but the attack on Taranto was similar in many respects to a destroyer action – relatively small and inexpensive forces (aircraft) attacking a far larger enemy under cover of darkness, and hoping to escape because of the confusion caused by damaging hits. The concept of an attack by carrier aircraft on Taranto had been mooted as long ago as 1935 when Mussolini invaded Abyssinia, and it was resuscitated in 1938 when Hitler's invasion of Czechoslovakia threatened all-out war. Admiral Sir Dudley Pound, Commander-in-Chief of the Mediterranean, believed his carriers would be highly vulnerable in time of war and wanted to get the best out of them before they were sunk. Captain A. L. St G. Lyster of the carrier *Glorious* was all for such an attack, and training was started. It came to nothing, but Pound took the idea with him and recommended the concept to his successor, Cunningham. Then in August, 1940, the new carrier *Illustrious* joined Cunningham's fleet, bringing with it Rear Admiral Lyster, who had lost none of his enthusiasm for the raid on Taranto. Cunningham may not have been a technical wizard, but he did not need to be. His every urge was to hit the enemy with anything that came to hand, and the air attack on Taranto had been placed in front of him almost ready-packaged.

The attack was hidden from enemy eyes by being buried in a mass of convoy and other naval activities, typical of a busy day in the wartime Mediterranean. No less than six separate British forces were at sea when the attack was launched, covering the arrival of four convoys and the passage of a naval force including the battleship *Barham* to Alexandria. The risks to the British operations are simple to catalogue. If surprise was not achieved and *Illustrious* was spotted close in to the mainland then she was a dead duck. There was no heavy support and inadequate numbers and quality of aircraft to beat off the determined attack that could be expected so near to the Italian mainland and Italy's major naval base. The aircraft involved in making the attack had to face a huge barrage of flak and a limited number of attack positions because of barrage balloons moored in both the inner and outer harbours; it was expected they would sustain a fifty percent casualty rate. As it was a total of twenty-one aircraft set out from *Illustrious* in two waves. It should have been more, but the carrier *Eagle* had to be withdrawn from the operation because of mechanical failure brought on by age and hard usage, and three Swordfish aircraft had crashed as a result of taking on board contaminated fuel. Given that there had also been a near-disastrous hangar fire in *Illustrious* that had activated the hangar sea-water sprinklers, necessitating the stripping-down and rebuilding of almost every aircraft, it was a wonder that any attack was launched. The twenty-one aircraft, armed with torpedoes, bombs and flares, hit three Italian battle-ships. *Conte di Cavour* was sunk and never made active service again: two other battleships were severely damaged, and though both were refloated and eventually made seaworthy again (*Littorio* in March, 1941, *Caio Duilio* in May, 1941), Italian battle-ship strength had been halved at a crucial period in the war. In exchange two Swordfish were lost.

The reasons for the British success, apart from their daring and training, are clear. The very complexity of the operations surrounding the attack and the presence of no less than six Allied forces at sea drew a cloak of confusion over the operation, under which *Illustrious* hid and surprise was achieved. The Italian fleet did not possess enough torpedo netting to guard its vessels and was not willing to lay all that it had because of the extent to which it interfered with manoeuvring. It needed 14,000 yards, had 4,593 yards in position and 3,171 yards waiting to be laid. A gale had torn away a significant number of barrage balloons before the attack; of ninety balloons, only twenty-seven were in position on the night of the attack. Despite an awesome collection of anti-aircraft guns both on shore and on the warships moored in the harbour, at night time these were instructed to fire on a 'blanket' principle, rather than at specific targets. The British Duplex torpedo warhead was able to run under enemy vessels and explode magnetically, thereby hitting the weakest part of the vessel; in this instance, without rough weather to interfere with it, it seems to have performed well. Finally, the antiquated Swordfish aircraft was suited for this form of attack better than almost any other. Its lack of speed did not matter in a night attack when it was shielded from fighter harassment, and its 'paper and string' construction allowed flak to pass through the fuselage and wings without crippling the structural integrity of the aircraft.

Taranto was a major victory, but far more of a victory for British naval planning and earlier generations of Staff Officers than it was a victory for Cunningham. It was the Navy as a whole which had decided to allocate scarce resources to the development of a carrier arm in the inter-war years, for all that design and procurement of both carriers and aircraft was seriously flawed. It was an earlier generation that had conceived the idea of the raid, and detailed planning of a type that Cunningham did not like that had brought if off. If Cunningham can claim relatively little of the success for the raid, then he can also claim little responsibility for what could be seen as its relative failure, the fact that so few aircraft were available to make the attack. The pitifully small number of aircraft available was the result of pre-war failures, as was the obsolete nature of the aircraft used. There was a weakness that lay at the door of all the Staff involved in planning the raid, namely the presence of only twelve torpedo-carrying aircraft in the force of twenty-one. The 250lb semi-armour-piercing bomb carried by the Swordfish was an ineffective RAF design, and even had it been effective it was unlikely to do much damage to heavily-armoured capital ships. It is difficult to see, with hindsight, why any Swordfish were armed with bombs, apart from the fact that there were limited torpedo-launching positions in the crowded anchorage.

Cunningham was not above gilding the lily. In his autobiography he states: 'They [the aircrews] clamoured to repeat the operation the same night,'[49] whereas the survivors themselves record only vast relief at having survived the first attack, and equal relief at not having to make another.[50]

At Taranto Cunningham was given the right vessels in the right place at the right time to carry out a pre-existing plan of excellent quality. He was man enough to take the opportunity thus offered to him. At Taranto, and at Matapan, good fortune had much to do with Cunningham's success. Napoleon's comment that he wanted above all generals who were lucky found no better justification than the career of Cunningham.

5 Matapan, Crete and *Bismarck*

Chronology of Events

1941

10 January. Dive bombers of the German X Air Corps hit carrier *Illustrious* with six bombs; *Illustrious* limps into Malta.

22 January. German battlecruisers *Scharnhorst* and *Gneisenau* leave Kiel for commerce raiding cruise (Operation Berlin).

1 February. German cruiser *Admiral Hipper* sails from Brest on commerce raiding cruise.

4 February. *Scharnhorst* and *Gneisenau* pass unnoticed through Denmark Strait.

9 February. Force H bombards Genoa (see Chapter 4).

11–14 February. *Admiral Hipper* attacks two convoys, sinks several ships and returns safely to Brest.

22 February. *Scharnhorst* and *Gneisenau* sink five merchant ships. *Admiral Scheer*, on separate raiding cruise, spotted by British forces, but escapes.

15–16 March. *Scharnhorst* and *Gneisenau* sink thirteen ships, are sighted by the battleship *Rodney*, but succeed in escaping.

17 March. U-boat aces Schepke captured and Kretschmer killed; Prien killed 7 March.

22 March. *Scharnhorst* and *Gneisenau* put into Brest, having sunk twenty-two ships totalling 115,622 gross tons.

28 March. Battle of Matapan. Italian battleship *Vittorio Veneto* damaged by Swordfish torpedo attack, heavy cruisers *Pola*, *Zara*, *Fiume* sunk, with two destroyers.

1 April. Admiralty regain control of Coastal Command from RAF; *Admiral Scheer* reaches Kiel after operational tour of

147 days and sinking of twenty-five ships totalling 115,026 tons.

24 April. British begin evacuation of Greece. Main burden taken by Somerville's Force H; more than 50,000 troops evacuated.

30 April. Commerce raider *Thor* ties up in Hamburg: 329 days at sea, twelve ships sunk. Improved air cover severely reduces capacity of German ships to break out unseen.

8 May. Commerce raider *Pinguin* sunk by cruiser *Cornwall*: previously *Pinguin* had sunk or taken as prize thirty-two ships totalling 154,619 gross tons.

9 May. British capture intact German *U110* with entire Enigma-M enciphering machine and attached documentation.

18 May. German battleship *Bismarck* and heavy cruiser *Prince Eugen* put to sea for commerce raiding.

20 May. German airborne assault on Crete starts.

22 May. Heavy British shipping losses off Crete.

24 May. *Bismarck* and *Prince Eugen* sink HMS *Hood*.

26 May. *Bismarck* crippled by torpedo hit from one of *Ark Royal's* Swordfish.

27 May. *Bismarck* sunk by *King George V* and *Rodney*.

28 May–1 June. Hostilities in Crete end; troops evacuated with heavy British losses.

On 10 January, 1941, Cunningham lost his only aircraft carrier from the Mediterranean Fleet. The damage done to *Illustrious* by German Stuka dive-bombers was a serious blow to him and all he had hoped to do in the Mediterranean. Dudley Pound had taken to heart the lessons of the Norwegian campaign, which suggested both to him and to Phillips that surface vessels required their own air cover if they were to be defended successfully against enemy air attack. We noted earlier Pound's belief, as expressed to Cunningham, that the Taranto attack would be the last dying fling of the Mediterranean carrier, and so it proved to be. Cunningham dismissed these worries, in the same way that he had always been inclined to dismiss air and submarine threats. He was to learn his lesson about aircraft the hard way with *Illustrious* and have it rubbed in with the devastation of his command in the evacuation of Crete. Similarly with the submarine, he lost the battleship *Barham* on 25 November, 1941, to torpedoes from *U331*, and had his two battleships *Queen Elizabeth* and *Valiant* sunk at their moorings by Italian midget submarines less than a month later.

Cunningham was not the only person who had painful lessons still to learn. Taranto had proved (and Pearl Harbor confirmed) that against moored battleships the best possible weapon was the air-launched torpedo. The attack on *Illustrious* showed what Midway was later to confirm, that the dive-bomber was the most effective weapon against fast-moving carriers. Cunningham and his fleet may have been lulled into a false sense of security by their recent experience of Italian high-level bombing, which had been largely ineffective, and by the effectiveness of British carrier aircraft in doing what they had been designed to do, namely to knock down enemy reconnaissance aircraft. There was nothing in the war to date to suggest the lethal efficiency of the experienced German pilots, trained specifically to attack naval targets.

If there were local conditions that allowed Cunningham to underestimate the threat from aircraft, so did his own background and the naval culture in which he grew up. He was a traditionalist, and that meant he saw naval air power as being useful for reconnaissance, for knocking down enemy reconnaissance and spotting for the big guns. It was this philosophy in the inter-war years which led to the Royal Navy placing such undemanding specifications on its naval aircraft requirements, and which allowed it to accept a complement of aircraft almost two-thirds less than that being built for the Japanese and American navies. In addition the Royal Navy in the 1930s had placed too much reliance on the multi-barrelled pom-pom, or 'Chicago Piano', as a mode of anti-aircraft defence. Cunningham was very much of this period. His papers show no awareness of what the Royal Navy was missing in terms of modern aircraft, or how desperately short of existing aircraft it was. In contrast Somerville's papers show a pressing awareness of the inadequacies of British naval aircraft, such as his comment on the Barracuda aircraft that it was 'a thorough misfit'.[1]

However, *Illustrious* was not helped by her design. Her much-vaunted armoured flight deck (actually an armoured box surrounding the hangar) reduced her carrying capacity of aircraft to a meagre thirty-six aircraft.[2] This was not enough to mount an effective combat air patrol, and even had more aircraft been available they would have been of inferior specification and performance. The armoured flight deck had a major weakness: the lifts between flight deck and hangar could not be armoured because of the problems that the extra weight would cause in allowing the lifts to be moved. This proved *Illustrious's* Achilles heel, together with the fact that the German bombs were heavier than the upper hangar armour had been designed to withstand.

Two months after Cunningham lost *Illustrious* he gained the new carrier *Formidable*, a vessel of the same class as *Illustrious*. Despite Taranto, Cunningham faced a tricky situation in the Mediterranean. Both Malta and the territory gained by General Wavell's December, 1940, offensive in North Africa demanded supplies. In March, 1941, it had been decided to send troops from Libya and Egypt to support Greece, and this would place a heavy demand on Cunningham's forces as all troops would have to go by sea along very vulnerable routes. German involvement in the Mediterranean war was increasing, as was shown by the fate of *Illustrious*. The Battle of Matapan was to prove almost the last fling of the Mediterranean Fleet before it entered a long dark time of the soul, which may even have broken Cunningham's spirit.

Cunningham had a number of factors on his side. First and foremost was a new fleet carrier, but he could add to this two fully-modernized battleships, *Warspite* and *Valiant*, the lightly modernized battleship *Barham*, and nine destroyers. The modernized battleships had a relatively low top speed of twenty-four knots, but in every other respect were excellent vessels – and *Valiant* was the proud owner of a Type 279 radar set. Secondly, the Government Code and Cypher School at Bletchley Park had cracked the Luftwaffe 'Enigma' codes and the little-used Italian naval equivalent. Thus the Admiralty knew that the Italians, under German prodding, planned an operation into the Eastern Mediterranean on 26 March. Convoys were re-routed, a force of four light cruisers and four destroyers sent out ahead under Vice Admiral Pridham-Wippell, and Cunningham himself set sail (one carrier, three battleships, nine destroyers) on the evening of 27 March after a flying boat reported Italian cruisers and destroyers at sea. Intricate steps were taken to ensure secrecy.

Not enough steps were taken to keep *Warspite* clear of a mud bank, with the result that she clogged her condensers and was reduced to a top speed of twenty knots.

Considerable confusion attended the whole battle. There were two British forces at sea, Cunningham's main battle fleet and Pridham-Wippell's cruisers, and no less than three Italian forces – one consisting of three 10,000-ton cruisers and three destroyers, a second of three 10,000-ton cruisers, two 8,000-ton cruisers and six destroyers and a third comprising the battleship *Vittorio Veneto* with four destroyers. The first Italian group was spotted by an aircraft from *Formidable*, but Cunningham discounted the sighting because of its proximity to the likely whereabouts of Pridham-Wippell's cruisers. *Formidable's* observers were not experienced, and both British Admirals and the Italian Admiral Iachino were to discount aircraft sighting reports because of the known difficulty of keeping an accurate navigational chart in an aircraft.

Then an aircraft from the Italian battleship spotted the British cruisers and, sensing a convoy, pressed on after them. The first group of Italian cruisers spotted the British cruisers, which turned away and headed for the main British fleet, being chased all the while by the Italians whose 8″ guns outranged the British. Cunningham did not appear unduly worried by the plight his cruisers were in. He ordered *Valiant* and two destroyers ahead to support Pridham-Wippell, but held back a torpedo strike ranged on *Formidable's* deck in the hope that the Italian cruisers were merely the curtain-raiser and that an Italian battleship was at sea somewhere nearby. It was a massive gamble, but, like all Cunningham's gambles to date, it worked: no British cruisers were directly hit and eventually the Italians turned away, hoping to draw the British cruisers on to *Vittorio Veneto* coming up behind. The British cruisers were ordered to shadow the Italians, and Cunningham called back *Valiant* to the main fleet. Cunningham had used his cruisers as live bait, gambling on bigger prey below the horizon. He was right.

Neither the British nor the Italian commander knew that there were enemy heavy forces at sea. Both discounted sightings made by their aircraft. At 0939 on 28 March Cunningham finally sent off his aircraft strike force (a meagre six torpedo aircraft and two fighters was all that his carrier could muster) against the Italian heavy cruisers. Just over an hour later *Vittorio*

Veneto hove into sight and promptly opened fire on the British cruisers at sixteen miles' range. The British cruisers did a smart about-turn and headed back towards the British main fleet, some eighty miles distant. The situation was looking quite desperate for the British cruisers when *Formidable's* strike force appeared, missed the battleship, but forced it to turn for home: Taranto had left its mark. Emerging from their smoke screen to find an empty sea, the British cruisers joined up with Cunningham and were stationed some sixteen miles ahead of his main fleet. The combined British force was chasing the Italians for all it was worth. Unfortunately at a top speed of twenty-four knots (*Warspite's* tubes had been persuaded to listen to reason) it was not worth enough. At their closest the Italian fleet had been forty-five miles away from Cunningham's battleships and had a six-knot advantage over the British. The British maintained intermittent air contact with the Italian fleet.

Now was the time for a massive air strike against the Italians, after which the big ships would come in and finish off the disabled Italian vessels. Unfortunately *Formidable's* total complement was thirteen fighters and fourteen torpedo-bombers, and all that could be launched (the remainder being out of service for a variety of reasons) were five torpedo-carrying aircraft. Admiral Iachino still did not know that a major British force was ranged against him. Cunningham had ordered land-based bomber attacks on the Italian fleet, and by a lucky coincidence these arrived on the scene just before *Formidable's* second strike; the latter took time to take up position as with a thirty-knot Italian speed, a thirty-knot headwind, and a top speed for the Swordfish aircraft of only ninety miles an hour, the aircraft only had an actual speed relative to the Italians of thirty knots. The land bombers were ineffective but distracted the Italians and let the torpedo-bombers make close runs. Tragically, Lieutenant Commander Dalyell-Stead, the leader of the flight, was cut down with his crew trying to cut across the bows of the Italian battleship. Nevertheless, a torpedo hit *Vittorio Veneto* astern, stopped her dead in the water and let in 3,500 tons of water. Cunningham immediately ordered a third all-out strike for dusk, and sent his cruisers on ahead to act as shadowers. In the meantime the Italian damage control parties were working wonders, and in about two and a half hours the battleship was under way again at sixteen knots. Quite rightly fearing a destroyer attack, Admiral Iachino bunched all his vessels round his wounded flagship. A smokescreen, searchlights shining into the eyes of the aircraft pilots, and a massive anti-aircraft barrage split up the ten attacking aircraft, but a hit was scored on the heavy cruiser *Pola* which forced her to slew out of line, dead in the water.

Here Admiral Iachino made the mistake that lost him the battle. He decided to send back two heavy cruisers, *Zara* and *Fiume*, with four destroyers to render assistance to *Pola*. Their path was leading them straight to the British battle fleet fifty miles away.

Cunningham thought he was chasing a crippled Italian battleship proceeding at thirteen knots. He was actually chasing one proceeding at nineteen knots, and one which made a major course change that threw off the shadowers. He ordered his cruisers to fall back and shadow the enemy, and denuded his own force of destroyers, sending the second and fourteenth destroyer flotillas ahead to mount a torpedo attack on the Italians. In the meantime he plunged ahead into the dark.

The outcome is well known. The British battle fleet ran into the Italian force sent back to help *Pola* and blew two heavy cruisers to pieces at point-blank range. In the mêlée two destroyers were sunk, and the *Pola*, the cause of it all, was also put out of her misery and sunk. It was a famous victory. It was also a flawed one.

The first flaw concerns Pridham-Wippell's cruisers. After engaging the Italian cruisers Cunningham signalled for all forces not engaged with the enemy to withdraw to the north-east – his aim being to leave the field clear for his destroyers to attack the Italian battleship which Cunningham at that time still believed to be in range. This signal was not intended for Pridham-Wippell's cruisers but it was received by them, and they broke off contact with the Italian fleet, which remained lost to British eyes thereafter. The fault was shared between two admirals, one for a confusing signal, the other for not querying it and thereby breaking the golden rule of never losing contact with the enemy. However, Pridham-Wippell was no coward and the signal explicitly commanded those *not engaged* with the enemy to withdraw. Perhaps in this incident the intellectual indolence of Cunningham can be seen. There are times when thought is more productive than hitting someone; Cunningham could hit magnificently, but his intellectual processes began and ended with the idea of turning towards the enemy. He simply did not realize the interpretation that others would place on his signal, and he did not have the excuse to offer that he was working with unfamiliar commanders or a fleet that had not had the opportunity to exercise and work together.

The second flaw was the idea of detaching the destroyers to go for the Italian fleet. The idea of a destroyer attack was sound, albeit horrendously risky, but the presence of a cruiser and a destroyer force ahead of the main fleet cramped everyone's style and reduced the effectiveness of both forces, fearful as they were of mistaken identity resulting in an all-British battle. Detaching the destroyers had all the hallmarks of Cunningham's famed aggression, but it opposed the destoyers with a far superior force and lay Cunningham's main fleet open to attack. It created more confusion in an already confused situation. Here again it was the decision of a man with tunnel vision. It threw a fast force with a weapon (the torpedo) that could sink a battleship against the enemy, but it ignored the realities and the complexitity of the situation. It was the order and plan of an egocentric personality. It assumed that the non-destroyer forces would understand instinctively and without questions the intentions of the commanding officer. The signal which diverted Pridham-Wippell's cruisers was the signal of a man who found it easier to dismiss officers than to understand them.

The third flaw was in reconnaissance. For a fleet commander with land-based aircraft, carrier aircraft and radar at his disposal Cunningham was too often in ignorance of what the enemy was and where they were. The main fault lay in difficult wind conditions, inexperienced observers and the inherent difficulties of navigation and course and speed estimates of surface vessels from the air. Cunningham's ignorance of the enemy's whereabouts also begs the question of what the situation would have been in a Fleet trained by that most air-minded of Admirals, James Somerville. No one could accuse Cunningham of having spent too much time organizing effective training programmes for his aircrews, or indeed for his anti-submarine officers.

There is a fourth issue that is not so much a flaw, more a point of interest. Cunningham was prepared to charge off into the gathering dark after a supposedly crippled battleship that might or might not be where it was expected, and in the process strip himself of much of his destroyer escort. His Staff opposed this on the grounds of the strength of Iachino's force, the possibility of submarine and destroyer attacks and the danger from German aircraft on the following day. They might also have added that, though the British Mediterranean Fleet had been practising night action since the days of Admiral Chatfield in the early 1930s and had the flashless cordite and the training the Italian fleet lacked, their training in night action was rusty, and that at night a large element of luck creeps into any action. Cunningham states that he 'paid respectful attention to this opinion'[3]; another commentator records that he called his Staff a 'pack of yellow-livered skunks', went off to have dinner and came back determined to press forward[4] with the action. Cunningham's aggressive tactics won the battle – but only because *Ajax* and *Valiant* had radar. It was the former vessel's set which first picked up the *Zara* group heading back to help *Pola*; the latter's Type 279 radar picked up *Pola* six miles away, and it was the forty degree alteration of course made on *Valiant's* report that brought the Italian force across *Warspite's* bows. With flashless cordite and radar the British were sighted men in a world of the blind. Even more, they could retain their sight whilst fighting. It was technology that won the Battle of Matapan as well as the aggression of the commander. It was human error, and the efficiency of the Italian damage control parties, that removed the chance of an even greater victory.

As a footnote, it is interesting to see that James Somerville made exactly the same mistake that cost Admiral Iachino the Battle of Matapan when, during Operation Tiger in the Mediterranean, he turned back his force to escort the destroyer *Fortune* which was restricted to twelve knots. Somerville justified this action, which could have had disastrous consequences, by writing:

> I couldn't leave my little boats unprotected, though I
> suppose in cold blood I ought to have. If Dad does not take
> a chance in helping the boys, the latter will inevitably lose
> confidence.[5]

It was the above sentiment that contributed to one of Somerville's more remarkable actions, as will be seen later. 'Dad' was so concerned about some men from his Eastern Fleet that he risked the whole fleet in order to save them. Both incidents were examples of a different type of gamble from those which Cunningham habitually took. Cunningham's gambles risked lives, Somerville's saved them: both commanders were immensely popular, an irony which needs a psychologist to explain it, not a historian.

Cunningham commented about the Mediterranean:

Things went well for us out here up to a point, in fact as long as we pursued one object. When we started pursuing two or more at the same time catastrophe resulted, not very surprisingly.[6]

The above extract points to one of Cunningham's weaknesses. He tended to oversimplify complex issues. As we have already seen, in his thinking a faulty technical device can be mended simply by sacking an officer; if a First Lieutenant does not get quick results, he is disposed of; if students dare to be dissident they are rendered docile by hard labour. Comments and actions such as these portray a delightfully simple world, but not always the real world. Every naval commander in history must have yearned for the luxury of pursuing only one object, but the Mediterranean theatre of war was always going to require an admiral to fight off a surface, air and submarine threat from two enemies, the Italians and the Germans, and require also naval forces to convoy essential military and civilian supplies. In addition, action in support of landings and troop advances were an inevitable duty, as was the possibility of defending against enemy landings. Catastrophe in the Mediterranean was not the result of the Allies pursuing more than one object. Involvement in Greece and Crete was merely an extension of existing objects. The problem was that it over-extended available resources and placed surface vessels in a situation where the air power mustered against them was always going to result in crippling naval losses. Cunningham's version of events is typical of many of his comments. It has a spurious and attractive simplicity which dissolves on closer examination, and it manages to place the blame for what happened on someone else.

Cunningham's conduct was amost faultless when the action started. His failure lay in not bringing more pressure to bear on having the whole Greece and Crete campaign called off before it started. To his credit he was initially against the expedition to Greece, but appears to have acquiesced when Eden, sent out by Churchill, placed convincing political reasons in front of him. Admiral Tom Phillips, the subject of a later chapter and the object of much ire and ridicule from both Cunningham and Somerville, was wholly opposed to the Greek fiasco and lost favour with Churchill as a result of this and of his opposition to the bombing of Germany. Cunningham was not a politician, but he must take some of the responsibility for Greece and Crete. His great strength was that he held the Fleet together almost by force of willpower alone throughout the Crete operation; his great failing was that he did not do more to stop it taking place.

With hindsight the attempt to protect Greece seems like yet another sideshow pushed by Churchill, so concerned with aggression on the fringes that he grossly overdrew the central bank balance of men and stores. The first troop convoy transport to Greece took place on 4 March, 1941. A few weeks later 50,672 soldiers were evacuated from Greece, some 1,600 of them unfortunate enough to be allocated to garrison Crete, where a German invasion was seen as imminent. Significant though the losses were, the evacuation of Greece was only a curtain-raiser for the folly of Crete. As one commentator has said:

> It is difficult to judge which was the greater folly, the
> British decision to defend Crete or the German decision to
> seize the island.[7]

The Cretan battles were of two types, those aimed to stopping a sea-borne invasion and those involved in the evacuation of the troops. The net result was a butcher's bill of three cruisers and eight destroyers sunk, two battleships, one aircraft carrier, five cruisers and seven destroyers seriously damaged. The Royal Navy did not have the reserves of ships or men to cope with this level of damage (even at the time of the French collapse sixty-six out of 178 British destroyers were undergoing repair), and these staggering losses had heavy repercussions.

It is from the Greece and Crete expeditions that a mess-deck song dates:

Roll out the *Nelson*, the *Rodney*, the *Hood*,
Since the whole bloody airforce is no bloody good![8]

and the apocryphal story of the rating blowing up his lifejacket
with the comment, 'This is the only bloody air support I'll get
this trip'.

The RAF claimed that they could not operate because the
Army had lost them all their bases. The truth is that the RAF
never sent enough aircraft to Crete or Greece, and that inter-
service co-operation between the three forces was abysmal.[9]

Cunningham refers to this as follows:

I was quite sure that if the soldiers [in Crete] were given
two or three days to deal with the airborne troops without
interference by sea-borne powers, Crete could be held. And
at great cost to themselves we gave them their three days
. . . but quite in vain. Our badly-equipped troops
handicapped by a want of preparation for which as one of
the three C-in-C's I must accept a sense of the
responsibility (chiefly for not being rude enough to the
other two) just couldn't hold the well-equipped Hun. . . . A
fact, which you may keep to yourself & a sad one was that
in some ships the sailors began to crack a bit.[10]

Here again Cunningham manages to disclaim much of the
responsibility for the débâcle. To say that his fault lay in not
being rude enough to the other Commanders-in-Chief ignores
the fact that Cunningham knew from the start what risks the
operation ran and let himself be argued in to not opposing it. It
is also clear on his own admission that he was ignorant of the
true state of efficiency of British troops. Bad equipment and lack
of preparation are not things which happen overnight. His
tunnel vision again did not let him see the true state of affairs
until it was too late to stop a disaster. He also did not realize
that the German airborne troops who took Crete were at their
last gasp, and expected their final assault to be a suicide mission.
They found instead the Allied positions abandoned. It was a
close-run thing, but this time the British lost.

Cunningham's personality was instrumental in holding the
Royal Navy to its duty when it was being knocked to pieces off
Crete. At one stage in the battle there were only four serviceable

aircraft on *Formidable*, and by mid-May there were only seven aircraft left on Crete. At a moment when it seemed that the damage to men and ships would not cease until not a single Allied vessel was left afloat, Cunningham made the signal:

> It takes the Navy three years to build a ship. It would take three hundred years to build a new reputation. The evacuation will continue.[11]

This is an inspiring signal, and a flawed one. What it does not state is how long it takes a navy to lose a war. The losses off Crete could have brought that date significantly closer, particularly as the one campaign that could have lost Great Britain the war (the Battle of the Atlantic, against the U-boat) was suffering from a chronic shortage of vessels and men. Cunningham's signal is magnificent. It is also tunnel-visioned in that it sees only one object as worth pursuing (the situation Cunningham always tried to work himself into) and an oversimplification. The finest ships in the world may only take three years to build. It takes longer to train officers and men to the pitch where they can fight and handle those ships in the best tradition of the Royal Navy. Crete lost the Royal Navy its most valuable resource, trained men. In forcing some of them to crack, not surprisingly, it came near to threatening the morale and belief in itself that had helped to make the Royal Navy what it was. It showed that in the final count Cunningham viewed men as disposable items. It is nonsense to suggest that the reputation of the Royal Navy would have been lost for three hundred years if the evacuation of Crete had been finished earlier. It takes a very great man to write such convincing nonsense.

The battle for Crete brought Cunningham to such a low ebb that he offered his resignation, believing that the affair might have 'shaken the faith of the personnel of the fleet in my handling of affairs'.[12] Perhaps he too had begun to 'crack a bit'. The strain on him had been immense. For the first time his aggression had bought no victory, but rather a smashing defeat with no silver lining whatsoever to its cloud. Cunningham was not a good loser, but his forces never had a chance when faced with the problems of landing and evacuation, limited water for manoeuvring and a skilled and very determined air force. It was Norway writ large, and to terrible effect. Such mistakes as were made seem to lie more at the door of Rear Admiral L. E. S. King. He had taken over from Admiral Rawlings when the forces commanded by the two joined up, as he was senior officer, but the move emphasized the dangers of a change of command in the middle of a battle. King detached the cruisers *Fiji* and *Gloucester* from his main force to stand by the sinking *Greyhound*, in another unwitting echo of Matapan. He was apparently unaware of their crippling shortage of anti-aircraft ammunition. This shortage was a major factor in their eventual sinking. Under the full fury of the Luftwaffe King also retired from the Aegean when theoretically he was capable of attacking a second invasion force. Judgements exercised by armchair historians in the warmth of home are most at fault when they concern events such as those Admiral King fell prey to. Suffice it to say that Cunningham saw King's detachment of the cruisers as a 'mistake', because a concentrated fleet mustered a greater concentration of anti-aircraft fire[13] and his decision to retire from the Aegean as a 'faulty one'.[14]

Privately Cunningham confessed:

I have always had the feeling that he [Admiral King] was a better office wallah than sailor. He wants everything cut and dried and most precise order, doesn't exhibit such initiative at sea.[15]

Cunningham's reputation as a martinet who dismissed people at the drop of a hat may have had something to do with King's caution. Some people responded well to his aggression; one wonders if others did not respond by the type of legalistic caution that Cunningham cites as King's major weakness. Cunningham pointed the finger at himself when it came to his ability to judge those immediately beneath him in rank:

Personally I think that as one rises in the service one is apt to underestimate the abilities of the officers junior to us.[16]

Cunningham's error, and uncharacteristic loss of aggression, came on 1 June, when Pound signalled him to evacuate more troops that night if there was any reasonable prospect of a substantial number of men embarking. Cunningham said no, arguing that he did not have enough ships, there was moonlight so night bombing was possible and fighter cover was thin and unreliable. He was also suspicious because the number of troops supposedly available for disemarkation had risen from 5,000 to 10,000, and this made him wonder if anyone knew the real figure. The most authoritative account of the Crete campaign states:

> By the same high standards which Cunningham applied to
> these actions, his own decision to terminate the
> evacuation on the night of May 31st must be judged
> 'unfortunate'.[17]

Cunningham's offer of resignation was the closest he came to admitting that he had not lived up to his own high standards, but it was phrased in a way that would have made it very hard for the Admiralty to act on it. It did not state that Cunningham had got anything wrong (as indeed he had not, at least not until the end), but offered as the reason for his resignation the fact that the Fleet might have lost confidence in him. As it had not, Cunningham's offer was immediately invalid. His failure to carry out the final evacuation shows the extent to which he was a favoured son of the Admiralty. James Somerville had faced a Court of Enquiry for beating off a superior Italian force at Spartivento; Cunningham faced nothing for failing to carry through an evacuation. The fact remains that Cunningham was absolutely right not to carry out the final phase of the evacuation. Enough damage had already been done.

The fighting around Crete and the simultaneous battle to sink the German battleship *Bismarck* were wholly separate affairs, but both hinged round aircraft. In command of the Home Fleet at the time of the *Bismarck* foray was Admiral John Tovey (pronounced 'Tuvvy'). He was yet another officer destined for distinction who came from an army rather than a Navy family: his father was a Colonel in the Engineers. He was born in 1885, and from Preparatory School went into *Britannia* in January, 1900.

It was perhaps no surprise that Cunningham and Tovey struck up a close friendship in later years. Both were of the same generation, both were outwardly fearless, and above all both were destroyer men through and through. Tovey's first command was the oil-fired destroyer *Jackal* in 1915. He then went on to earn a reputation for immense courage in command of the destroyer *Onslow* at the Battle of Jutland. The DSO in 1919 and special promotion to commander for persistence and determination in attacking enemy ships marked him out clearly as a rising star, even at the young age of thirty-one. A year at the Royal Naval Staff College, Greenwich, and two years in the operations division in the Admiralty (1920–22) confirmed that impression, as did promotion to Captain in 1923. Shore appointments and appointments as Captain (Destroyers) then followed. The intertwining of his and Cunningham's career was again evident. When Tovey's destroyers were based at Port Edgar, Cunningham was captain in charge of the base. Between them they developed a new training scheme which was a significant improvement on the old one, and which increased the amount of time spent at sea. Tovey then spent a year at the Imperial Defence College, and two years as naval assistant to the Second Sea Lord at the Admiralty, before being given command of the battleship *Rodney* in 1932. Cunningham had commanded *Rodney* in 1929 and gone straight on to command the Royal Navy barracks at Chatham. Tovey followed exactly the same path, taking over at Chatham in 1935 and being promoted Rear Admiral in the same year. He became Rear Admiral (Destroyers) in the Mediterranean in March, 1938, and Vice Admiral in May, 1939. He thus served under Cunningham when the latter became Commander-in-Chief of the Mediterranean and worked closely with him from the outset. Cunningham made Tovey commander of all Allied light forces in the Mediterranean and second-in-command to himself. Tovey's destroyers were superbly handled in the action at Calabria on 9 July, 1940, when a single long-range hit by *Warspite* on the Italian flagship sent the Italian fleet scurrying for home. Ten days after Calabria Tovey's forces sank the Italian cruiser *Bartolomeo Colleoni*.

Tovey was described by Somerville as:

a *first-class* fellow who sees the daylight bright and clear.[18]

Tovey was almost the identikit picture of the type of naval officer most favoured by traditional senior officers. Like Cunningham, he had magnificent fighting qualities, a down-to-earth, no-nonsense approach, and a fund of practical seamanlike experience. A friend of Cunningham's wrote to him:

I'm glad you've got Tovey. I thought the world of him in the last war especially one day, gallant resourceful & quick as lightning flying at their throats.[19]

Cunningham was unstinting of his praise:

I am so glad Tovey has been selected for the Home Fleet though I shall badly miss his sane and optimistic outlook out here.[20]

The praise was reciprocated:

In the early part of the war when they took away all my [Tovey's] command but apparently had no use for me, I found myself losing my self-confidence and it has only been your friendship and trust in me that has helped me to regain it.[21]

The break with Cunningham came in 1940 when Tovey was given the acting rank of Admiral and transferred to relieve Sir Charles Forbes as Commander-in-Chief of the Home Fleet. It was in this post that he met and sank the *Bismarck*. Some of Pound's bitterness at the criticism levelled at him comes over in his comments on Tovey's appointment:

Tovey takes on the day after tomorrow and I am sure he will be a success, but it is a difficult job to do anything spectacular in, and a lot of people think that Admirals are doing nothing if they don't put up spectacular shows.[22]

In fact Tovey did achieve two very spectacular things – the loss of *Hood* and the sinking of *Bismarck*, but before these took place there were clear signs of strain developing in the all-important relationship with Churchill. Tovey wrote a long and occasionally hilarious letter to Cunningham, describing the time he spent with Churchill before the Home Fleet job was finally offered. At their first meeting Tovey spoke his mind:

As you know I never require much encouragement to give tongue to my opinions . . . [Churchill said] he didn't mind my being absolutely outspoken.[23]

But Tovey and Churchill had a major disagreement later at Chequers when Churchill made the fatuous remark that British unpreparedness in 1939 was more the fault of the heads of the fighting services then it was of the politicians. Tovey took issue with this, and for a while it appeared that he was not, after all, to become Commander-in-Chief of the Home Fleet. This decision was changed, but disputes were to surface later. After the *Bismarck* saga Churchill, and possibly Tom Phillips, wanted the captain of *Prince of Wales* court-martialled for turning away from the enemy. Tovey threatened to resign and act as 'prisoner's friend', and no more was heard of the matter. Later Tovey disagreed vehemently with Churchill about the need for and wisdom of the Arctic convoys. Tovey had the misfortune to be right when he said that the scattering of the infamous convoy PQ.17 could be 'sheer bloody murder'[24]: it was. Tovey also launched a vigorous campaign for more long-range aircraft in the Atlantic and objected to Churchill's schemes for combined operations against the Norwegian coast. The end result was predictable. Churchill described Tovey as 'a stubborn and obstinate man'[25] and referred to his 'naturally negative and unenterprising attitude of mind'. Tovey, on the other hand, gave a far more reasoned vision of Churchill:

> To me [the strategic control of the war] appears to have been based on expediency and bright ideas without any real governing policy behind it. WC as Prime Minister is magnificent and unique, but as a strategist and tactician he is liable to be most dangerous. He loves the dramatic and public acclamation. He has, to my knowledge, put up some wild schemes and, again without knowing details, I disliked intensely his original scheme for a second front.[26]

When Cunningham was called home from the Mediterranean Fleet it was part of an attempt to get rid of Tovey and appoint Cunningham in his place. Cunningham said he would take over from Tovey if and when Tovey dropped dead on his bridge. Cunningham went instead to Washington and Tovey was sent to command the Nore. His problem was that when his big chance came he failed to win that smashing victory that would have made him too expensive to dispose of.

That opportunity came when the new German battleship

Bismarck and the cruiser *Prince Eugen* set sail on a raiding cruise. The details of this engagement are well enough known to need only the briefest of summaries here. The British had ample warning of the cruise through ULTRA, through other intelligence and from air reconnaissance, not to mention reports from neutrals. After being spotted by two British cruisers the German vessels were intercepted by the new battleship *Prince of Wales* and the old battlecruiser *Hood*. After only a few salvoes *Hood* blew up. *Prince of Wales*, hit several times and with defective main armament, retired to shadow the German force. It split up, *Bismarck* having received a hit forward that severed fuel lines and gave her leaking tanks and quite severe flooding. The British then lost *Bismarck*, and found her again only at the last minute as she was nearing Brest. A final fling from *Ark Royal's* Swordfish put a torpedo into *Bismarck's* rudders, allowing her to be finished off the morning after by British battleships and cruisers. In one sense the engagement was a draw, one battleship each. In another sense it was a British victory, as the Germans could afford the loss of a battleship far less than the British. In a far more real sense, it was a defeat for the British, because 'the mighty *Hood*' was more than a battleship, almost the symbol of British naval might – an illustration, if nothing else, of the danger of letting any one vessel become a public-relations symbol of a fleet's might. It was also clear that the resources needed to bring about *Bismarck's* destruction were absurdly out of proportion, and that a large element of luck contributed to the final sinking.

As Commander-in-Chief Home Fleet, Tovey bore the greatest responsibility for the action. His conduct of it was flawed, though, in fairness to a great fighting sailor, there were many areas where the odds were stacked against him. The most obvious of these was in *matériel*. The British had never made effective arrangements for refuelling at sea, perhaps the spin-off of a Navy brought up on the concept of Empire and convenient coaling stations. To compound this fault, they insisted on designing vessels with comparatively limited endurance, of which the 'King George V' class battleships were an example. Tovey had three capital ships immediately available to him in Scapa – two 'King George V' class battleships and *Hood* – with the battlecruiser *Repulse* available from the Clyde. His apparent strength – twenty 14" and fourteen 15" guns against eight 15" and eight 8″ for the Germans – was entirely deceptive. *Repulse* had a light armament of only six 15″ guns, and, though fast, was very lightly armoured and relatively unmodernized. *Hood*, for all her beauty, was a bastard design. Essentially a battlecruiser, she had been reworked while on the stocks after three similar vessels had blown up at Jutland. The result was that more armour had been slapped on to her, but some of it was in the wrong places, and little of it suitable protection against plunging fire or bombs: her deck armour was known to be inadequate and shortage of resources meant that her planned refit never took place. There were three other features about *Hood* that made her a potential death trap. Firstly, she was carrying the 'Unrotated rocket Projectile' weapon at the time of her death, a harebrained idea for launching parachute mines against air attack. Ammunition for this weapon was stored in thin metal lockers topside. Secondly, there is some evidence that in her recent Mediterranean cruise considerable quantities of ready-use 4″ ammunition had been allowed to be stored out of secure magazine space, to speed up rate of fire, and there is no evidence that this order was rescinded. Finally, she carried eight torpedoes on board for her above-water tubes, protected only by relatively thin 3″ armour. The explosion that tore her apart was sixty-five feet away from the nearest magazine, but in a position entirely in keeping with the torpedo warheads going up in sympathy after hits from either of the German ships.

In theory the two 'King George V' class battleships should have been much better. Modern in design, they carried ten 14″ guns of a new design, two of them in quadruple turrets. They had excellent armour protection, a reasonable speed of twenty-eight knots and an innovative and acclaimed secondary armament of dual-purpose 5.25″ guns. Much has been made of the fact that *Prince of Wales* was not fully worked up, and indeed never had the chance to do so fully right up until the time of her sinking by the Japanese. It now seems as if the significance of that fact should be played down, at least relative to the significance of other factors. The major factor is that the new quadruple turret was a disaster. Ironically, one of the reasons for its inadequacy was an obsession with magazine safety. Complex safety interlocks and insufficient clearances made the quadruple turrets gluttons for jamming. The jamming crippled *Prince of Wales*; it affected her sister ship *King George V* almost as badly when *Bismarck* was sunk. One turret was out of action for half an hour, for seven minutes her fire power was down to twenty percent, and for twenty-three minutes to sixty percent. In December, 1943, the figures for *Duke of York* when she sank *Scharnhorst* were not much better. Other problems with the class were their low freeboard and the absence of what the Germans called an 'Atlantic bow'. It was a design requirement that the main armament of these vessels should be capable of straight-ahead fire, but the low bow this made necessary was a killer in bad weather. In *Duke of York* a favourite cry was 'Seals in the shell-room', because deck fitting forward tore away in heavy seas and let large quantities of water into bow compartments. Throughout the war German capital ships had both higher speed than their British counterparts and the capacity to maintain this speed more effectively in bad weather. In fairness to the designers, as had already been mentioned, the class had been designed round the 1936 London Naval Treaty. That was not much comfort to Tovey when considering his options. In addition to his other worries, he had the carrier *Victorious* with him in Scapa, but she was not fully worked up either, and had only nine Swordfish and six Fulmar aircraft embarked, the remainder of her space being taken up by crated Hurricanes.

Tovey's initial dispositions were beyond criticism. He knew through ULTRA that German reconnaissance aircraft had been paying special attention to the ice pack off Greenland, and he stationed two heavy cruisers in the Denmark Strait between Iceland and Greenland. He sent *Hood* and *Prince of Wales*, with a destroyer screen, to patrol the Iceland-Faeroes Gap. He then brought his flagship *King George V* to short notice for steam, together with the aircraft carrier *Victorious*. Clearly he wanted to keep his flagship in harbour as long as possible so that he could have at least one fully-fuelled battleship ready to react to events, and so that he could maintain telephone contact with the Admiralty for as long as possible in what might well be a very confused situation. The combination of *Hood* and *Prince of Wales* was also an obvious one. *Hood* was not well-protected, but she was a proud ship with a heavy main armament and was fully worked-up. *Prince of Wales* was not fully-worked up nor had she a competent main armament, but she was as unsinkable in armour terms as any capital ship outside the Japanese

Yamato. This combination might indeed have worked if Vice-Admiral L. E. Holland had not got several things wrong. Firstly, he hauled his force round to the south-east when contact was lost with the Germans for three hours, fearing that the Germans had reversed course or passed behind him in order to break out into the Atlantic. Had he held his nerve his vessels would have been the top of the 'T', the Germans its stem. As it was, he came in sight of the German force when almost parallel to them, and turned inward enough to restrict his fire to forward guns only, whilst allowing the German to give him their full broadside. Tovey considered signalling Holland to put *Prince of Wales* in the van to absorb punishment, but refrained. He was absolutely correct, and it is an irony that in a naval war dotted by wrong-headed interfering signals for the Admiralty one that might have helped never got sent. For reasons best known to himself Holland sent in *Hood* first, tied *Prince of Wales* so closely to his track that the vessel actually had to swerve to avoid running over the remnants of *Hood* when she sank, and failed to involve the two heavy cruisers he had nearby to divert enemy fire.

Tovey's mistakes were twofold. There were two possible breakout points for a German force, the Denmark Strait or the Iceland-Faeroes Gap to the south. German reconnaissance by air had been of the northern route; it was the furthest away from Scapa Flow and the figures for British battleship endurance were presumably known to the Germans; the last German breakout had been by *Scharnhorst* and *Gneisenau* through the northern route, the Denmark Strait, although as far as I can ascertain Tovey did not know that the commander, Lutjens, was the same for both operations. A gambler would have staked his all on the Denmark Strait passage. It was clear that the first force sent out was the most likely one to meet the Germans, and the most balanced combination for that first striking force would have been *King George V* to meet *Bismarck*, *Hood* to haul off out of range of *Prince Eugen's* 8" guns and pound her to pieces, then turn her attention to *Bismarck*. *Victorious* should have sailed with the two capital ships to provide reconnaissance, to launch a long-distance strike if the gamble had proved wrong and the Iceland-Faeroes Gap route been used, and to launch a strike on *Bismarck* when she was engaged with the British vessels, having hauled off with the destroyer screen when

Bismarck was first sighted, out of 15″ gun range. With this arrangement, *Prince of Wales* and *Repulse* would have been the back-up-force, able if the worst came to the worst to shadow *Bismarck* until a greater concentration of force could be achieved.

The *Bismarck* episode needed someone with the courage to put all his power into the first punch. Tovey left too much of it in Scapa and paid the price. He was also let down by Holland, who was over-cautious in his decisions, but if any man paid the full price for his mistakes, it was Holland, who went down with *Hood*.

Tovey made three other mistakes in the course of the operation. Firstly, for too long he missed the fact that *Bismarck* was heading towards Brest. Secondly, Tovey had with him two destroyers when he set out equipped with radio-direction-finding equipment. He thus insisted that the Admiralty signalled to him 'raw' bearings from any shore station which could be converted to suggest an actual position by the trained staff on board the destroyers, rather than the position any such bearing might suggest. The destroyers had left to refuel in Iceland; the bearings on *Bismarck* when they were received were wrongly plotted on board *King George V*, which did not have the trained staff of the destroyers. The result was that for vital hours Tovey steamed as if the German ship was heading back through the Iceland-Faeroes Gap, instead of towards Brest. He was only saved by *Ark Royal's* disabling strike. The third error never evolved into disaster but how easily it might have done so. When it was confirmed that *Bismarck* had been hit and was apparently only able to steer to the north, Tovey declined a night action, let Admiral Vian's destroyers harry *Bismarck* instead and opted for a dawn engagement with *Bismarck* silhouetted against the rising sun. During this night action no less than sixteen torpedoes were launched at *Bismarck* and it may well be that none hit. Furthermore, *Bismarck* was lost to sight twice for considerable periods of time, in either of which she might have mended her rudders and been proceeding towards Brest at twenty-two or twenty-five knots; her engines were undamaged, as were her shafts. It is interesting to speculate what would have happened if she had tried to proceed at full speed to Brest *in reverse*, something which modern-day opinion believes might have been possible. Tovey took a tremendous risk in leaving *Bismarck* alone for the night.

It was not as if the Germans made no mistakes. *Bismarck* was not the perfect design her defenders have sometimes claimed. Her 'soft' forward end and the disposition of oil tanks rendered her liable to just the sort of damage *Prince of Wales* was able to inflict. In the final conflict with *King George V* and *Rodney* she was finished as a fighting ship very early on, landing not a single hit on the British ships. One reason was that her fire control systems were bunched together amidships, the natural aiming point for all hostile fire, and with these gone early in the action she was effectively crippled. Also, the two-tier, antiquated armour protection of *Bismarck* allowed communications and electrical systems to be destroyed very easily, whilst preserving watertight integrity and magazine and engine-room space: the vessel stayed afloat long after it was finished as a fighting unit. If *Bismarck* had design weaknesses, Lutjens' command of the operation was also significantly flawed. Despite announcing that he would not do so, he had allowed his force to loiter in the Norwegian fjords well within range of British reconnaissance: while loitering had failed to refuel, an error that was to become crucial after the damage inflicted by *Prince of Wales*. When he had sunk Britain's most prestigious warship, he failed to turn round and go back home when the field was clear, and at the same time failed to chase after *Prince of Wales* when he had a glorious opportunity to do for her as well. He sent long and loud radio signals back home when radio silence should have been observed.

Tovey's actions illustrate perhaps what happens when a dashing and daring destroyer commander is placed in command of a Home Fleet. Nelson's dictum was that no commander can do much wrong if he lays himself alongside an enemy and blasts the hell out of him. Life for the Commander-in-Chief of the Home Fleet in 1941 was rarely that simple. The frustration of Tovey is evident in a letter he wrote to Cunningham:

> How the devil do you get in touch with the blighters?
> That's what I want to know, so please let me into the
> secret.[27]

Tovey was 'a very able commander. He was like Cunningham, but approachable. Anyone who served with him loved him . . .

when appointed C-in-C of the Home Fleet it was a tremendously popular appointment.'[28]

Yet somehow this was not enough. The responsibilities of the Home Fleet seemed to weigh him down, turning the all-dash-and-daring destroyer commander into a cautious, even fearful Admiral. Churchill did not help. The marvellously straightforward fighting sailor had to cope with an interfering Prime Minister as well as interminable convoy duties and the niggle of an idle fleet stuck to its anchors in Scapa Flow. No one can doubt Tovey's capacity as a fighting admiral; as a thinking admiral he was less impressive, and he shows, more than all the others, that aggression, personal charm and utter integrity are not enough for a truly successful commander: ruthlessness, intellectual agility and, above all, good luck are equal factors in the balance of success.

If there was a real hero of the *Bismarck* episode it was James Somerville. His Force H was never really allowed to do what it had been set up for, and it was hauled north into the Atlantic at a moment's notice. It was Somerville's *Sheffield* that made contact with *Bismarck* and stuck to her. It was Somerville's *Ark Royal* who came straight from the Mediterranean and its flat calm, and launched a strike against the enemy when the deck rise and fall was measured at fifty-two feet. The first strike launched by *Ark Royal* actually attacked *Sheffield*, through no fault of their own. It was *Ark Royal's* maintenance crews who were able to prepare a second strike in time, and *Ark Royal's* aircrew who were able to find *Bismarck*, and possibly hit her no less than three times. It is surely too much of a coincidence that the most air-minded of British Admirals was in charge of the carrier that crippled *Bismarck*, and too much of a coincidence that the British Admiral who had an obsession about full training and working-up commanded the vessel whose crew proved beyond all doubt that they at least were fully worked-up. The chase for *Bismarck* was a saga of refit and repair. *Prince of Wales*, through no fault of her own, was an inefficient vessel. *Rodney*, when she met *Bismarck*, was on her way to America for refit, way below her design speed and full of stacked crates of spares and convalescent soldiers. Force H played the crucial part in the sinking of *Bismarck*. Its commander, Somerville, was perhaps the man who most of all sank the *Bismarck*.

6 *Prince of Wales* and *Repulse*

Chronology of Events

1941

22 June. Operation Barbarossa, German attack on Soviet Russia, starts.

21 August. First Russian convoy sails.

25 August. Force K (Admiral Vian) attacks Spitzbergen.

27 August. German *U570* captured, to be commissioned as HMS *Graph.*

16 September. First group of German U-boats ordered to Mediterranean.

23 September. German dive-bombers sink Russian battleship *Marat*, the first battleship ever to be sunk by dive bombers.

24 October. British destroyer *Cossack* sunk by U-boat. On board is *Bismarck's* cat, Oscar. Oscar is taken over by *Ark Royal.*

27 October. Admiral of the Fleet Sir Roger Keyes replaced by Lord Louis Montbatten as head of the Directorate of Combined Operations.

31 October. US destroyer *Reuben James* torpedoed and sunk by *U552.*

8/9 November. Force K (Admiral Vian) attacks Italian convoy and sinks seven transports and two destroyers.

13/14 November Ark Royal. torpedoed and sunk; Oscar, *Bismarck's* cat, seen as a bad sea-going risk, dies ashore in the Home for Sailors, Belfast, in 1955.

19 November. German commerce raider *Kormoran* and Australian cruiser *Sydney* sink each other.

25 November. British battleship *Barham* torpedoed and sunk in Mediterranean by *U331.*

7 December. Japanese carrier aircraft attack Pearl Harbor.

10 December. British battleship *Prince of Wales* and
    battlecruiser *Repulse* sunk by Japanese land-based aircraft.

Perhaps only the sinking of *Hood* and *Bismarck* has rivalled the
loss of *Prince of Wales* and *Repulse* in terms of high drama and
tragedy. Four major books have been written on or around the
episode, and just as Cunningham has become one of the comparatively few widely-known British Admirals because of his
association with two famous victories, so the Admiral in command of Force Z, Admiral Tom Phillips, has become uniquely
associated with this disaster.

One view of Phillips has achieved wide notoriety since the
tragedy of the sinking of Force Z. In this view Phillips is the
jumped-up Staff Officer, the brilliant brain with no human
touch and a dogmatic manner. While salty old sea dogs like
Andrew Cunningham and James Somerville clucked in disapproval, Phillips was promoted over the heads of those considered
more worthy. Most of all, Phillips set his heart against air
power, believing that the battleship ruled all. Then, irony of
ironies, he was sent out to face the might of Japanese air power
and led his two fine capital ships to the slaughter, victims of
bigotry and an outdated worship of the capital ship.

This view finds its most concise expression in one of the best-
known of the books written about the sinking, Middlebrook and
Mahoney's *Battleship*:

> The facts speak for themselves: these two great ships and
> many good men were lost because one stubborn old sea-
> dog refused to acknowledge that he had been wrong.[1]

It is all nonsense. Phillips was one of the greatest losses the
Royal Navy suffered in the war. His ships were doomed from
the moment they were sent to the Far East. In losing them
Phillips was obeying the very best traditions of the service he
revered. He made mistakes in the way he handled his two
capital ships, almost inevitably, but many fewer than he might
have done. In the final count, he was unlucky. For all the
rantings of historians and academics, there is a quality that
cannot be summarized in a footnote or secured by reference to a
learned authority, and that quality is luck. It ran against Tom

Phillips on 10 December, 1941, and that fact should not be allowed to damn him, especially when his actions were entirely in keeping with the character and personality of two of his staunchest critics, Cunningham and Somerville.

Tom Spencer Vaughan Phillips was born in 1888, the son of a colonel and the grandson of an admiral, illustrating the point yet again of the existence of a 'pool' of military families from which so many top commanders came. He attended *Britannia* and was promoted Lieutenant at the early age of twenty, largely as a result of his obvious intellectual brilliance after obtaining the maximum number of five 'firsts' in his courses. Even his worst enemies could not deny Tom Phillips the quality of intelligence, but his intelligence was not always his best friend. He did not suffer fools gladly and could be very remote; in some accounts these traits have been used against him, ignoring the fact that both were held by the most successful British admirals of the war. He specialized in navigation, was present at the Dardanelles, but was 'marooned' on board *Lancaster* in the Far East for much of the First World War, missing Jutland. In a varied and successful career, he attended the first RN Staff College course after the war and became Staff Officer to Admiral Sir Roger Keyes in the Mediterranean. Keyes was a fire-eater and never easy to please; Phillips' capacity to work with hard masters is a skill rarely commented on. He had two periods of roughly five years in all, commanding destroyer flotillas and one as captain of a cruiser, but Admiralty appointments were more common, even though when he was promoted to Rear Admiral in January, 1939, it was as Commodore commanding the Home Fleet Destroyer Flotillas. A favourite of Churchill's, he was made Deputy Chief of Naval Staff on 1 June, 1939, in succession to Cunningham, the post being renamed Vice Chief of Naval Staff in April, 1940. He was to become a close personal friend of Pound's and his most valued aide. The Official Historian, Stephen Roskill, seems to see Phillips as an all-big-gun and big-ship man. There appears to be no evidence for this view; if anything, Phillips learnt his trade in destroyers.

The odium heaped on Phillips by a string of commentators seems grossly unfair and ill-advised, but before attempting to explain that interpretation it is perhaps as well to present the conventional view of Phillips and the loss of *Prince of Wales* and *Repulse*. His intellectual brilliance has already been noted, but he lacked the 'common touch'. A very small man, he was known as 'Tom Thumb' or 'Titch Phillips', and some of those who knew him (though none who are prepared to be quoted) believed that he fell into the conventional psychological cliché of being the little man who had a point to prove, and was thus unnaturally aggressive and forthright in defending himself. His brilliance had seen him receive early promotion as a staff officer, but the up-and-at-'em brigade of the Royal Navy had never had much time for staff officers and saw Phillips as a good brain but a bad seaman, an arm-chair warrior with far too little seagoing experience. Cunningham wrote to a fellow admiral:

What do you think of the Far East? What about *P of W* & *Repulse*. Why & oh why did they not send out someone of experience or at least have Geoffrey Layton who is a well-tried sailor & full of determination?[2]

Layton was the commander superceded by Phillips, who had to take over again after the loss of the two ships.

Somerville referred to Phillips as the 'pocket Napoleon'[3], and said that he had 'all the tricks to learn & no solid sea experience to fall back on,'[4] while Cunningham wrote to another friend:

What on earth is Phillips going to the Far Eastern Squadron for? He hardly knows one end of a ship from the other. His only experience is eight months as RAD [Rear Admiral, Destroyers] and then he had the stupidest collision. However, if you have a seat on the board you can generally manoeuvre yourself into a good job – I did![5]

The Official Naval Historian hammered another nail into Phillips' coffin:

Rear Admiral Tom Phillips, the Deputy Chief of Naval Staff, who had no first-hand experience of the deadly effect of unopposed dive-bombers on warships, insisted that all that was needed to deal with them effectively was greater courage and resolution; and he took it very badly when told that such ideas were unjust to those officers who had the experience, and were in fact far from the truth. . . . Phillips *would* not accept that it was suicidal to send warships to operate off an cncmy-held coast without air cover.[6]

It may have influenced Roskill's judgement that he was one of the officers who tried to tell Phillips the truth about the Norwegian campaign; and that he received sharp treatment in so doing. Middlebrook and Mahoney state as fact that Phillips 'had no great opinion of the effectiveness of the modern aeroplane or the danger it posed to warships,' and then remarked that, while he was not alone in this, 'it is probable that Phillips' views were considerably more out of touch and mistaken than those of most of his contemporaries.'[7]

Another historian confirms Phillips' contempt for aircraft as a threat to well-defended capital ships:

It was his conviction that all warships at sea, if properly equipped with anti-aircraft armament and well-trained gun-crews, could repel air attack, even from shore-based aircraft.[8]

A number of works cite the story that one of Phillips' friends (the name of the friend varies with the source) became so exasperated with his inability to realize the damage aircraft could do that he announced that when the first bomb hit a ship commanded by Phillips, Phillips would exclaim, 'My God, what a hell of a mine!'[9]

Phillips has also been seen as a favourite of Churchill's and Pound's, owing his command in the Far East to favouritism more than aptitude:

Phillips' nomination to such an important appointment . . . is to be attributed chiefly to Pound's admiration and gratitude for a man who had served him well at the Admiralty.[10]

It is not widely known that the original plan was for Vice Admiral Holland, killed in *Hood*, to become VCNS, and for Phillips to receive a seagoing appointment. It was always Phillips' hope that he would go to sea after his period as VCNS, and he placed considerable pressure on those around him at the Admiralty for this to become true.

The background to the sending out of what came to be known as Force Z has been well-documented elsewhere. With the growing likelihood of war with Japan no one at the Admiralty was opposed to reinforcing the Far Eastern Fleet, if the vessels could be found – but the Royal Navy was hopelessly over-stretched, and the most that could be offered at short notice was a squadron of old 'R' class battleships. Some of these were to find their way out to the Far East when Somerville became Commander-in-Chief there and were to prove a total liability. They were slow, weakly armoured, gluttons for fuel, old and unreliable, short-ranged, appallingly ventilated and without adequate facilities for preparing fresh water. In fairness to the Admiralty, the vessels were seen as participants in trade protection, not as something designed to take on the Japanese fleet. Churchill described them as 'floating coffins'[11] and there is no doubt that he was right. His idea was to send a deterrent force to the Far East, based on his belief that Japan would wage a war against trade and not launch a direct assault on the Malayan peninsula. The actual mechanism by which the modern battleship *Prince of Wales* and the largely unmodernised battlecruiser *Repulse* ended up at Singapore with minimal destroyer escort has still not been satisfactorily explained, but against the wishes of the Admiralty and presumably at Churchill's prompting these were the two vessels that became Force Z. It could be that a major factor in Churchill's decision to send a modern battleship to the Far East may have been the desire to impress Australia and New Zealand, cementing their commitment to what was still at that time a European war. Churchill was obsessed by the impact *Tirpitz* was having on British dispositions and mistakenly assumed that a 'King George V' class battleship in the Far East would have the same effect on the Japanese.

Force Z was sent to the Far East because it was the only readily available way of reinforcing the garrison at Singapore, which was quite unprepared for war; because it was hoped its two capital ships would deter the Japanese; because it was hoped it would be a rallying gesture for Australia and New Zealand in exchange for their commitment to the war in Europe; and because Indonesian and Malaysian natural resources, as well as trade with India, were vital. In all, bar the effect on Australia and New Zealand, the gesture was doomed. Singapore had suffered badly from British penury in the inter-war years. It

10 'Cunningham was a firm traditionalist, and a stickler for uniform in particular.' This photograph compares interestingly with that of Fraser in plate 20.

11 'Gallant, resourceful and quick as lightning flying at their throats.' Tovey boarding *Prince of Wales* to take over the Home Fleet.

12 The loss of the *Hood*.

13 *Bismarck* in flames.

had neither the fortifications, the men, nor the aircraft to withstand a determined assault: the plans existed, but the money did not. The Japanese were committed to a war of conquest and expansion, not a trade war, and the presence of one new and one old capital ship would cause hardly a flicker on the strategic scales.

Much has been made of the fact that in the original dispositons Force Z would have included the carrier *Indomitable* Unfortunately *Indomitable* had grounded while working up in the West Indies and hence was unable to join Phillips. She carried twenty-one fighter aircraft in all, composed of Fulmars and Hurricanes.

The main reason for sending of Force Z disappeared on 7/8 December when the Japanese attacked Pearl Harbor; deterrence had clearly failed. Phillips could stay in Singapore and face inevitable air attack, retreat to Australia, hide in the islands, or try to disrupt the Japanese invasion forces. He chose the last option, and no commentator has disputed that this was the right decision. He sailed on 8 December, 1941, in the hope of attacking Japanese invasion forces off Singora on the morning of 10 December. He asked for air cover off Singora, but was told in a signal of 9 December that it would not be possible. He pressed on but was spotted by submarine and by aircraft from Japanese cruisers and broke off to return to Singapore. He then received a signal suggesting that the Japanese were invading Kuantan, easily within range on his course back to Singapore. He set course to investigate, but made no signal to Singapore announcing his change of course and intention. Force Z was sighted by the Japanese and bomber and torpedo shore-based aircraft launched against it. These failed to find Force Z, but did find the destroyer *Tenedos* detached from Force Z through lack of fuel.

In the meantime the tail-end of Japanese reconnaissance had spotted Force Z and a massive shore-based air attack was launched. Phillips arrived at Kuantan, found no sign of invasion, waited to investigate some suspicious ships, but broke off and headed for home when he received the signal from *Tenedos* saying she was under air attack. Neither at this juncture nor at any time during the action did Phillips call for air cover from Singapore.

Japanese air attacks on the two British ships sank them both. In the first attack *Repulse* was hit by a bomb which exploded on her armoured deck and did little damage. The real damage was done by torpedo aircraft. These first of all crippled *Prince of Wales* by damaging hits on her stern, then sank *Repulse* after she had put up a marvellous fight, then put paid to *Prince of Wales*. Tom Phillips could almost certainly have saved himself, but went down with *Prince of Wales*. Captain Leach of *Prince of Wales* also died with his ship. Captain Tennant of *Repulse* went down with his ship, but, much to his surprise, came up again after it had sunk, and lived to fight another day. The loss of these two vessels was a disaster for the Royal Navy, its impact lessened only by the fact that it was sandwiched between the horror of Pearl Harbor and the loss of Singapore itself shortly afterwards.

Given a bare recital of the facts, it is all too easy to see Phillips as a man lacking in practical experience who led his force unwittingly into the jaws of Japanese air power and paid the price of his own ignorance. The truth is rather different. The odds were stacked against Phillips' before he went near the bridge of *Prince of Wales*. In the eyes of the Royal Navy and its leading Admirals, he was guilty of three cardinal sins. Firstly, he achieved a double promotion to Vice-Admiral and then Admiral in a very short space of time while still comparatively young, which caused much jealousy. Cunningham in particular appears to have taken against Phillips on this count, as a contemporary noted:

> There was probably a considerable element of jealousy in the dislike [by Cunningham of Phillips]. I often noticed, with surprise, a strong streak of jealousy where other 'up and coming' Flag Officers were concerned. Surprising in a man of such sterling qualities.[12]

As is well known, there was considerable antagonism between Cunningham and Admiral Fraser, and it seems probable that the jealousy noted above was quite a strong feature in Cunningham's make-up. It is interesting to note that when Pound criticized Cunningham's friend Somerville over the action off Cape Spartivento, Cunningham defended Somerville, but without mentioning him by name, and without any of the fervour that Somerville showed when he put his head on the block over Admiral Dudley North, or that Tovey showed when resisting the court-martial of Captain John Leach over the *Bismarck* and *Prince of Wales* episode.[13] Cunningham did defend Pound, but Pound's reputation never approached that of Cunningham, and some of his defence of Pound manages to make it quite clear what Pound's failings were. Cunningham was willing to give praise to commanders such as Tovey, Vian and Ramsay, but, with the possible exception of the last, the praise somehow never seemed to suggest that these other commanders were anything other than highly effective subordinates. Cunningham did not like to share the stage.

In any event, Phillips' meteoric rise had provoked jealousy. Somerville had an axe to grind, in that he might very reasonably have expected the appointment instead of Phillips, and indeed was to receive it after him. Tovey was not likely to support Force Z when it cost him one of his very few modern battleships to go off on a wild goose chase to the Far East, while *Tirpitz*, *Scharnhorst*, *Gneisenau* and *Prince Eugen* were all capable of breaking out into the trade routes.

If Phillips' youth provoked jealousy, then a triple dose of petrol was added to the flames by the fact that Phillips was so closely associated with the Admiralty, with Churchill and Pound and with Staff work.[14] As we have already seen, none of these were automatic recommendations among other fighting Admirals. In fact the link with Churchill had cooled almost to animosity by the time Phillips took command of Force Z (though Churchill was clearly deeply moved by Phillips' death), and this cooling of relations may have been one reason why Phillips was given the job. Originally Churchill had conceived a great affection for Phillips, referring to him as 'that little cock sparrow on the edge of his chair and not caring a damn what I say'[15], but from Spring, 1941, Phillips appears to have said too much. He expressed his opposition to the mass bombing of Germany, a view which history is increasingly coming to agree with but which angered Churchill. The final straw was Phillips' impassioned opposition to the Greece expedition. He considered this a wasteful sideshow and felt that reinforcing the Mediterranean was far more important. Ironically, this opinion might have put him on the same side as one of his great enemies, Cunningham, but Cunningham either did not know of Phillips' opposition or chose not to show his knowledge of it. Again, Phillips was right, but being proved right was never a way to

Churchill's heart. Cunningham, who did not support the expedition to Greece but gave in when political pressure was brought to bear, was perhaps the better politician, even if he was a worse strategist. As a contemporary commented:

> The PM had not even spoken to him for 8 months; and my recollection – a most untrustworthy authority! – is that he [Phillips] had been relegated to Coventry because of his refusal to endorse the expedition to Greece.[16]

In the First World War when Churchill was at the Admiralty he had fallen out of with Rear Admiral Sir Doveton Sturdee, but did not wish to offend Fisher, so sent Sturdee to hunt the *Scharnhorst* and *Gneisenau* off South America, thus getting rid of a nuisance while preserving the peace. It is possible he was trying a variation of the same trick with Phillips. Whatever the truth, Phillips was far from being a stooge or lackey of Churchill's; if anything, he fell into the opposite camp.

He was young, associated with the Admiralty and people there who were unpopular with some fighting admirals – and he was seen as a bad seaman. The old guard of officers placed tremendous value on seamanship and an officer's capacity to handle a ship. Phillips lacked seagoing experience and the image of him as a desk admiral was based on a collision between *Encounter* and *Furious* when Phillips was firstly Commodore and then Rear Admiral (D), Home Fleet, in 1938–9. There was no Board of Enquiry into the collision and no real evidence to suggest that he was anything other than a competent seaman. In any event, very few senior officers had extensive experience of handling major squadrons in Far Eastern waters at that time. There is a cruel irony in the accusation quoted above that Phillips was a salty old sea dog: it was the salty old sea dogs who most hated him, and he was far from being of their kind.

Phillips has been accused of bad tactical ship-handling in the early stages of the encounter. This charge is based on the fact that he tried to manoeuvre his two vessels as one in close order when the first bombing aircraft made their run. *Repulse* was hit by one bomb but not seriously damaged in this attack (all armour-piercing bombs had been requisitioned for Pearl Harbor), and Phillips rapidly changed his orders so as to allow both ships freedom of manoeuvre. By the time the attacks which sank his ships came, he had therefore scrubbed the only serious error in the handling of his ship of which he was accused. However, even this is not the whole story. High-level bombing had been notoriously inefficient in the Mediterranean and British attempts to bomb German battlecruisers in France had fared no better. By keeping his ships together and thus concentrating his anti-aircraft fire Phillips may have had much more right on his side than he has been given credit for. *Repulse* was hopelessly under-gunned in terms of anti-aircraft weapons, while *Prince of Wales* had long-range 5.25″ high-angle guns. By keeping close order Phillips was keeping his weakest vessel under the umbrella of his greater fire power and ensuring clear firing arcs for his own long-range guns.

The jealousy of other officers can be understood, and explained. It can also be largely dismissed. There were good reasons for sending Phillips out to command Force Z, far better reasons than there were for sending the Force itself. Phillips had an excellent brain and was well able to take decisions. The First Lord, A. V. Alexander, took 'great comfort' from the appointment, and he was no fool.[17] As an independent and sharp-witted man, Phillips could be expected to take decisions far away from the Admiralty or any hope of reinforcement, but because of his knowledge of the Admiralty he could also be expected to act in sympathy with its philosophy. He could probably not have docked *Illustrious* in Malta Harbour at twenty-three knots without the use of a tug while an air raid was going on, but he had experienced and capable captains to manoeuvre his ships under fire, and his wide historical knowledge and instant grasp of strategy was likely to be of more assistance to him than any amount of seamanship.

The Official Naval Historian, Captain Stephen Roskill, was in general hostile to Phillips, whereas his great rival, Professor Arthur Marder, viewed him in a more benign light. The family and other papers pertaining to Admiral Sir Tom Phillips are unusual in that they are still held by the family and not lodged with any of the major institutions to which such collections usually go. The papers are not extensive, but they are informative. Roskill did not consult these papers. Marder did, and quotes extensively from them in his comments on the sinking of Force Z. One fact highlighted in the papers is the deep respect that Phillips could command from his subordinates, an important factor when trying to justify his appointment, especially as so many others suggest only dislike for him. Certainly he was not an easy man. Like Pound, he was a tremendous centralizer, hated delegation and took far too great a work load on himself, checking draft after draft of documents and picking out the smallest details for correction. He thought he was always right, and tended not to listen to others before making up his mind. He could be abrasive, was short-tempered and obstinate. He seldom smiled. But there was much more to him than this. He frequently *was* right, and he was extremely hard-working, thorough, quick, and decisive – no bad features for a fighting admiral. He revered the Royal Navy and lived for it. He had a tremendous ability to impress people outside the Navy. It is well known that Force Z visited South Africa and General Smuts on its way to the Far East, and well known that Smuts predicted the possibility of a first-class disaster when the British and the Americans each had two inferior fleets in the Far East. It is less well known that Smuts was extremely impressed by Phillips, and Smuts was a very hard man to please or flatter.[18]

Phillips also appears to have been good in dealing with women and very popular with them, and in sharp and intelligent society a woman as powerful as Lady Diana Cooper admired Phillips' social and intellectual ease. It is clear that at one stage Marder considered that he might have been taking drugs or stimulants: extensive research revealed the truth, that he adored chocolate and stored large quantities of it in his desk!

The Phillips papers contain tributes to the Admiral which paint a very different picture from the vicious comments of other senior admirals. For instance:

It is futile for me to tell of the Admiral's genius or of his kindness and humility. I early surrendered to him my whole devotion.[19]

My husband was serving as Flag Lieutenant to your husband and I had two letters from him this week posted Cape Town, saying he had never had such respect and admiration for anyone as he had for 'his admiral', and that he was a really *great* man. My husband did not give his heart freely, and I feel much comforted to feel that he lost

his life serving such a man. It seems the only spark of
brightness in what is a very sad time to me.[20]

As you know I loved Sir Tom, but I never realized when I
last wrote to you what the nation lost when he was killed.
He was the one man who might have saved the situation
in Malaya and heaven knows how many people have told
me that in these last few months. We're still in a pretty
pickle in this part of the world, and I often feel that his
vision and drive are what we are all missing.[21]

Phillips' tremendous capacity to impress those outside of the
Navy is frequently emphasized:

Your Tom was a very outstanding character. . . . [He had]
character and charm in quite a different form and degree to
that of any other Naval Officer or man in other services
that I had ever met. In his own way he was just in a class
by himself.[22]

He was not short of the ability to impress those working inside
the Navy either. Tennant of *Repulse* was an outstandingly
successful captain of an extremely happy and efficient ship.
Unusually for a naval officer of the time, he was a great nature-
lover. Even more unusually, he found on the desk of his sea
cabin one day at sea on his birthday a large vase of flowers, with
the message 'From the Stokers'. A man who could receive that
kind of tribute from stokers was remarkable. His comment on
Phillips was 'he was very charming and good to work with'.[23] It
is clear from these comments and many others that Phillips had
the capacity to arouse intense loyalty and affection from those
with whom he worked. He could not do this on a large scale
with a ship's company for insance – nor could he do it with
many of his fellow senior officers. However, it is time that the
image of him as an aloof and angular intellectual, devoid of
personal human skills, must be laid to rest.

This leads on to the other great feature of the Phillips myth,
namely his belief that capital ships were proof against air attack
if correctly handled. There seems no doubt that for some years
before the war, and for at least a few months into it, Phillips did
not believe that the aircraft posed an overwhelming threat to a

well-defended surface ship. There are two significant facts here: firstly, going by what was known to the Royal Navy in 1939, Phillips was correct in believing that the threat from aircraft was overrated. Secondly, the evidence that he had changed his mind by the time of the sinking of Force Z and was seriously concerned about the threat posed by aircraft is overwhelming.

From the viewpoint of an intelligent man looking at the evidence of pre-war experience and the first months of the war, the air threat to surface ships was able to be contained. Italian high-level bombing in the Mediterranean had been singularly ineffective, as had torpedo attacks from shore-based aircraft. At Taranto success had been achieved in a surprise attack against moored ships at anchor in harbour. *Bismarck* had been crippled by one hit only, having shrugged off at least one other, and had no destroyer or cruiser screen to augment her anti-aircraft firepower. British bombing of German ships in France and Germany had been largely ineffective, despite a vast expenditure of effort, as had similar German bombing raids on Scapa Flow and other bases. There was every reason to believe that well-defended ships able to manoeuvre freely had a good chance of avoiding damage, at least from high-level bombing. If Phillips underestimated the threat to capital ships from the air, he had logic and some experience to back him up.

Furthermore, no one in British intelligence was aware of the highly advanced Japanese torpedo and aircraft designs, and in particular the techniques which allowed the Japanese to drop torpedoes at a height and air speed that would seem a taunting dream to any British pilot of a Swordfish torpedo bomber. As one historian has written:

> The opinion prevalent in British intelligence circles was that the combat worth of Japanese aircraft was well below that of their British counterparts.[24]

As we now know, the exact opposite was true.

Nevertheless, Phillips was above all an intelligent man, and what he felt in 1939 was not what he felt in 1941. Narvik and, to a far greater extent, Crete and Greece showed him the way the wind was blowing. Phillips urged Churchill to send Hurricane fighters to Malaya in 1941, well before his appointment to Force Z, but Churchill favoured sending the fighters instead to

Greece and to Stalin, leaving Malaya with the antiquated Brewster Buffaloes. Marder sums it up:

> The Tom Phillips of the Autumn of 1941 was therefore not the Tom Phillips who had made light of the air danger in the Norwegian operations a year and a half earlier.[25]

There is ample evidence from contemporaries to back up the fact that Phillips was more than aware of the air threat:

> My wife and I send you our deepest sympathy and you may care to know that I am taking every measure in my power to point out that Tom clearly appreciated the air risks, but had to do the best he could with what he had. The answer to the fools who say that without air protection the ships should have stayed in Singapore is quite simple. If that had happened these same critics would have demanded that he be shot for neglect of duty.[26]

This comment is also interesting because it reveals the implicit assumption on the part of those serving in Force Z that once out of Singapore it would be devoid of air cover. Much has been made by historians of the fact that Phillips failed to call for air cover, yet, as will be shown later, he had every reason to believe it would not be available. Phillips had been aware for years of the value its own air service would bring to the Royal Navy:

> Tom and I have always deeply resented the failure of successive governments to allow the Navy its own air service.[27]

At the conference Phillips held before Force Z set sail the air threat and the absence of air cover was clearly laid out as a major risk:

> We all of us (that is, the assembled Admiral's Staff, and commanding officers) fully appreciated that, lacking air cover, we should, on the morrow, find ourselves in an extremely hazardous way.[28]

Again it is made very clear that all those involved in the command decisions for Force Z did not believe that adequate air cover was available from the RAF. Other writers comment on Phillips' appreciation of the air threat:

> What seems to me to have been such hard luck is that old Tom should have gone out in circumstances so contrary to all his convictions. As you know he was all for a lot of smaller ships with a large air arm in support – he had *neither*.[29]

There were greater ironies than this. As VCNS Phillips had actually been responsible for stating the Admiralty opposition to the sending of Force Z, as at the time he was deputizing for Pound.[30]

Far from being unaware of the air threat, Phillips had drawn up plans when he was VCNS for just such a situation as the ships had found themselves in and reached the conclusion that the only sensible thing for them to do would be to withdraw to the nearest safe harbour so as to pose a distant threat to the Japanese[31]. Any decision to withdraw from Singapore once war was declared and invasion imminent could not be left to the man on the spot, who would in all certainty have then been accused of cowardice. It had to be ordered from Government: but no order came, and it was the absence of that order that sealed the fate of Force Z and its commander. Furthermore, he was almost obsessional about trying to arrange air cover before Force Z set sail. Almost his first action on arriving in Singapore was to raise the question of air cover with Sir Robert Brooke-Popham, the RAF Commander-in-Chief. He specifically asked his Staff if they thought it wise to set sail, bearing in mind that air support could not be counted on and might not be forthcoming[32]. He asked for three elements of reconnaissance and fighter cover before he set sail, and was so concerned about this being provided that he sent a reminder:

> I am not sure that Pulford realizes the importance I attach to fighter cover over Singora. I'm therefore going to send him a letter stressing this point again and asking him to let me know as soon as possible what he can do for certain.[33]

In summary, it is clear that Phillips had pressed for modern fighters to be sent to Malaya. He had argued forcibly against the sending of Force Z. He had made air cover one of his main priorities when reaching Singapore, pushing his concern over it almost to the point of rudeness. He had made it unequivocally clear to his Staff that he was concerned about the threat from aircraft and the weakness of his fleet in terms of air cover, had invited their views and found them unanimous in supporting his decision to set sail. It is difficult to think of any improvement that he could have made on his conduct of operations up to this point. Furthermore, his actions prove that he was fully aware of the necessity for air cover.

This leads on to the actual operation itself. As in so many areas, the odds were stacked against Phillips. He should have had a fleet carrier in attendance, but the grounding of *Indomitable* made this impossible. It has been suggested that the presence of the carrier would simply have added to the butcher's bill, with any fighter cover the British could have provided likely to be overwhelmed by the Japanese. To an extent this is true. A carrier would probably not have saved Force Z from destruction, but its fighters would certainly have had an effect on the battle and may have drawn off the Japanese attackers from the battleship and battlecruiser. The survivors would almost certainly have perished at a later date, unless withdrawn, but the disaster of Force Z might have been lessened. Historians have tended to comment on the absence of a carrier and ignore the other deficiencies in Phillips' 'fleet'. His destroyer escort was paltry in the extreme. Cunningham was ordered to detach two destroyers to form part of Force Z. Despite a rather sickening amount of humbug explaining why he sent *Jupiter* and *Encounter*, the facts were that the former took on a 10° list when fully loaded with oil, and the other had what was described as a 'corrugated bottom'. Both were in a desperate state. With an effective destroyer screen acting as an advanced picket and breaking up air attacks the story of Force Z might have been very different. As it was, the feeble escort provided to two capital ships placed them at severe risk from submarine attack, a risk which Phillips was clearly aware of as, in his discussions with Admiral Hart, he requested extra escorts from Singapore. These were despatched: they were not to arrive in time.

Nor was Phillips well served by the capital ships he did have. *Prince of Wales* was not a particularly happy ship and had never had the opportunity to work up fully. There were no aircraft to provide anti-aircraft practice for either vessel on the voyage out to the Far East and *Prince of Wales* lacked the experience of vessels with Norwegian, Greek or Mediterranean service in fending off concentrated air attack. In theory *Prince of Wales's* anti-aircraft fit was highly advanced; in practice things were a little less rosy. Her 5.25″ high-angle secondary armament may have suffered fire-control weaknesses, but it was virtually wiped out at an early stage in the action when electrical power failed to all but a handful of the turrets. Her pom-poms were short-range weapons anyway, but suffered throughout the action from jamming caused by premature separation of the cartridge case and shells in the belt-fed ammunition. *Repulse's* anti-aircraft armament was a joke; she was of a largely unmodernized First World War design that, from her earliest days, had suffered from inadequate armour protection. The two best ships in the world would have faced disaster in the Far East even if Nelson had been leading them: these two were far from the best. Furthermore, Phillips had no opportunity to exercise as a squadron and clearly felt worried at his inability to work up his two vessels and their escorts.

No one denies that he was right to attempt to intercept the invasion barges off Singora. No one denies that he handled his ships well on the outward leg, maintaining radio silence, and withdrawing when it became clear that he had been spotted and could no longer achieve surprise. It took immense moral courage to back away in this manner. Then Phillips received a signal from Rear Admiral A.F.E. Palliser, his Chief-of-Staff at Singapore, stating that a Japanese invasion force was reported to be attacking Kuantan, virtually on his route home. Had this signal not been sent Force Z would in all probability have made it back to Singapore and lived to fight, and be sunk, another day. The tone and content of the signal made it inevitable that Phillips would make the slight detour necessary to investigate Kuantan. Palliser failed to tell Phillips that the report of an invasion was unsubstantiated, and failed to arrange air cover over Kuantan. Phillips was obsessional about radio silence. He has been criticized for this, but right was on his side. We know now that Japanese radio-direction finding was not particularly effective; Phillips had no cause to underestimate his enemy in this area, and given the unreliability of RAF cover he quite rightly made surprise and avoiding detection his first priorities. He had been told before he left Singapore that air cover was doubtful, and so his aim was to avoid detection. Radio silence was an essential part of that. Phillips did not signal Palliser to arrange air cover over Kuantan. He had every right to expect that, having sent the signal, Palliser would automatically have arranged air cover for the area. A further fact that has not, to my knowledge, been commented on before is that if an invasion was taking place in an area easily within range of the Singapore air bases, Phillips had every right to expect aircraft from Singapore to be over the area anyway. He had already received a signal from Palliser stating that fighter protection would not be available on 10 December for Force Z. It did not specify a specific area for the non-availability of cover, but he knew that aircraft availability from Singapore was at best uncertain and technically inadequate even if it came. After sailing, he had been told that air cover would not be available because of the collapse of outlying airfields. His chance of any air cover, always uncertain in his mind anyway, was diminishing by the minute. He dare not reveal his position by signalling and had two separate reasons for supposing there would be air cover over Kuantan – firstly, Palliser presumably knew that his signal left Phillips no option but to make the easy diversion to Kuantan. Secondly, even if Palliser had not ordered aircraft there to cover Force Z, they should have been present anyway over an invasion area within easy range of Singapore. In other words, if air cover was at all avilable, it should have been ordered out to cover Kuantan. If it was not available, there was no point in giving away Force Z's position by radioing for it.

Phillips arrived at Kuantan and saw no sign of invasion. He has been criticized for dawdling too long at Kuantan, for not relying on his aircraft reconnaissance report that the beaches were clear, for sending in a destroyer to check, and then taking more time to check out a group of junks the fleet had passed shortly before dawn. It is hard not to think that Phillips was correct in all he did. In disbelieving the evidence of his air reconnaissance he merely took a wise precaution. Japanese air reconnaissance throughout the operation showed its own share of confusion and the confusions and mistakes of air reconnaissance in the war to date had been legion. Did not a number of highly-trained British aircrew attack one of their own cruisers, *Sheffield*, thinking she was the *Bismarck*, only a short while earlier? Had not both Cunningham and Iachino at Matapan disregarded aircraft sightings because of their known unreliability? Phillips was right to check his air sighting; what a fool he would have looked if his aircraft had failed to spot vital evidence, or if the Japanese had already taken Kuantan, and the calm of the beaches been merely the aftermath of a painless Japanese victory. His search after the junks was again merely prudence. What if the reported invasion had merely been a preliminary reconnaissance and the real invasion fleet was on its way to Kuantan? Phillips was 500 miles away from the Japanese-held Saigon airfields, clearly not threatened by enemy warships and well within range of his own air cover.

Earlier, Phillips had detached the destroyer *Tenedos* to refuel. At 1030 she signalled that she was being bombed by enemy aircraft. He immediately spotted the writing on the wall, altered course to the south-east, increased speed to twenty-five knots and sounded action stations.

It is easy to see why he did not call for air cover when he received *Tenedos'* signal. It would have revealed his position for one thing. The other major reason is discussed at length below: he had good cause to believe that air cover was not available.

His second opportunity to call for air cover came at 1015, when a Japanese reconnaissance aircraft was sighted, and his third at 1115 with the first high level bombing attack which landed one ineffective hit on *Repulse*, so he had every reason to think that he could handle a string of such attacks. *He had no reason to think that efficient shore-based torpedo bombers were available to attack him*. Had he known this he would have been justified in calling for air support. When the fact was forced on him, it was too late.

Even then, it was appalling bad luck that crippled *Prince of Wales* and effectively sank Force Z. One torpedo hit on the stern had delivered *Bismarck* to the British. One last-gasp shell-hit similarly delivered *Scharnhorst*. A stern hit nearly lost the Italian fleet *Vittorio Veneto* at Matapan. One or possibly two torpedoes hit *Prince of Wales* near the outboard propeller strut. The distorted shaft thrashed a huge hole through the guts of the ship, causing massive flooding. The shock of this and other hits knocked out a large part of the battleship's electrical power, effectively cutting off power to the rear half of the vessel for the duration of the action. The result was disastrous. Without power, damage-control parties could not be directed to the most effective areas. Many of the high-angle turrets were put out of action, thus rendering useless the ship's most powerful weapons for this kind of engagement. Pumps to contain the flooding were put out of action. Steps were subsequently taken to protect the electrical systems on board the 'King George V' class against shock damage, but that was too late to save *Prince of Wales*. The torpedo hit on the stern sank her as surely as it sank *Bismarck*. It was far more a cause of her loss than any deficiencies on the part of Admiral Tom Phillips. Once *Prince of Wales* was crippled the older and less well-defended *Repulse* was doomed; it was only a matter of time. Despite being brilliantly handled, and surviving more hits than any First World War design had a right to expect, *Repulse* succumbed.

Middlebrook and Mahoney, two of Phillips' fiercest critics, cite him as having made four 'major errors'. Firstly, when a suspected Japanese plane was seen off Kuantan on the morning of Force Z's arrival, Phillips did not signal for air support. The validity of this accusation is then removed by the admission that no one knows to this day if the aircraft was Japanese, and it certainly submitted no sighting report. Secondly, Phillips is criticized for sending *Express* inshore to check if landing was taking place when *Prince of Wales's* Walrus aircraft had reported no sign of activity. As discussed earlier, he would have been a foolish admiral to have relied on the spotting capacity of one aircraft with a not particularly experienced crew. Thirdly, the turn to the north-east is damned, taken as it was to investigate a small vessel towing some barges. This complaint is also rendered invalid by the authors' admission that it made no difference to the sighting of Force Z by reconnaissance aircraft a few minutes later. Furthermore, Middlebrook and Mahoney ignore the fact that a Walrus aircraft cannot take prisoners, and the opportunity to interrogate whoever was on the barges provided Phillips with one of the few opportunities to find out what was actually happening, if anything, off Kuantan. The fourth error, and the most serious, was the failure to ask for air cover at 10.15 when the reconnaissance aircraft mentioned above sighted the force. Phillips' reaction was to turn away, go to twenty-five knots and call action stations. As far as is known, he did not call for air cover. There is one very obvious reason why no call went out. Just after sailing from Singapore Palliser had signalled Phillips:

> Fighter protection on Wednesday 10th will not, repeat not, be possible.[34]

We now know this meant fighter protection off Singora – *but that was not the message given*. The message clearly stated that fighter protection was not available on that day. Phillips knew that fighter bases were collapsing like pins in a bowling alley all around him. He had arrived at a suspected invasion site to find no air cover when the reported invasion and his presumed presence there should have made the presence of aircraft inevitable. Little wonder then that Phillips presumed he was on his own, as the Royal Navy had so often been left when relying on the RAF for air protection. Middlebrook and Mahoney consider this interpretation, but dismiss it and say:

> It is more likely that Admiral Phillips was confident that his ships could defend themselves and that he was determined not to ask for the help of another service.[35]

Why is it 'more likely'? This interpretation simply cannot be treated as fact. The fact is that Phillips was told unequivocally that fighter protection would not be available on the 10th. What we know about Phillips and his concern for air cover before setting sail make it far 'more likely' that he considered the RAF unable to provide help and that by asking for it he would merely be telling more of the Japanese where he was. The Middlebrook and Mahoney interpretation also ignores two other vital factors. Firstly, before leaving Singapore Phillips had been pressed by the RAF to stick to a predetermined course 100 miles or so off the coast in exchange for air cover. Phillips quite rightly dismissed this limitation on his freedom of action as ludicrous – and even had he agreed to it the collapse of RAF bases which had been signalled to him made the proposed plan untenable. In other words, the RAF had first asked Phillips to restrict his movements in a most dangerous and foolhardy manner, and, had they succeeded, he would have taken all the risks and still found himself without air cover. It is hard not to believe that this fact reduced the credibility of the RAF even further. Secondly, Palliser had signalled to Phillips that enemy land bombers could reach him *five* hours after his being sighted. In fact it was just over *one* hour after the reconnaissance sighting that major Japanese forces appeared, but, given the information available to him, Phillips had every reason to consider time was on his side.

Even Middlebrook and Mahoney agree that the decision to break off the action against Singora took immense moral courage and a very astute reading of the situation. The only valid complaint that can be lodged against Phillips throughout the whole course of the action is his failure to call for air protection when he had been spotted. The official account of the action states that it was believed:

> Japanese aircraft encountered would not be carrying anti-
> ship bombs or torpedoes and that the Force on retirement
> would only have to deal with hastily organized long-range
> bombers from bases in Indo-China.[36]

Thus Phillips had every reason to believe that only inadequate Japanese aircraft were available, that these were over 400 miles away from his force and that the RAF were unable to provide air cover for him. Given these facts, the condemnation of Phillips is armchair history at its worst. It is far more satisfying, and a much better story, to see Phillips as the stubborn sea dog refusing to acknowledge the power of aircraft. The only unfortunate thing about this view is that it is untrue.

The last words should be left to those who knew Phillips. Pound, possibly his closest friend, admitted to having been worried about his failure to call for air cover, but advanced some sound reasons for it:

> I hold most strongly that, placed as he was, he was
> absolutely right to do as he did up to a certain moment,
> and that was when he was sighted at 6.45 in the morning
> by an aircraft which presumably was an enemy one. I see
> no reason why he should not then have asked for fighter
> cover but he may well have been influenced by the fact

that he was 400 miles from the established enemy
aerodromes, that the Army was fighting hard in Malaya
and wanted all the air it could get, and that as, not
knowing the time of the attack, all he could ask for was a
standing patrol and what they could have sent him would
really have been little good.[37]

We now know in addition that Phillips had been told air cover
was not available and had seen direct apparent evidence of that
over Kuantan. Palliser has most often been condemned for not
realizing the need for air cover over Kuantan: he can more
justifiably be damned for sending the signal that told Phillips he
could have no air cover at all, and it is this signal that seems to
be the crux of the whole affair.

A 1977 letter from Captain S.E. Norfolk to the *Sunday
Telegraph* shows up, on the basis of personal experience, many
of the loopholes in the conventional image of Phillips and seems
to strike as true a note as any:

> The attempt by the writers of the articles on the loss of the
> *Prince of Wales* and *Repulse* to put the blame on Admiral
> Sir Tom Phillips and their portrayal of him as a stiff-
> necked, obstinate, out-dated old sea dog is utterly untrue.
> He was a clear thinking, up-to-date, reasonable, and
> approachable man, devoted to the service.

The letter goes on to blame Winston Churchill and Dudley
Pound, who gave way to Churchill's pressure to send the ships
to the Far East, against the advice of the naval staff, led by
Phillips when he was Vice Chief of the Naval Staff:

> Accepting, regrettably, the overall responsibility of
> Winston Churchill, the man with the professional
> responsibility for the loss of the ships was the then First
> Sea Lord, Admiral Sir Dudley Pound, on two counts – he
> gave way to Churchill's pressure to send the ships to the
> Far East against the advice of the Naval Staff led by
> Admiral Phillips, then Vice Chief of the Naval Staff, and
> he failed to give the necessary order for putting into effect
> the accepted policy for the disposition of naval forces in
> the Far East in the event of a Japanese attack on Singapore,

which required naval service units to be withdrawn to a secure base to pose a potential threat to the Japanese lines of communication.

This failure sealed the fate of Force Z, which Admiral Phillips must have known, as he had been the architect of the policy for dealing with this eventuality when he was Director of Plans at the Admiralty in 1937.[38]

There are few greater tragedies in the Second World War than a fine man condemned for his failure to call for air support of dubious validity when in receipt of a signal stating it was not available in any case.

Two footnotes need to be added to this episode. On 27 February, 1942, took place the Battle of the Java Sea, when a combined Dutch and British force was wiped out by the Japanese. The power of Japanese aircraft had by then been proven. The Dutch Admiral, Doorman, asked for air support for his fleet, but Allied Headquarters:

> ordered the only striking force available (nine old torpedo-bombers of No.36 Squadron of the RAF, escorted by eight Buffalo fighters) to attack the Japanese transports, which had turned away from Java as soon as naval action seemed imminent.[39]

It is perhaps not surprising that Phillips had no faith in air cover arriving. And, even if it had, the Official History goes on to provide an interesting statistic of the likely result if it had come. When the Japanese attacked Colombo on 5 April, 1942, they sent ninety-one bombers and three dozen fighters. They were opposed by forty-two British fighters, Hurricanes and Fulmars. The Japanese lost seven aircraft; the British lost nineteen[40]. In the face of modern British shore-based aircraft the Japanese airforce emerged triumphant. With even older aircraft, it is highly unlikely that off Singapore the outcome would have been any different.

7 The Channel Dash and Sirte

Chronology of Events

1941

25 November. Battleship *Barham* torpedoed and sunk in Mediterranean.

7 December. Japanese carrier aircraft hit Pearl Harbor. Two battleships are a permanent loss, three sunk but later re-commissioned and three more damaged.

14 – 19 December. First Battle of Sirte and related convoy activities.

15 December. Admiral Somerville appointed to command Far Eastern Fleet.

19 December. British battleships *Queen Elizabeth* and *Valiant* sunk in Alexandria Harbour by Italian midget submarines.

21 December. Escort carrier *Audacity* sunk in battle for Convoy HG76, but five U-boats and two Kondor aircraft are lost in exchange for two merchant ships.

1942

11 – 13 February. German battlecruisers *Scharnhorst* and *Gneisenau* and heavy cruiser *Prince Eugen* sail from Brest and force passage up the English Channel, all arriving safely in Germany.

27 February – 1 March. Battle of the Java Sea. British lose cruiser *Exeter*, veteran of the River Plate, and destroyer *Electra*; Dutch lose two cruisers and a destroyer.

March. Lord Louis Mountbatten appointed Vice Admiral and Chief of Combined Operations; preparations begin for St Nazaire and Dieppe raids.

6 March. Home Fleet under Admiral Tovey fails to intercept

Tirpitz as she makes a brief foray from Trondheim against Arctic convoys.

22 March. Admiral Vian wins second Battle of Sirte.

28 March. Raid on St Nazaire.

April. Admiral Cunningham relinquishes Mediterranean command to Admiral Sir Henry Harwood and is appointed to Washington as representative on Joint Chiefs of Staff Committee.

5 April. British heavy cruisers *Cornwall* and *Dorsetshire* sunk off Ceylon by Japanese carrier aircraft. British carrier *Hermes*, a destroyer and a corvette sunk by the same force on 9 April.

5 – 9 April. Japanese carrier planes attack Ceylon.

18 April. Doolittle raid from American carriers against Tokyo.

7 – 8 May. Battle of the Coral Sea. Americans lose one large carrier (*Lexington*) to one Japanese small carrier (*Shoho*), but Japanese also have *Shokaku* damaged and *Zuikaku* denuded of aircraft, both of which factors are crucial in affecting the later Battle of Midway.

In many respects the end of the 1941 and the start of the 1942 marked the nadir of Royal Navy fortunes in the Second World War, excepting only the war against the submarine, which followed a timetable of its own.

The temporary loss of *Queen Elizabeth* and *Valiant* was a strange affair. Had it occurred to any Admiral other than Cunningham the odds were that the Admiralty would have had him smartly removed, but Cunningham was insulated by the power of his victories, his media status and his significant political skills. The relative weakness of ships moored 'securely' in their home ports had been amply illustrated by the loss of the *Royal Sovereign*, the attack on Taranto, the attacks on the German vessels in Brest and by Pearl Harbor. The British were to show they had learnt the lesson later when they disabled *Tirpitz* by midget submarine attack. The attack on the cruiser *York* in Suda Bay much earlier, though different in the type of vessel used, had illustrated the Italian skill in one or two-man semi-suicide missions. There was no shortage of courage in the Italian Navy, for all the jokes that circulated about the moral fibre of the Italians.

Any harbour is vulnerable. Cunningham cannot be blamed for the fact that his two battleships were sunk: that was a risk facing any vessel at any time. He can be blamed for his parsimony in allocating money and resources to harbour defence[1] and for not attempting to move both vessels out of their berths once frogmen had been discovered. Harbour defences were not Cunningham's strong point, smacking perhaps too much of the 'desk wallah'. Vian's comment on Cunningham that he was heaven at sea and hell in harbour speaks for part of this. The aggressive spirit goes for the jugular with minimum delay and maximum effectiveness. It does not countenance the existence of a beast that does not have a jugular, and when there is no beast within talon range it turns, like evil in a Shakespearian tragedy, on to itself or those nearest. The junior officers who felt the savage blow of Cunningham's tongue, or lost their chance of promotion in the Navy because of his disapproval, were facing the same man who leant over the deck of his bridge and yelled 'Give the buggers some more!' at Matapan. It was the same man who poured that aggressive spirit into reducing expenditure and snarling at Staff Officers who dared raise doubts about base security. With Admiral Vian, who had much the same aggression but far less basic humanity than Cunningham, the Admiralty found the answer, which was to keep him at sea for the whole duration of the war. It is difficult to see, even with the famed hindsight of historians, what other option there is, but it does help to explain why all navies tend to promote very different men in wartime from those they promote in time of peace.

If December, 1941, was not a good time for Admiral Cunningham, it was a bad time also for Admiral Ramsay. In charge of the Dover Command, Ramsay suffered the only blot on his escutcheon by the escape of three major German warships up the Channel from Brest. The story of the 'Channel Dash' would be incredible if it were the subject of a wartime thriller.

Scharnhorst and *Gneisenau* had made it to Brest after their commerce raiding trip, *Prince Eugen* after the *Bismarck* episode. Constant aerial bombardment had winged the vessels, but not seriously enough to put them permanently out of action. It was clear, however, that their time was limited, and in Brest they were a wasting asset to the German Navy, so Hitler initiated the Channel Dash. He spotted, quite rightly, that in the long term the ships were doomed in Brest. He was already beginning to become nervous about what was to become an obsession, the Allied invasion of Norway, and wanted naval reinforcement for that area. He spotted, quite rightly, that the British lacked the ability to respond to crisis situations with decisiveness and efficiency. He felt that an escape up the Channel would catch the British with their trousers down, and he was right.

The infuriating thing was that the British had spotted their own weakness, and what the Germans were likely to do. Shipping movements, and the existence of what we now know to have been a spy in Brest, had alerted the Admiralty to the likelihood of a move by the big ships. Their appreciation, produced on 2 February, 1942, noted that an Atlantic sortie was unlikely because after so long in harbour the vessels could not be fully worked up for sea (unlike the British, the German attention to detail and plain common sense made them obsessive about not sending vessels into proper combat unless they were fully worked up); that the ships would have to be moved to a quieter harbour and that the most likely route for them was up the Channel, because, ironically, it was the least defended, and the shortest route home. The appreciation ended with:

> We might well find the two battle cruisers and the eight inch cruiser with five large and five smaller destroyers and ... twenty fighters constantly overhead ... proceeding up Channel.[2]

This was exactly what did happen, with a slight reduction in the number of fighters. The British even had the day predicted almost exactly. So why did the British fail to intercept effectively?

A major reason was that the German plan, devised by Vice-Admiral Ciliax, was superb in every respect, from progressive jamming of British radar stations, so that jamming on the night and day of the breakout would not be noticed, to the arrangements for surface and air cover. A good plan coincided with several British weaknesses.

The Royal Navy was hopelessly stretched, and it was deemed impossible to bring capital ships of the Home Fleet down south to be within range of German aircraft. Furthermore, such a transfer would have left the field free for a breakout by *Tirpitz*.

It was therefore recognized that, while some smaller vessels could be allocated to guard against a breakout, the main burden of attack would come from the air. The Nore Command was told to keep six destroyers with torpedo armament at short notice in the Thames and reinforce the six MTBs at Dover with six more. Two fast minelayers, *Manxman* and *Welshman*, were allocated to lay mines in the Germans' swept passages. Submarines were in appallingly short supply, as a result of heavy demands from the Mediterranean, and only the modern *Sealion* was available to try to penetrate Brest roads. Admiral Ramsay, on his own initiative, arranged for the six Swordfish torpedo aircraft of 825 Fleet Air Arm Squadron to move from Lee-on-Solent to Manston, Kent. Finally, Force H was signalled to take account of the possibility of a break-out by the German ships into the Atlantic or down south.

The naval weapons available were pin-pricks. The balance of forces was weighted heavily in favour of the RAF and Coastal Command. Fourteen Beaufort torpedo-bombers were available in Scotland, waiting for *Tirpitz*. They were ordered south to Norfolk, but suffered because of freezing weather and snow in East Anglia. Twelve more Beauforts in Cornwall and seven more near Portsmouth were ordered to be ready for the break-out. Twelve Hudson bombers were on or near the East Coast, and a further 240 aircraft suitable for day bombing were available at various airfields. The problem was that the Beauforts appear to have been under-trained; the 240 RAF aircraft had no training in attacking surface ships and the co-ordination between the attacking forces and fighter cover (a theoretical 550 aircraft) was laughable.

Ramsay's fault was a very simple one, and it was the only one he made. As the following will show, his error faded into relative insignificance when put side by side with the appalling errors committed elsewhere on the day of the break-out. In common with most other Naval sources, Ramsay believed that the German ships would attempt to force the Dover Straits at night. The maximum number of British forces would be available in the Dover Straits and it was reasonable to assume that the uncertainty of night would do most to negate the advantages of these forces. In fact the Germans had realized on closer examination that the opposite was true. They had ample air and surface cover for their fleet. The confusion of a night engagement would render this excellent cover ineffective, the confusion of darkness hindering the Germans as much as it helped them. If the German force had not been able to provide adequate air cover, if its vessels had been without adequate anti-aircraft armament, if a flock of small coastal vessels had not been available for escort duties, and if the passages the German ships would have to use had not been swept, then darkness would have helped the Germans. As it was, darkness was far more useful for covering their escape from Brest and delaying discovery.

Five factors in all contributed to British failure. Firstly, British plans envisaged the German force being in the Dover Straits in darkness. Secondly, the British agent in Brest, codenamed 'Hilarion' and later to become Admiral Phillipon, had not been briefed on the possibility of a Channel break-out; had he been he might have got his warnings off earlier. Thirdly, an obsessive secrecy was maintained about the operation. Air forces in general were not briefed on what they might have to attack, and one illustration of that fact was the comment of a British reconnaissance pilot when he caught sight of the German force: 'I didn't think we had such beautiful warships!' 'We' didn't. Fourthly, for a fortnight before the break-out a signals exercise had been planned known as 'Tiger II', which began with the news that the two German battlecruisers had broken out of Brest and were proceeding up the Channel. This exercise was not cancelled when it was realized that the exercise and the real thing might coincide. The result was that when the signal for the real 'Operation Fuller' arrived in Corps Signal Office, without the prefix that would have made it an exercise, it was assumed that this was a mistake, that it was the exercise, and the signal put to the bottom of the pile, with neither the RAF nor the Admiralty being informed. Fifthly, the RAF resented its bombers being taken off the bombing of Germany and put aside for 'Fuller'. In a unilateral decision, without informing the Air Ministry, Fighter or Coastal Command, 200 bombers were removed from stand-by and the remaining 100 placed at four hours' notice. Underlying most of these crucial errors was one fact. Liaison between the intelligence services, the RAF, Coastal Command, Bomber Command, the Royal Navy and the Army were laughable. It was this that Hitler had spotted, and this that was to make a nonsense of British preparations for the break-out. When a suspicious British officer tried to telephone his worries through, someone in the local telephone exchange had put two plugs into one socket, thus delaying connection. At another stage in the battle a fleet of Hudson aircraft were frantically circling Manston airfield seeking instructions on how, when and where to attack, using radio telephone (R/T), while Manston was frantically signalling to them, not having been told of their conversion to R/T, in Morse (W/T). Without the tragic loss of life that was to follow, the whole episode could have had elements of a Whitehall farce; with that loss of life it took on more the quality of a Senecan tragedy.

The details of the engagement need not to detain us long. There were six levels of reconnaissance that should have spotted the Germans. A bombing raid on Brest failed to notice the departure of the vessels. The submarine *Sealion* had to withdraw to recharge her batteries at night and missed the departure of the German squadron. There were three Coastal Command patrols that should have spotted the German ships. Two suffered from radar failure; the third was recalled an hour early because of fog shrouding its base at exactly the time the German ships passed through its patrol area. Radar and other failures were partially excusable; what was not excusable was that no one was told of the large amount of time the patrol areas had been left unwatched as a result of these cumulative failures.

The first confirmed sighting of the German squadron was made at 1109 by two Spitfires who had been taken out 'unofficially' in the hope of finding something to shoot up. As radio silence was strictly observed, the report was not made until the Spitfires landed. It took until 1210 for the first shots to be fired at the Germans, from the 9″ battery at South Foreland. Under-trained and almost out of range, these guns made no hits. MTBs and MGBs were ordered out. Partially crippled by engine failure (a continual feature with British light forces throughout the war), these vessels either failed to make contact or had to launch their torpedoes early through the escort screen, to no effect. The six Swordfish from Manston sacrificed themselves, also to no effect. Surface and air units launched thirty torpedoes at the German ships. Not one hit, nor was there a single bomb hit on a German capital ship, cruiser, or destroyer. The six British destroyers (reduced to five when *Walpole* stripped a bearing) launched a heroic attack on the Germans, but failed to strike. There was no lack of courage from the British forces. Bomber Command launched 242 aircraft against the Germans, of which thirty-nine found the enemy and fifteen were lost. Thirty-five Coastal Command Hudsons and Beauforts were launched, and 398 fighters. Despite this overwhelming superiority, not a single torpedo or bomb hit was made against the German major vessels, and the sum total of this major effort was *one* bomb hit against the German torpedo boat *Jaguar*. The only British response that was in any way effective was minelaying. *Gneisenau* hit one mine, *Scharnhorst* two, and the latter was quite seriously damaged by the second shock.

Ramsay made an error of judgement, but it is difficult to see in this a cause of the débâcle. The cause was that Coastal Command had been starved of resources, and too often sent overseas when fully operational, and Bomber Command had no training in attacking moving surface vessels. The job of sinking the German ships was given to forces which had neither the training, skill, nor resources to answer the need, and in so doing the British appeared amateur by comparison.

The truth about the Channel Dash was that the Admiralty was not geared to facing a threat from capital ships on its own doorstep, was too stretched to allocate surface vessels to this eventuality, and so passed responsibility over to the RAF with predictably disastrous consequences. Tovey refused to let any elements of the Home Fleet go south to meet the likely threat. As with all commanders in the war, successive losses, political pressure and native caution conspired to make this decision. It was not one that would have been taken in 1939, and one wonders if a Tom Phillips or a Somerville in command of the Home Fleet would have let it ride. After all, its main justification was the threat from *Tirpitz* and other German heavy units in the north. The Channel Dash gave the Home Fleet the opportunity of a stab at three such units on home ground. It was a pity that Tovey's nerve had been drained by the cold in Scapa Flow and that he did not pick up the gauntlet. It is an illustration of what happens to a fighting sailor when he is deprived for too long of the opportunity for aggression.

Tovey had bad luck on 6 March. *Tirpitz*, flying the flag of Vice-Admiral Ciliax, the man who had planned and led the Channel Dash, made one of her rare forays out of Trondheim with three destroyers, chasing after convoy PQ 12. Tovey had two 'King George V' battleships, *Renown*, the carrier *Victorious*, the cruiser *Berwick* and twelve destroyers. The German and British forces passed within eighty or ninety miles of each other but remained ignorant of each other's presence: reconnaissance ordered from *Victorious* which would almost certainly have found *Tirpitz* could not be flown off because of the foul weather. After much fruitless chasing, Tovey decided *Tirpitz* had passed to the south of him, whereas in fact she was still to the north and capable of posing a serious threat to the convoy. The search was intriguing in that Admiralty ULTRA intelligence had *Tirpitz's* position right, while Tovey had it wrong. Twice the Admiralty signalled Tovey to change course, and on the latter occasion the change brought *Tirpitz* in range of *Victorious*. The Albacores from the carrier failed to make a hit. They launched their attack on *Tirpitz* from a bad position, astern and to leeward, and allowed themselves to be spotted well in advance. *Victorious* had failed to slow down *Bismarck* and failed even to hit *Tirpitz*. Her aircrews did not lack courage, but they did lack training – the leader of the Albacore Squadron had only just taken over command and had not flown previously with the Squadron. All his crews lacked training, though why this is so is less clear. The Albacore itself was an 'improved' version of the Swordfish, with an enclosed cockpit, but flight engineers who worked with the Albacore disliked it intensely and considered it too heavy, giving it a tendency to stall at awkward moments and 'drop out of the sky'[3]. The Fleet Air Arm had expanded dramatically in the space almost of months and the number of trained men in its squadrons was continually being diluted by new pilots. The problem was one shared by the U-boats and by the escorts that were striving to sink them.

It is also interesting to note that only one strike was launched against *Tirpitz*. When that failed she anchored off Narvik and the Home Fleet went home. It was clear that she might attempt to return from Vestfjord to Trondheim, but the submarine and destroyer dispositions made by Tovey were a day too late and *Tirpitz* made it back unscathed to Trondheim. Undoubtedly bad weather, and the extreme range for effective air reconnaissance, made Tovey's job more difficult. He was incensed by the whole business. He was under instructions to make the protection on the convoys his first aim, which he considered a major cramping factor in his attempts to bring *Tirpitz* to action. He was also ordered to provide fighter protection for all capital ships when in range of enemy shore-based aircraft. This meant he had to operate carrier and battleships as one unit, sometimes without a destroyer screen in hostile waters. Thirdly, he complained about the 'detailed instructions for the handling of his forces' that had come from the Admiralty – a very old issue, and one that had not gone away, though this time there was no Phillips to blame. Some of Tovey's complaints were the product of pure frustration, but all were based on common sense. One problem was that ULTRA did not always make life easier for either the commander at sea or the Admiralty. Admiralty knowledge of an enemy's intentions was always likely to be better than that of the commander at sea, yet the Admiralty had to be extremely cautious in the signals it sent in order not reveal the source of the information. Thus the commander at sea could not know if the orders he received were based on accurate intelligence or simply Pound meddling again with the freedom of discretion of the man on the spot. It did not make for easy relations, particularly as with hindsight we can see that Pound was starting to show the symptoms of the illness that was to kill him in 1943.

Tovey will now disappear from the pages of this work, relegated later in the year to the Nore Command. His career is an interesting one. He had considerable intelligence, personal charm and good leadership qualities. He was friendly with the right people, had the aggressive spirit so beloved of Churchill and seamanship so beloved of the old guard. He had a magnificent fighting record – and yet sadly his single victory was the flawed one of *Bismarck*, gained only after savage loss and with a very considerable element of luck. There was a bitter aftertaste to that victory with the attempt to court-martial Leach. If 4 March had gone his way, Tovey would have become the Man Who Sank The *Tirpitz*, as later Fraser was to become the Man Who Sank The *Scharnhorst*. Such a victory would not have automatically ensured his further progression and fame: the Man Who Sank The *Graf Spee* was booted out of the Mediterranean Command when one of his aggressive ventures went wrong, supposedly for his failure to clear Tripoli Harbour. Later history suggests that Harwood was very badly treated, and that he did all and more at Tripoli that could be expected of him. However, sinking the *Tirpitz* would have come near to giving Tovey the kind of unassaillable position that Cunningham had. So why did it all go wrong?

There can be no doubt that Tovey went the way of many other commanders who argued with Churchill. Individual instances have been cited already, including the one that nearly stopped Tovey being offered command of the Home Fleet in the first place. Secondly, the job with the Home Fleet was in many respects the most bitter and unenviable of the top jobs that the Navy had to offer. One of its main tasks was to safeguard against the potential ravages of the German capital ships, and their caution built up an immense frustration. The remainder of the job was calculated to shorten tempers – swinging aimlessly around at anchor in the God-forsaken hole of Scapa Flow, continually fighting off those who cast envious eyes at the vessels moored there in 'idleness', unable to bring an enemy to battle and hampered by having vessels of short range and no capacity for refuelling at sea.

However, Tovey seems to have lacked that extra dimension that protected Admirals such as Cunningham, Somerville, Ramsey, Horton and Vian. Of all the great Admirals of the war, Cunningham perhaps used his intelligence least, but he had a native shrewdness, the survivor's instinct of the canny Scot. His complaints to Pound always have a slight sweetener at the head or tail, where Tovey's appear strident in comparison. Both Cunningham and Tovey could appear as bulls in the china shop, but Cunningham's bull chose which china to break very carefully. Somerville and Ramsey had a capacity to disarm people, the former of his sense of humour and the sheer sparkle of his personality, the capacity he had to make people feel that with him life was being lived to the full, while with the latter it was a quiet charm compounded of high ability, endless patience and natural good manners. Vian and Horton were bullies, personalities of immense power and aggression who were lucky enough to be given the right battles to fight, and who were utterly ruthless. Neither of them was required to come into direct contact with Churchill overmuch, so their capacity not so much to call a spade a spade but rather to hit people over the head with the sharp end of it did not lead to political trouble. Tovey was too unflinching. He belonged to a service which bred extreme loyalty and favoured among its officers a no-nonsense, commonsense approach. Frustration at the ills being wreaked on that service and an inability to be a politician were bad bedfellows in the climate of naval operations for the Second World War. Tovey suffered by having both, possibly to excess. Very rarely, if ever, were his complaints anything less than well-founded. His reward was to be posted to relative obscurity, but what is impossible to quantify is the value that his complaints and objections had in holding back some of the wilder excesses of Churchill. The same is true of Pound, and both Pound's and Tovey's true glory may lie more in what they stopped than in what they did.

It would be wrong to end discussion of Tovey without mentioning the tragedy of Convoy PQ17. Here, as in many other areas, Tovey was proved right, and PQ17 must remain as an unremovable black mark against Pound's reputation.

Convoy PQ17 sailed on 27 June, 1942. There were four German heavy ships in the north – *Tirpitz, Hipper, Scheer, Lutzow,* with ten destroyers between them. Tovey wrote, quite rightly, 'The strategic situation was wholly favourable to the enemy.'[4]

The German vessels were out of effective bombing range, often out of effective reconnaissance range because of the weather, and fast enough to slip the limited number of submarines that could be kept guarding their exit routes. Relatively short endurance on the part of the British vessels added to the problem, as did the fact that one 'King George V' class battleship was not a match for *Tirpitz.*

It is clear that Tovey and Pound were involved in extensive arguments over PQ17. Tovey believed, rightly as it turned out, that the Germans would not risk *Tirpitz* again in the Barents Sea after the unexpected shock of meeting *Victorious's* Albacores off the Lofoten Islands. Tovey disagreed violently with the Admiralty rules governing the use of cruisers on the Russian convoys and was horrorstruck when the idea of scattering a convoy if faced with surface ship attack was mentioned to him. Here again, Tovey's seagoing experience seems to have pointed him in the right direction. There were some indications that *Tripitz* and other vessels had set sail to attack the convoy, so Pound ordered it to scatter. In fact, as we now know, the German vessels did briefly set out, but turned back when it became quite clear that German aircraft and submarines were doing a very effective job on the dispersed convoy. Convoy PQ17 was massacred and the echoes of that defeat have rolled on down the years, complete with lawsuits and bitter recriminations. The basic facts are clear. The action was in opposition to everything that Tovey held holy and was a serious error in judgment on the part of the Naval Staff, who were implicated in it just as much as Pound himself. It is hard not to believe that something snapped in Tovey's faith at that moment.

The loss of *Prince of Wales* and *Repulse*; the sinking of *Queen Elizabeth* and *Valiant*; the Battle of the Java Sea; the escape of *Scharnhorst* and *Gneisenau*; the failure to bring *Tirpitz* to action – these were a true catalogue of doom and it took Admiral Vian to bring along some cheerful news.

Phillip Vian was almost a generation after Cunningham and Somerville, starting as a naval cadet at Osborne in 1907, and passing out from Dartmouth in 1911. He was yet another destroyer man, serving in one at the Battle of Jutland, specializing in gunnery and spending the first two years of the war as Captain (D) of the 4th Destroyer Flotilla. He first became famous in February, 1940, when he took the destroyer *Cossack* into Josing Fjord to rescue 200 British seaman on board the *Graf Spee's* supply ship, the *Altmark*. Of all the Admirals discussed in this work, Vian is one of the hardest to come to terms with. He has the distinction of having written one of the most tedious war memoirs of any major figure in the Second World War, *Action This Day*. To be so tedious when the subject was involved in the *Altmark* episode, the sinking of the *Bismarck*, many major actions in the Mediterranean including being the leading figure at the Battle of Sirte, at Salerno, commander of major naval forces for Overlord, and then commander of the British carriers working with the Americans in the Pacific Fleet is in itself a major achievement. Many people saw Vian as insufferably cruel:

> He was a man of great courage, but also a cruel man, even
> sadistic. Anyone who worked for him swore he led with
> the whiplash. He made life for his secretaries absolute hell:
> some of them cringed when he came in.[5]

Few would deny that Vian was ruthless, extremely hard-driving, and virtually without any softer personal features. Yet it has to

14 Somerville: 'An
enormously human person'.

15 'Tovey was sent to command the Nore'. Fraser (right, standing front of
the quadruple 14-inch turret he developed) takes over as C-i-C Home Fleet
from Tovey. Both men were in contention for the post of First Sea Lord;
the third contender, Cunningham, got the job.

16 'That little cock sparrow sitting on the edge of his chair and not caring a damn what I say.' Churchill and Phillips (beyond him), with Professor Lindemann on the left.

17 'Why & O why did they not send out someone of experience or at least have Geoffrey Layton who is a well-tried sailor & full of determination.' Fraser (left), Layton and Somerville, the former taking over as C-i-C Far Eastern Fleet.

be said that he viewed himself with the same intolerant harshness that he viewed others. Buried in the Public Record Office is an insignificant report from Vian when he was a Captain (D):

> 'Gurkha' was in the hands of an inexperienced commanding officer, and became detached: he should not have been allowed to become detached: the responsibility for failure to call him in is wholly mine: I have not, I regret to report, any explanation worth recording to account for this omission.[6]

Similarly, Vian blamed himself for the loss of the cruiser *Naiad*, claiming that he hesitated momentarily when the torpedo track was sighted, and thus ensured that the torpedo hit on the bulkhead between two engine rooms, the one place where a single torpedo was liable to sink a 'Dido' class cruiser.

If Vian was capable of blaming himself, his conduct of operations was not without criticism from others. When boarding *Altmark* he made no attempt to silence or jam its radio. In the chase for *Bismarck*, he was ordered to join the Commander-in-Chief with his destroyers, but worked out that he had the only surface force capable of contacting *Bismarck* before nightfall on 26 May. Vian knew that he was leaving *King George V* and *Rodney* with no destroyer escort, but still he headed straight for *Bismarck* and did not break radio silence to tell Tovey of his decision.[7]

He was promoted Rear Admiral at the end of June, 1941, in an early promotion scheme introduced by Pound but thought to be unpopular with the rest of the Navy. In command of the 15th Cruiser Squadron in the Eastern Mediterranean from October, 1941, he again showed his tendency to carry out independent action. The bombardment of Derna was one such:

> The bombardment of Derna had not been specified in orders issued to the Rear Admiral commanding the 15th Cruiser Squadron, but was carried out on his own initiative. This action probably had useful moral effect; it had the not unnatural result of drawing down a series of air attacks which, fortunately, caused no serious damage.[8]

Vian's response was that he would have been spotted anyway, and might as well have a go first.

As has already been mentioned, Admiral Ramsay had grave doubts about Vian, particularly when they were working together on Overlord:

He is d – d temperamental & at times a great annoyance
. . . he is always apt to work against rather than with me.[9]

P. Vian has been on my mind for some time owing to his peculiar behaviour. I think he is not quite normal at times.[10]

Ramsay was able to work with Cunningham and Montgomery, so his concern over Vian is therefore all the more telling. On the other hand, Cunningham had nothing but praise for Vian as 'a fighting sailor'.[11]

The Battle of Sirte was based, as was so much of the action in the Mediterranean, round the need to supply Malta. Convoy MW10 consisted of an oiler and three other merchant vessels. There were meant to be twenty-three escorts, including five light cruisers. Cunningham had no aircraft carriers or battleships operational, and no heavy cruisers. The strength of Vian's escorting force was deceptive. Of his cruisers only one, *Penelope*, was fitted for surface action, and then with only six 6" guns. Of the remainder, three were 'Dido' class anti-aircraft cruisers, with twenty-eight 5.25" high-angle, dual-purpose guns between them, whilst the last cruiser, *Carlisle*, was a Great War design converted to carry eight 4" anti-aircraft guns. This was not a strong force for coping with Italian battleships and cruisers, even though all bar one cruiser had torpedo armament. The British cruisers were for the most part functioning more as large destroyers. The escort also included six 'Hunt' class destroyers. Designed as convoy escorts (Cunningham had played a large part in their design), these had a relatively slow top speed of around twenty-five knots, good anti-aircraft armament, but no torpedoes. Given the vessels available to him, Vian's dispositions were excellent. He divided his force up into three, a striking force to harry the expected Italian surface vessels, a smoke-laying force to cover the convoy, and the majority of the 'Hunts' in close escort for anti-aircraft defence. It is daunting to realize that on the Malta run the convoy would expect to face attack from Italian battleships, cruisers and destroyers, bombers, torpedo-bombers and submarines. With this in mind the predominance of escorts over merchant vessels is explained. Vian was also for the most part commanding battle-hardened veterans, and his plan of action took account of the realities of combat in that the minimum of signalling was required, each vessel being told exactly what it had to do at the pre-convoy briefing. Fear may have had something to do with the success of this approach – captains only made a mistake once with Vian – but it was also made possible by the experience of most of the commanders in his force.

The Italians mustered a 15" gun battleship (*Littorio*), two heavy cruisers, one light cruiser and seven destroyers. The first contact was with the cruiser force, the second with the combined Italian fleet. The weather was on Vian's side – the wind, a strong one, blowing the smoke made by the British forces directly towards the Italians. If Matapan was won by radar, Sirte was won by smoke. The Italians made hesitant thrusts towards the British, who in their turn dipped in and out of their own smoke threatening torpedo attack and harrying the Italians. To Vian it seemed obvious that the best plan for the Italians would be to work round the British smoke to leeward, and on three separate occasions he led a major part of his force in this direction to head off the Italians if that was where they were headed. This left the Italians with the opportunity of coming round to the convoy the other way, to its west, and on one occasion this very nearly happened, with only the bravery of the remaining British destroyers heading off the attack. It was at times a close-run thing, but Vian's force held off the Italians until nightfall. He was not to know it, but the gale that was rapidly brewing added to the Italians' discomfiture by causing two destroyers to founder and the light cruiser to be so damaged that she fell easy prey to a British submarine. However, all the luck was not to go the British way, despite their forces having escaped any serious damage as a result of the encounter. The sad fact was that, through no fault of Cunningham's or Vian's, the object of his expedition failed to be met. Of the four merchant vessels, two were sunk or grounded before they reached Malta, and the remaining two destroyed shortly after they had arrived by bombing in Malta Harbour. Some of their cargo was saved. A number of British destroyers had also been damaged, enough to make Cunningham uncertain that another convoy could be run to Malta without more destroyers. Cunningham, Vian and every other fighting Admiral was paying the price for two things – firstly, the lack of money for warships in the inter-war years, and secondly, the priorities for shipbuilding at that time. The 'Hunt' class escorts has been sponsored by Cunningham when he had been at the Admiralty in 1938, the idea being for a small and cheap escort with a good anti-aircraft fit that could be produced in reasonable numbers in time for the war. With hindsight these vessels were not as a great a success as Cunningham had hoped. Their actual anti-aircraft armament was good but it far outran these small vessels' magazine capacity, with a result that the commander of any heavily-engaged 'Hunt' always had his mind on the amount of ammunitiion he had remaining, something shown at Sirte. Secondly, the relative low speed of the vessels made them good anti-aircraft escorts for a merchant ship convoy, but was a serious drawback when it came to helping out with warships. A junior officer wounded on the destroyers that tried to stop *Scharnhorst* and *Gneisenau* commented with some bitterness that his destroyers had 'Hunts' attached to them for air support, but that his main memory of the class was seeing them vanish into the mists behind the faster destroyers as they headed into air attack. A major advantage could have been reaped in the inter-war years if time and resources had been allocated to the development of a dual-purpose destroyer main armament: it was a perpetual complaint of Vian's that the standard British 4.7" gun was limited to forty degrees elevation, rendering it useless for anti-aircraft fire. Dual-purpose armament was developed for capital ships and cruisers – the 5.25" mounting – but too much time was spent on developing firstly the 16" guns for *Rodney* and *Nelson*, and then the quadruple 14" turrets for the 'King George V' class, neither of which repaid their investment, and both of which were plagued with problems throughout their life.

Sirte was the type of action at which the Royal Navy excelled. The enemy were in plain sight. The dash, courage and daring of Beatty welded to the dogged persistence of Jellicoe produced a resounding victory, all the sweeter because it was in the best traditions of the Navy by being against a superior enemy force. It was the type of action that Cunningham, Somerville or Tovey would have given their Admiral's rings to take part in. It was only in the Mediterranean that this type of action was possible, one reason why the Admiral who had the Mediterranean command at the outbreak of war was one of the most fortunate of them all.

Vian's further career is worth examination, at the risk of breaking from strict chronological sequence. Outwardly, it was a career of immense success. He went in charge of five carriers to the Salerno landings and was offered the head of Combined Operations in succession to Mountbatten by Churchill. It is not hard to see why Churchill made this offer. Vian had shown all the dash and daring which Churchill so admired. He was no respecter of persons (or, for that matter, of orders) and had the slightly piratical feel to him that seems to have gone along with Combined Operations, typified by Keyes and Mountbatten. An extraordinary element is added to this offer by Vian telling how the First Lord, A.V. Alexander, took him aside and asked him to refuse Churchill's offer, because he was needed as Deputy Commander-in-Chief of the Naval forces for Operation Overlord, the invasion of France. However, Alexander insisted that Vian did not tell Churchill what he had said. As it turned out, Vian did refuse and became Naval Commander of the Eastern area of Overlord, working under Admiral Ramsay. The success of Overlord is well known, and from it Vian went on to command the carriers in the British Pacific Fleet in 1945. He was knighted after Sirte, appointed 5th Sea Lord, then Commander-in-Chief Home Fleet, and finally promoted Admiral of the Fleet in June, 1952.

This apparent success does nothing to cloud the obvious reservations that many people felt about him. No one doubted his ability as a fighting admiral, but, as these pages have shown, the most successful admirals were required to do rather more than fight. Vian appears to have been capable of working under orders when the command structure was clearly defined. When it was not quite so clearly defined, then he could be troublesome. The point is made by Fraser's biographer:

> Though he never made a major issue of the fact, Fraser
> could certainly have coped more easily with this tension in
> the [Pacific] Fleet if he had had more effective support from
> Admirals Rawlings and Vian. The two officers did not get

on, and Fraser had to blend tact and firmness in replying to the confidential letters each was wont to send him about the other.[12]

Vian could be a tricky customer to work with, as both Ramsay and Fraser testified. He was excellent with a fighting fleet at his command, though he ruled by fear to a far greater extent than Cunningham. Possibly one reason for Cunningham's affection for him is that Vian was never going to rival Cunningham in terms of popularity or general status, for all the respect afforded to his fighting skills. Vian was never given full autonomy, but always a command where the final responsibility rested elsewhere. It is interesting that when Rawlings went home from the British Pacific Fleet and Vian became straightforward number two to Fraser, the problem ceased: Vian could cope with a hierarchy, but not with parallel tracks.

The Mediterranean lost Cunningham in April, 1942, to Washington, where he became the Royal Navy's permanent representative on the Combined Chiefs of Staff Committee. Four months earlier his friend Somerville had been taken away from Force H and given command of a new Eastern Fleet: neither Admiral relished their new post. The truth was that Cunningham left the Mediterranean when there were precious few ships left for him to do anything with. His replacement was Admiral Sir Henry Harwood, the victor of the River Plate, and as has already been discussed, this was not a happy appointment for him. He faced a strong enemy in the Mediterranean, with Malta on its last legs, and what few vessels remained to the Mediterranean fleet quite literally cracking up with the strain of extended service. There are accusations that Cunningham's weak Staff work left a trail of problems for Harwood, and certainly Cunningham did not leave trailing clouds of glory. He had allowed his capital ships to be sunk in harbour, and not long before he had also faced the loss of the veteran battleship *Barham*. Essentially an unmodernized First World War design, *Barham* was hit by three U-boat torpedoes and blew up dramatically. It became clear that the anti-submarine training of some of Cunningham's destroyers was not up to scratch, and after the loss of *Barham* efforts were made to improve it. Cunningham confessed to Pound:

[the submarine that sank *Barham*] was actually pinged by
one of the destroyers who unfortunately disregarded it as a
non-sub echo.[13]

Cunningham must take some blame for the fact that training
was not up to standard, though typically his comment to Pound
puts the blame on the destroyer and no one else. Vian, for all
his unpleasantness, took blame where it was due. Cunningham
was more reluctant so to do. He told Pound that 'our anti-
submarine vessels are sadly out of practice'[14], but does not
remark on the responsibility of the Admiral commanding for
ensuring that such vessels were not out of practice. Cunningham did not like submariners at the best of times, particularly for the manner in which they offended his dress sense, but
there were few excuses for a commander to neglect anti-
submarine exercises in the Mediterranean, infested as it was
with both Italian and German submarines. Nor did Cunningham readily accept blame for the sinking of his two battleships in Alexandria harbour. Instead, he admits that he knew an
attack of such a type was possible, that he warned his vessels
and arranged for patrolling boats to drop small charges at the
harbour entrance at regular intervals. As we already know,
Cunningham had been pestered to improve defences, but had
turned this down on the grounds of expense. Commenting to
Pound on the steps taken *after* the event to secure the harbour,
Cunningham writes:

It is costing a lot; but we must have this harbour really
secure.[15]

Yes indeed, just as one must have one's escorts worked up to
detect submarine attack. Cunningham's protestations with
regard to the defences of Alexandria are really a little too much,
given his known parsimony and unwillingness to spend such
money.

His views on things being 'too velvet-arsed and Rolls-Royce'
did not extend to his own conditions and pay when he went to
Washington. He complained vociferously and won himself a
significantly better deal than any previous representative. It did
not add to his enjoyment of the post:

I am rather horrified by the jealousy and suspicion between the USA Navy Office & our Admiralty. I can find no joint Staff anywhere. It is true there are liaison officers but nowhere are our two staffs sitting together and studying war problems on a broad basis. We have divided the world into spheres of influence & each country is fighting its own war in its own sphere & resents the other poking his nose into or even examining the problems in the sphere in which he is predominant. Worse, the USA Army and Navy, when not fighting each other, are each fighting a separate war. We, however, can claim no virtue in that respect as it is clear that the RAF are also fighting their own war without much regard for the needs of the other two services. . . . I am little better than a pillar box for our Admiralty to post their letters in.[16]

In Washington Cunningham had to come to terms with the famous Admiral Ernest King:

A man of immense capacity and ability, quite ruthless in his methods . . . not an easy person to get on with. . . . He was tough and liked to be considered tough, and at times became rude and overbearing. . . . He was offensive, and I told him what I thought of his method of advancing allied unity and amity. We parted friends. . . . Not content with fighting the enemy, he was usually fighting someone on his own side as well.[17]

It is difficult to judge Cunningham's effectiveness in this job for it was soon superseded by his appointment as Allied Naval Commander Expeditionary Force for the TORCH landings in North Africa. Ramsay had been mooted for this post, and one view has it that American pressure gave Cunningham the job – quite likely, as a victor of Cunningham's stature *and* his being a man they already knew made him a powerful candidate. Ramsay had reason to feel disappointed. He had appeared to be heading for the top post and had in fact been given three months to complete the naval plans for TORCH and issue the operational orders. By the time consent was given for the TORCH landing on 24 July, 1942, Ramsay had done much to stake his claim. He had been given the grand title 'Naval C-i-C,

Expeditionary Force' in July, 1942, together with the acting rank of Admiral. There had been initial problems with Mountbatten, Chief of Combined Operations, but Ramsay solved these by a personal meeting. He had met and made friends with Montgomery, and spotted the weaknesses of his American allies:

> Things have been in a proper mess in higher direction
> circles, owing to the American desire to do something
> quickly, yet not knowing what it is possible to do.
> Consequently their perspective is all wrong and they have
> to be shown it. . . . The Yanks are new at the game and
> have the enthusiasm of beginners. . . . However, they are as
> good for us as we are for them![18]

The last sentence sums up Ramsay. He was extremely perceptive at spotting the weaknesses of individuals or organizations, but managed to do so without any feeling of personal pride or jealousy being involved. He was utterly immovable when fixed on a point, but also utterly polite and unflappable, and hence a most difficult man to get angry with: he simply wore down by the repeated application of common sense many of his would-be opponents. Finally, and perhaps an even more important reason for his success, his awareness of people's weaknesses was always leavened by an open, fresh and hugely enthusiastic awareness of their strengths. Hence his genuine admiration for the energy and enthusiasm of the Americans and his capacity to respond to it. Hence his comment on Montgomery:

> I've had a most invigorating time with the Iron General.
> He is without doubt a tiger of a man, full of ideas and
> opinions . . . and fairly stirring everyone up.[19]

Ramsay adored energy, enthusiasm and drive, and in his quiet way let his adoration show. He never patronized or fussed, and also had a sense of humour. His remarkable capacity to get on with people is illustrated by the fact that he disagreed strongly with Mountbatten over the Dieppe raid, which turned out to be a disaster, but remained on speaking terms with him after the event. He even managed to disagree with Churchill without losing his favour:

Yesterday morning the P.M. sent for me to 10 Downing Street, where I spent an hour and a half in discussion, and had to argue with him when he was incorrect in his facts or assumptions. Conferring with him always produces a desire in me to smile, because there is something irresistibly comic about him.[20]

Churchill's support for Ramsay is witnessed by the fact that it was pressure from Churchill that made the Admiralty put Ramsay back on the active list, something he valued more than almost any honour that came to him in the war.

At least in his later years Ramsay did not show resentment at those who sought to steal his fire, unlike Cunningham. One reason for the intense dislike of Mountbatten among some naval officers was what was seen as his unfailing attempts to get publicity, and credit, for himself where the work had been done by others. Cunningham wrote to Ramsay after TORCH:

Have you read Mountbatten's puff on the news page of *The Times* on the 18th? I see he lays claim or an American pressman does for him to have made the plans for TORCH. Really he ought not to be allowed to advertise like this. If you see the CNS you might point it out.[21]

Ruffled feathers from Cunningham, but none from Ramsay; one of the few disparaging comments he makes about Mountbatten, and that in his private diary, is that good officers were wasted serving with him[22].

It seems clear that a vast amount of the credit for the planning for TORCH and its success must go to Ramsay. Cunningham was not a good Staff officer and acknowledged his weakness. Ramsay was masterly, as someone who worked with both reported:

I had to deal more with Cunningham than Ramsay. The latter was very polite and meticulously accurate in his planning; the exact opposite to the former![23]

Ramsay's letter to Cunningham when the latter went off to the TORCH landings is model of its kind, and powerfully moving. It is from an officer who has been pipped at the post for a major job, required to work under his rival for the duration and seen much of the credit for the success go to that other officer. In addition it is from an officer who has been sorely tried and tested by the Royal Navy, but still given it his unfailing devotion:

Dear Andrew,
. . . It wasn't easy to see you go without giving a thought to what might have been, but any such thought is swamped in no time by the knowledge that what is, is for the best, and had I been the authority in power I would have ordered things to be as they now are. There is no one I would rather have done my work for than you, and I have done it with real pleasure. I'm confident that success awaits you. . . . I've watched the progress of the various convoys with interest and some anxiety, but so far all our decisions have proved successful and therefore I hope correct. . . . I'm just going down to bid everyone farewell at the station. Again it will mean some natural feeling of being left out in the cold, and it is damned cold here. . . .
    The best of luck and every possible success,
       Ever yours,
       Bertie.[24]

Greatness can take many forms.

8 Barents Sea and North Cape

Chronology of Events

1942

4 June. Battle of Midway; four Japanese carriers lost to one American.

27 June. Convoy PQ17 sets out, is ordered to scatter by Admiralty when attack from German surface vessels is feared and is largely destroyed by German air and submarine attacks.

10 August. Malta Convoy Operation 'Pedestal' sets out. Five ships get through in exchange for one carrier, two cruisers and a destroyer sunk, one carrier and two cruisers badly damaged.

19 August. Dieppe raid.

10 September. British occupy Vichy-French island of Madagascar.

14 October. German raider *Komet* sunk off Cherbourg.

8 November. Operation TORCH, landing in French North Africa.

31 December. Battle of the Barents Sea. *Admiral Hipper* and *Lutzow* fail to score major victory against Convoy JW51B: Hitler demands an end to German surface fleet; Grand Admiral Raeder resigns, Dönitz takes over. Elements of surface fleet reprieved.

1943

1 January. Cruiser *Ajax* of River Plate fame severely damaged in Bône harbour by JU87s.

20 February. Admiral Sir Andrew Cunningham resumes his old post as Commander-in-Chief, Mediterranean Fleet.

May. Admiral Tovey moves from Home Fleet to Nore
  Command. He is succeeded by Admiral Sir Bruce Fraser.
10 July. Allied invasion of Sicily, Operation HUSKY.
3 September. Italy signs surrender document.
11 September. Admiral Cunningham signals to Admiralty
  arrival of Italian battlefleet in Malta.
22 September. *Tirpitz* disabled by midget submarine attack.
21 October. Death of Admiral Sir Dudley Pound, First Sea
  Lord. Post offered to Admiral Fraser, who declines and
  suggests Cunningham to Churchill.
26 December. Home Fleet under Admiral Fraser sinks
  Scharnhorst at Battle of North Cape.

As was noted in the previous chapter, Admiral James Somerville
was appointed at the end of 1941 to command the hastily-
mustered Eastern Fleet. It was not a post he viewed with
excitement:

> This damned appointed gives me no kick at all, and I keep
> asking myself why the hell I am here at my age.[1]

Somerville was up against Nagumo's carrier forces, arguably the
most powerful and efficient capital ships in existence anywhere
in the world at that time. At his disposal he had a superficially
powerful fleet – three carriers, two of them modern (*Formidable,
Indomitable, Hermes*), five battleships (*Warspite, Resolution,
Ramillies, Royal Sovereign, Revenge*), two heavy and four light
cruisers, and sixteen destroyers. Somerville's task required miracles of morale-boosting as well as miracles of leadership: his
fleet appeared as shaky as its likely fortunes. The carriers badly
lacked training and experience. British emphasis on armour
protection for their carriers meant that the two modern British
ships carried less than half the aircraft of a Japanese or American
fleet carrier, and inexperienced and untrained crews were in any
event flying aircraft that in general had significantly lower
levels of performance than their Japanese counterparts. Of the
battleships only *Warspite* had been reconstructed. The remainder were all First World War 'R' class vessels. They were pushed
to reach eighteen knots, at that speed had fuel only for three or
four days and water for less and were without air-conditioning

or adequate ventilation. The light cruisers were all First World War designs. The polite phrase for the destroyers, that they were 'in need of repair', covers the fact that they were for the most part semi-wrecks. Of course the fleet had had no time to exercise together as a squadron. Somerville's fleet was therefore composed of obsolete, inexperienced and often ill-trained ships, many of which were falling apart. It is no wonder that he compared it to the Russian equivalent at Tsushima. Force Z should at least have had the speed to run away: Somerville's lacked even that.

If there was a 'forgotten army' in the Far East, Somerville's fleet has a claim to be the forgotten fleet. It is difficult now to realize how great was the threat that faced the Far East when Somerville's fleet made its appearance there. Britain had suffered a string of appalling defeats from Japan and elsewhere, the Americans were reeling from Pearl Harbor, and there seemed every chance that Japan would continue her advance, capture Ceylon, and in so doing dominate the Indian Ocean and Britain's trade routes. The Battle of the Java Sea had left the Indian Ocean open and virtually undefended. Admiral Raeder wrote to Hitler on 13 February, 1942:

> Japan plans to protect this front in the Indian Ocean by capturing the key position of Ceylon, and she also plans to gain control of the sea in that area by means of superior naval forces. Fifteen Japanese submarines are at the moment operating in the Bay of Bengal, in the waters off Ceylon and in the straits on both sides of Sumatra and Java.[2]

Had Ceylon fallen there is some reason to think that it would have brought Churchill's government down with it. Somerville arrived in Ceylon on 24 March, 1942, and there were accurate predictions that a Japanese attack could be expected on 31 March.

Somerville divided his fleet into two squadrons, a fast and a slow, and cleared them from Ceylon immediately he realized the threat of an imminent Japanese attack. Fortunately Addu Atoll had been prepared as an emergency base, unbeknown to the Japanese, and it was here that Somerville withdrew to muster his fleet. He was not to go on without loss. By the evening of 2 April it appeared that the danger to Ceylon had passed and he ordered his two 8″ gun cruisers, *Dorsetshire* and *Cornwall*, back to Colombo, one to finish her refit and the other to escort an Australian troop convoy. *Hermes* and the destroyer *Vampire* were ordered to Trincomalee to continue preparations for the projected attack on Madagascar, with *Hermes* having only damaged aircraft on board. Somerville's relaxation was premature. When the Japanese force was sighted, the two cruisers were treated to one of the most savagely successful bombing raids ever launched and sunk within a few minutes, leaving over 1,100 men floundering in the sea. *Hermes* was ordered to sail from harbour and hide to the north-east, but was also found and sunk by carrier aircraft.

There are two areas of interest to Somerville's command – his conduct of operations while commanding the Far East Fleet and his later clash with Lord Louis Mountbatten when the latter was appointed Supreme Commander, South-East Asia. As regards the former, Somerville avoided a massive and humiliating defeat at the hands of Nagumo's forces and, though we now know that the Japanese were never to invade Ceylon, that much was certainly not clear at the time and there was precious little to stop them had they so chosen. It took guts for someone such as Somerville, accused effectively of cowardice at Spartivento, to refuse surface action and resolve that his only way of hitting the enemy was by night air attack. The Admiralty did recognize that his 'R' class battleships were the makings of a disaster and allowed them to be sent to Africa out of harm's way, but even then he could not win. Pound criticized his policy of not launching daylight attacks, mentioning in a reply to Somerville's signal from Mombasa outlining his Fleet in Being policy that he found this an 'unattractive policy', to which Somerville replied that he was forced into it by his 'unattractive aircraft'[3]. Admiral Sir Algernon Willis after the war was to criticize him for the other failing:

> I thought at the time . . . and I think so still that
> Somerville took unjustifiable risks & that his movements
> were not in line with the policy for the 'Fleet in being'
> which Admy has accepted. Although he did his best to
> avoid surface action & succeeded, the fleet was in great
> danger of overwhelming air attack, to counter which we

had a quite inadequate fighter cover. It was Providence
alone who saved us from this. . . . I am sure GL [Geoffrey
Layton, in command in Ceylon] realized that Somerville
was overreaching himself.[4]

This is a surprising statement from an officer committed to
Somerville. The risks referred to are presumably the two
occasions on which Somerville, evacuated from Colombo and
steaming around waiting for the Japanese attack, turned *east*,
that is towards the enemy. On 1 and 2 April Somerville steamed
east by night and west by day. On the surface this appears
foolhardy. The reason is that, firstly, no one believed that the
Japanese would detach their 'first division' to attack Colombo,
and the expectation was that the attack might be based on
cruisers; secondly, no one at the time had anything near an
accurate idea of the size, skill and efficiency of the strike force
that a Japanese carrier squadron could muster. It has to be
remembered that at Pearl Harbor the attack had been against
anchored vessels and minimal opposition, and obviously used
the whole weight of the Japanese navy, and that Force Z had
been sunk by shore-based aircraft. If a relatively light force *had*
been moving towards Colombo Somerville would have been
perpetually damned if he had not moved close enough to mop it
up with the superior power of his Fleet, and the aim of the
eastward move was to get close enough in to launch air attacks
at night, it being thought that the Japanese did not like to fight
at night.

This excuse does not stand for the second excursion east, after
two relatively modern 8" gun cruisers had been smashed to
pieces within minutes by a Japanese force. After that event
Somerville knew that the first team were definitely out on the
pitch and knew something of their power. To turn towards
them was flagrantly in breach of the Admiralty 'Fleet in Being'
concept, and ran appalling risks. Willis was not alone in reaching that conclusion. Commander Ralph Edwards, Chief of Staff
to the Eastern Fleet, went to see Somerville in his cabin to point
out the risks he was running by steaming east, and to ask him
to retire. He emerged from the cabin and went to Commander
Kaye Edden (now Vice Admiral Sir Kaye Edden), and said: 'I
can't shift the old bugger. Can you?'[5]

Edden went in and pointed out all the reasons why they

should retire, including the fact that they were heading towards the area where the survivors of the two cruisers were in the water, and the Japanese might even be using these men as 'live bait'. Somerville's response was to ask at what speed they were steaming. Edden replied eighteen knots: Somerville ordered it increased to twenty knots. In response to Edwards' query, Edden could only answer that the effect of his statement had been to increase speed in the wrong direction.

Somerville can only have been steaming east to rescue the men from *Dorsetshire* and *Cornwall*. Those closest to him believe that he knew full well the risks he was taking, and that he believed that if he failed to rescue those men the morale of the Eastern Fleet would never recover. Weeks later Edden asked some of the survivors in hospital how they had survived forty-eight hours in shark-infested waters. The answer from them all was that they knew Somerville would come to pick them up.

It is perhaps this moment, and Cunningham's turn towards the enemy at Matapan, that show the true qualities of a 'fighting admiral'. No one who knew Somerville doubts that he knew exactly the risks he was running – perhaps the fall of a government, certainly a disaster if it went wrong that would make Admiral Tom Phillips appear a victor by comparison. If the gamble worked, 1,112 men were rescued – and a bond of faith struck with his men that would never leave them. True fighting admirals are gamblers on a massive scale. Somerville gambled, and won. It is hard not to warm to him for so doing, as so many men who served with him warmed to him. His ability to go to a job he hated and to sustain the morale of men who knew they were serving in 'iron coffins' is one of the most underrated achievements of the war, in its own way worthy to be set by the side of Cunningham's similar maintenance of morale during and after Crete:

> Perhaps the most remarkable of [Somerville's] successes came after the Singapore disaster when he was made C-in-C East Indies with a scratch fleet made up in the main of the old R-class battleships. Morale was at a very low ebb after the loss of *Prince of Wales* and *Repulse*, and this was a scratch fleet which must have known it was completely outclassed by the Japanese. Yet by the time he got it out

into the Indian Ocean, he had built it up to a state of extraordinarily high morale. He was that kind of man.[6]

Both Cunningham at Matapan and Somerville in the Far East turned towards the enemy when prudence would have dictated that they turn away. There the similarity ends. When Cunningham turned towards a possible enemy force at Matapan he was turning towards possible glory and victory, as well as the risk of death and defeat. When Somerville turned he faced the risk of death and defeat, but no chance of glory: history gives little of that to those who save lives. Somerville put his life and his reputation on the line for the sake of other men's lives. In the opinion of this commentator that may not make his a better commander than Cunningham; it does give him an equal, but different, claim to greatness.

As a footnote, Willis explains one reason for his fear:

And still the RAF haven't got a Dive bomber nor a torpedo aircraft that's any good.[7]

and later:

I should not like to say what would have happened if we *had* encountered the enemy on these outings. The F/B reconnaissance was so thin as to be very misleading and even dangerous, and we just do not know what the enemy force consisted of.[8]

Somerville should not have ordered his two cruisers and *Hermes* away when he did, but he had some reason for thinking that the threat from the Japanese had gone away and that in any event it was not as concentrated and heavy as it turned out to be. Better air reconnaissance might have avoided the loss of the cruisers, and, while Colombo had been reinforced with Hurricanes, there were desperately few Catalinas for long-range reconnaissance. As mentioned before, the performance of the Hurricanes against Japanese pilots suggests that air cover for Force Z would have made no difference, even allowing for the absence of fighter cover for the Japanese on that day. Somerville's other mistake during his time of office was to avoid the institution of a convoy system, because of the lack of escorts, something which North

Atlantic experience had proved to be a wrong approach. Here again, it could be argued that destroyer escort for his capital ships was more important in the Far East than for merchant and other shipping. Against Somerville's failures must be set the fact that he kept the Fleet in Being and avoided exposure to an immensely skilful enemy, that he kept up morale in the Eastern Fleet to a remarkable extent and that in later months he acquiesced to the Fleet becoming merely a trade protection fleet. That required a degree of humility that some of his peers certainly did not have.

Somerville was preapred to lose his forces to theatres where he felt they could do more good. This was not a feature of Lord Louis Mountbatten at any time in his life, and from that starting point may be logged one of the many areas where these two powerful men fell out. It is no secret that Somerville and Mountbatten had very stormy relations and elements of the dispute have rumbled on in the post-war years. The conventional image, cultivated to an extent by Mountbatten himself, and further by his biographer, Philip Ziegler, is that Somerville was jealous of Mountbatten receiving such an appointment at forty-two years of age as a jumped-up naval captain, and that Somerville was in any event an aged crustacean ripe for retirement who received his just desserts in the face of Mountbatten's youthful blast of energy and drive. Despite Mountbatten's remarkable capacity to damage destroyers, he does not feature in this work as a fighting admiral – in naval terms he was merely a Captain (D) – and research into him for this section of the book has proved to be the most difficult area of all. Almost the only 'closed' files in this field are those concerned with Mountbatten, and those who have trodden the field before seem to have overlooked in certain cases fairly obvious pieces of evidence.

The case against Somerville can be stated quite simply. He had been and still was intensely irritated with the Admiralty, and Churchill in particular. The irritation may have stemmed from the fact that it was, in effect, Churchill who ordered him to bombard the French at Oran, and Mountbatten was to an extent Churchill's creature, as least as much as he was ever anyone's. Somerville could be stubborn to a fault, easily dismissive, and unwilling to change his mind, being prone to quick judgements. He could be intemperate in signals and correspondence, and where a dispute was involved sometimes refused personal contact and conversation for too long, a feature of his handling of the Oran affair. He disliked politicians, hypocrisy and 'publicity-seeking allied to brashness'[9]. However, it is clear that a major error was committed at the start, but not by either party: Whitehall appointed Mountbatten Supreme Commander but did not specify from the outset the distinction between his and Commander-in-Chief, Eastern Fleet's responsibilities. The model for Mountbatten's appointment was Eisenhower: the latter was not given operational control over the Mediterranean Fleet when he took up his corresponding position there. The absence of a clear directive meant a no-man's-land that one party or the other would have to conquer. It was not a good start. Cunningham, now in charge in London, and who at one stage had been considered as Supreme Commander[10], tried to pour oil on troubled waters, but a basic problem was that Somerville's area of responsibility extended outside that of Mountbatten, so Somerville believed his Fleet should fall under Mountbatten's direct command only for Combined Operations. Roskill, in *Churchill and the Admirals*, notes that Cunningham changed from supporting Somerville to coming down more on Mountbatten's side, which may or may not be another example of Cunningham's ability to change with the political wind, as he had done over Greece.

There is no truth to the story suggested in several sources that Somerville resented the appointment of Mountbatten. It is possible that he might have put up a public front of approval while inwardly resenting Mountbatten, but extremely unlikely, if this were the case, that he would have hidden it from those closest to him, or kept it a total secret in his private correspondence with some of his oldest friends. No one has ever accused Somerville of being a hypocrite. He clearly admired Mountbatten. To Cunningham in 1941 he wrote:

> I'm glad you've sent Dicky Mount B home to represent matters. He's forceful and has the gift for putting a case.[11]

To Pound he wrote:

> Dickie Mountbatten's appointment as Supreme Commander came as a bit of a surprise, but we all feel that

his imagination and drive will be of the greatest value. . . .
So far as the Naval side is concerned I feel quite confident
. . . since in all my past dealings with Dickie, I have found
that we see very much eye to eye on most matters.[12]

Both these extracts are typical and representative. Somerville
sent a warm and generous signal to Mountbatten which he
responded to with equal generosity and warmth:

Your typically thoughtful, helpful, and charming telegram
did more than anything else to reassure me and make me
feel that after all the Naval aspect of my task was going to
be made pleasant and easy for me.[13]

By this time Churchill seems to have forgiven Somerville and
responded warmly to the welcoming signal Somerville sent to
Mountbatten. All seemed set for a happy relationship, but things
started to go wrong later on:

Dickie is quite unable to resist the urge to have a finger in
every pie and to discuss even the most minute detail. . . .
As Dickie said to me, 'I hate to be presented with a fait
accompli.'[14]

Mountbatten seemed to take more authority on himself than
Somerville believed was his right. He also visited Somerville's
ships to address the crews without obtaining Somerville's consent, and arranged for maximum media coverage in which
frequent reference was made to 'Mountbatten's Fleet': Somerville, no mean publicist himself, was bound to resent this. Apart
from plain bad manners, the boost it may have given to Mountbatten's reputation was likely to be countered by the effect on
the way his Fleet viewed Somerville. Just as a dog can only have
one master, so with a Fleet: it was certainly one of the keys to
Cunningham's success in the Mediterranean. Mountbatten also
tended to have huge Staffs with him. Somerville insisted from
the outset that his own Staff were to treat Mountbatten's with
kid gloves[15], but Mountbatten's Staff, apart from its reputed
size, aroused bad feelings because of the way its contemporaries
saw it being full of men who were 'brilliant, ambitious, a bit
flashy'[16]; it also had a reputation for political intrigue, and

appears to have done nothing to make the job of Somerville's Staff any easier. Mountbatten also aroused resentment by the way he 'staged' certain events. Before visiting a ship, for example, he is reported to have gone into the most intimate detail about its crew, finding the names of anyone who had served with him, and then 'accidentally' recognizing the man in question. Somerville was not above arranging dramatic incidents, but Mountbatten's slickness of operation allowed some observers to see what he was doing as hypocritical manipulation. The difference between Mountbatten's efforts and a typical Somerville episode is shown when the latter sent a message on *Warspite* to his Commander (a Baronet) that he knew would go round the messdecks in record time:

> Dear Charles, I am well aware that as a Baronet you are indifferent to the suffering of mere Admirals, but would you mind having my lavatory unblocked?[17]

Two cruisers had been sunk and *Warspite* was steaming into very possible annihilation. Episodes such as this made Somerville part of the joke, diverted attention and suggested a *sang froid* on the part of the Admiral that could only boost morale. Here also lies the difference between Somerville's sense of humour and that of his friend Cunningham. Somerville always made himself part of the joke; Cunningham always made the joke at someone else's expense. There was an element of this in Mountbatten. His actions were seen as being for the benefit of Mountbatten; Somerville's were usually for the benefit of his Fleet. In some ways of course the problem was that both men were quite alike, for all the age difference. Both had an eye for the dramatic, both were far more familiar with technology than their contemporaries. Both had quick minds and respected minds which worked equally fast.

It may even be that Mountbatten had decided that Somerville had to go long before they met in the Far East:

> When Churchill made Lord Louis Mountbatten, Keyes' successor at Combined Operations, Supreme Commander in the Far East in 1943, the first question Mountbatten asked Dudley Pound (according to Mountbatten) was whether he was allowed to sack Somerville, twenty-three

years his senior, for whom he had conceived a powerful dislike. Once out in the East Mountbatten found it difficult to find an excuse for ridding himself of such an efficient and liked flag officer. However, at a fleet inspection Mountbatten considered that he had been treated with a lack of respect appropriate to his rank, and that was the end of the seagoing career, in August 1944, of one of the finest fighting admirals of the war.[18]

The dispute with Mountbatten was undoubtedly a major factor in Somerville being relieved from the Far Eastern Command, replaced by Admiral Bruce Fraser and sent to relieve Admiral Sir Percy Noble as Head of the British Naval Mission in Washington. Before he went, Somerville mounted two attacks on Sabang and Surabaya, both very successful, and both a fitting final fling for a fighting admiral. They made Churchill even more reluctant to have Somerville replaced[19], but did not change the fact of his posting.

Somerville had immense personal skills and was undoubtedly the most effective British Admiral to represent British interests in Washington. He started his job with utter distaste:

Nothing has occurred during the week that I have been here to change my opinion that this is a bloody awful job and Washington is a bloody awful place.[20]

This was the third post he had had which he treated with initial depression. For all its awfulness, Somerville was, as has been said, 'the most successful of all British admirals in handling 'Ernie' King.'[21]

In the meantime Somerville kept the Admiralty waiting four months before agreeing to go back on the active list. His given reason – he did not want to debar promotion to those beneath him – was undoubtedly genuine, but it is hard not to believe after all his arguments and plain talking with Whitehall that he did not enjoy the delay while he kept them waiting.

Washington was a rather strange end for an Admiral who had spent more time at sea than anyone other than Vian. He did it well, with a fair amount of bad language, a lot of signals, a lot of letters and a lot of humour; but that was to be expected. It was a mixture he had brought to a career which he and the

Navy had thought finished before war broke out, which restarted with an act of great generosity to a brother Admiral, and which ended with him taking on America's answer to King Neptune and being offered a seat beside him on the throne.

Somerville's replacement in the Far East by Fraser brings the latter into this story for the first time. Fraser is best known for the sinking of *Scharnhorst*, but that engagement links in with the earlier Battle of the Barents Sea, a curtain-raiser for it, and bringing to prominence another admiral, 'Bob' Burnett.

Robert Lindsay Burnett was born in 1887 of well-to-do Scottish parents, was clear in his own mind at least that he was going to join the Navy from the age of seven and entered *Britannia* in 1903. In some respects his career is typical – affluence, *Britannia*, service mainly in small ships with action in the Heligoland Bight and Dogger Bank affairs, command of a small vessel (a torpedo boat), and then destroyer command. Again one is reminded of the importance of destroyers as a training ground for the Admirals who were to command in the Second World War. In other areas Burnett's career was very different. He was a magnificent athlete and sportsman, but no great intellect. He was teased throughout his career for his lack of brains, and often used to thump the seat of his trousers and inform those listening that that was where his brains were. Until the late 1920's the majority of Burnett's appointments were in physical training of one form or another, but when Cunningham took over as Captain of the battleship *Rodney* in late 1929 he found as its Commander Burnett:

> a man with a good hold and an excellent way with the men
> . . . he . . . had been told that the ship had already as many
> brains as were needed and that was why he had been
> selected.[22]

As well as being an excellent athlete, Burnett had a passion for and great skill in amateur theatricals:

> Bob Burnett was a ball of fire and a great extrovert. He
> wrote and produced comic operas for us to put on. . . .
> There is a tale which *may* be apocryphal, though I believe
> it. ABC was giving a lunch party when we were at Gib. Bob
> dressed up as a female guest, in place of someone who had

fallen out, and was duly 'received' in the cuddy and got away with it.[23]

Another description of him was 'podgy Bob Burnett, a P.T. Specialist, with his eternal red-faced grin.'[24]

After a successful tour of duty in *Rodney* Burnett was made Captain and the remaining time from then until the war included command of a destroyer flotilla. Burnett often expressed surprise at his progressive promotions, but he was given the acting rank of Rear Admiral in November, 1940, and, as Flag Officer of the Home Fleet minelaying squadron, he was responsible for the deep minefield in northern waters. In 1942 he became Flag Officer, Home Fleet Destroyer Flotillas, and a year later Flag Officer 10th Cruiser Squadron.

Burnett played a leading part in the Arctic convoy battles and his involvement there was a rare vision of the right man in the right place. His simple philosophy of aggression and his optimism could take the combined battering of appalling weather, sometimes overwhelmingly unfavourable odds and unhelpful allies. His physical endurance helped him to cheer and raise the spirits, and the endurance, of others. His gut seaman's instinct and an element of natural guile served him well in out-thinking German air and submarine forces, and in waters where a man's life could be measured in seconds it is perhaps true that this relative lack of imagination did him no harm. He was a fighter, plain and simple, yet also an immense enthusiast, and a marvellous figure for keeping up morale on the convoy runs, as thankless and dangerous a task as faced any naval commander in the war. He was adored by his crews and understood his men in a way equalled only by Somerville. In December, 1942, the battered and overworked cruiser *Sheffield* hauled into Scapa Flow from the TORCH landings. The crew had had no leave for six months, and as a collision with the minesweeper *Cadmus* had left some damage there were high hopes that the necessary repair work would secure leave. However, welding equipment was brought on board and it was clear no leave was forthcoming. That night the welding equipment was mysteriously thrown into the Flow. Burnett came on board soon afterwards. Knowing he faced a disgruntled crew, he addressed them:

Last night in the starboard hangar you were singing 'I'm dreaming of a White Christmas'. Well, in the words of a famous comedian, 'you lucky people' because you're going to have one.[25]

That was Burnett's way of announcing the Russian convoy operation. There were no more disciplinary troubles.

The Battle of the Barents Sea was based round Convoy JW51B. After the disaster of PQ17 the convoys had been split into two and their designation changed. JW51B had a local escort of nine vessels, only two corvettes and two trawlers of which would go all the way with the convoy to Russia. They would be joined by seven fleet destroyers (Captain R. Sherbrooke in *Onslow*, in command of the 17th Destroyer Flotilla). Burnett in Force R (the 6″ cruisers *Sheffield* and *Jamaica*) was to give cover fifty miles to the south of the convoy, while there was a distant battleship covering squadron from Scapa led by *Anson*.

The Germans, for their part, were able to muster two heavy cruisers (*Hipper* and *Lutzow*) and six destroyers to attack JW51B. Though hampered by orders to use extreme caution, the German plan was simple, and it worked. The two German big ships would split up and meet the convoy at dawn. *Hipper* would draw off the escorts to the north, the convoy would dash to the south, straight on to the 11″ guns of *Lutzow*. That was exactly what happened.

German surface forces left to attack Convoy JW51B on 30 December, by which time the convoy was in a far from rosy position. Appalling weather had separated much of the port wing from the convoy, and Sherbrooke had lost contact with four escorts and two merchant ships. The battleship covering force was due to turn back and, more seriously, Burnett had no idea of the true position of the convoy. It had been blown off course and Tovey had signalled a position for it that was almost 150 miles away from its true position.

The Germans have often been criticized for their caution, but they were not alone in being affected by this doctrine. After the loss of the cruiser *Edinburgh* Tovey had set his heart against cruisers giving close escort to convoys because it put these valuable vessels too much in the firing line for U-boats, but in northern waters an escort fifty miles away was all too likely to lose contact altogether, or be too far away to help. Caution also dictated the battleship escort turning away so far to the west that it was of little use.

On 31 December Burnett thought he was crossing the wake of his convoy fifty miles astern; he was actually thirty miles north of it. The first shots of the battle were fired shortly after 0915 by *Hipper's* destroyers. Sherbrooke led out to defend the convoy and there then followed a dangerous game of tag in which *Hipper* dipped in and out of squalls, firing accurately, and sinking the minesweeper *Bramble*, while seriously damaging *Achates* and *Onslow*. The former was to sink later. In the meantime the convoy was headed straight for *Lutzow*. Her captain blamed bad weather and poor visibility for his failure to open fire until the last minute, and it may have been that his orders to break off after the convoy had been attacked in order to undertake a commerce raiding cruise made him unduly nervous about sustaining damage. Either way his delay threw away the German victory, for a few minutes after signalling *Lutzow* that there were no cruisers about (the German Admiral Kummetz's way of telling his other captain to get on with the job of sinking the convoy), 6″ shells from Burnett's Force R burst round *Hipper*.

By his intervention Burnett undoubtedly saved the convoy. *Hipper* was hit three times in quick succession, one hit getting under her armour belt and slowing her down. *Hipper* turned away. Burnet's cruisers then pulverized a German destroyer that appeared at short range out of the gloom (the destroyer thought *Sheffield* was *Hipper*, and signalled plaintively 'You are firing on me!'). The two German vessels briefly re-engaged, but finally broke off shortly before 0100.

Sherbrooke received the Victoria Cross for his defence of the convoy, in which he was seriously wounded, but his victory was a close-run thing, secured partly by his and his forces' heroism, Burnett's arrival at a crucial moment when really only one destroyer stood between the Germans and the convoy and the failure of *Lutzow* to go in for the kill. Burnett's handling of the action raised several question marks. He had become lost from the convoy through no fault of his own. At 0858 on the morning of the action he had decided to trail two vessels picked up on radar. They were actually two ships detached from the convoy, but he was right to be suspicious and treat the echoes as if they might be German vessels shadowing the convoy. At 0932 Force R spotted gunfire (the German destroyers firing at *Obdurate*), but dismissed it as AA fire. At 0946 heavy gunfire was seen (*Hipper* firing on *Achates*) and Sherbrooke's sighting report of three enemy destroyers received. It took nine minutes for Burnett to turn towards the gunfire and increase speed to twenty-five knots. He can be criticized for this, but he was in an appalling quandry. The gunfire could be miles away from the convoy he was ordered to protect, and by heading for it he could be heading away from the convoy and leaving it open to German heavy vessels. The two echoes he was trailing could be those heavy units; in practice, Burnett was hung on the horns of a dilemma and had to take a massive gamble. He chose, after nine excruciating minutes, to follow Nelson's ruling that no commander can do much wrong if he lays himself alongside his enemy, and headed for the sound of the guns. In so doing he proved Nelson right, and himself.

There were more serious complaints concerning Burnett's handling of his cruisers almost a year later in the action in which *Scharnhorst* was sunk. This time Burnett was in command of 'Force 1', consisting of the heavy cruiser *Norfolk* and the 6″ gun cruisers *Sheffield* and *Belfast*. Convoy JW55B was the bait for *Scharnhorst*. Again the weather was foul, though this time Admiral Fraser, with excellent intelligence of *Scharnhorst's* movements through ULTRA, was at sea with *Duke of York* and able to intercept the German vessel on her return home. Again Burnett was out of position, possibly as a result of being given a wrong position for the convoy earlier in the day. He was actually fifty miles ahead of the convoy, a position which allowed *Scharnhorst* to come between him and the convoy, threatening the latter very seriously. When he did deploy his cruisers it was in a manner that masked the fire of two out of the three of them. The fire opened by the cruisers was again very effective (two hits by *Norfolk*, one on the German ship's forward radar), but Burnett delayed in following *Scharnhorst* when she turned to port by eleven minutes. Then at 1014 Burnett turned away altogether, deliberately lost contact with *Scharnhorst* and headed back to the convoy.

Burnett had been criticized for thus losing contact, though Roskill backs him. Roskill's is the correct interpretation. Burnett was clearly prone to hesitation when major decisions had to be taken. Twice at a crucial time he hesitated, and twice he was proved right. Burnett gambled that *Scharnhorst* would come back again for another go at the convoy. It was all too probable that *Scharnhorst* hoped to draw the cruisers away from the convoy, lose them and then double back, making use of the capital ship's ability to sustain high speed in very bad weather. Burnett's breaking off contact with the German ship was taken badly by Fraser who was theoretically heading straight for *Scharnhorst*. He was appalled by the prospect of *Scharnhorst* simply carrying on past the convoy and proceeding in the opposite direction to *Duke of York* in order to mount a commerce raiding cruise. This was the dilemma that had faced every Admiral seeking to intercept heavy German surface units. It had contributed significantly to the sinking of *Hood*, and bedevilled the search for *Bismarck*. Despite this, it has to be said that Fraser's instincts were at fault. Increased air cover and saturation of the Atlantic by Allied navies meant that the days of the commerce raider were gone. Fraser was out of touch if he felt that *Scharnhorst* was ever likely to play a Lone Ranger role as a commerce raider. Burnett realized this and time was to prove him correct. At 1210 *Scharnhorst* reappeared on Burnett's radar exactly where he had predicted. The remainder of the battle is covered later in this chapter.

Burnett took vast risks, was prone to momentary hesitation and on two occasions was out of position when major surface forces threatened a convoy. The fact remains that on both occasions he got it right. He may have been steering and thinking with the seat of his pants, in which case one hopes some museum has preserved this part of his anatomy, as it played a crucial part in two major naval victories. Burnett had the 'x' factor – luck – so conspicuously absent from an outstanding Admiral such as Bonham-Carter: when two successive cruisers were sunk under him the ratings started to refer to lifejackets as 'Bonhams'. In all the war Burnett is the outstanding example of a natural leader with little or no capacity for strategic thought, but a basic fighting instinct that somehow always got him in range of the enemy.

There could hardly be two more contrasting figures than Burnett and Fraser, except that both were exceptionally popular with those who worked under them. One glimpse of Fraser sees him as:

> An exceedingly intelligent and sympathetic man, exuding
> an overpowering friendliness: he was not a man one was
> fearful of, and one felt one could trust him.[26]

The above is a far cry from Vian, from Horton and indeed from Cunningham. Fraser was born on 5 February, 1888, the son of a General who was a superb architect and engineer. The pattern is a familiar one: the 'pool' of families devoting their children to military service, the second son going into the Navy, the distant relationship with a powerful and perhaps even intimidating father. At Bradfield College Fraser was in the Navy class, his brothers in the Army class. In 1902 he passed fifth into *Britannia*, and passed out joint first. Unlike Burnett, there was no doubt of Fraser's intelligence; unlike Cunningham, there was no doubt of his willingness and ability to use that intelligence. Fraser is sometimes seen as the first of a 'new breed' of top commanders, well-versed in technical matters. This is true enough, except inasmuch as it denies the technical skill of an older man, Somerville, but it may well be that Fraser's natural intellect put him into this category as much as any major change in the Navy.

Fraser was different in other ways. He is one of the few Admirals who achieved fame in the war who was a gunnery specialist, attending Whale Island and achieving considerable distinction there, including compiling the Navy's handbook for Director Firing. He was *not* a destroyer captain, but did see active service on board the light cruiser *Minerva* between 1914 – 15. This gave him a taste of the type of experience Cunningham and the others had often had in colonial wars – patrolling Akaba, firing on forts, rescuing ditched seaplanes, cloak-and-dagger missions, taking landing parties ashore with field guns. He was even able to make one of the Navy's first heavy anti-aircraft guns by mounting a field-gun on a capstan. He had the distinction of being a Bolshevik prisoner in 1920 and oversaw development of the Navy's gunnery Fire Control Table. Much of his service in the inter-war years was with that cauldron of promotion, the Mediterranean Fleet, where for a period he was Fleet Gunnery Officer. As Director of Naval Ordnance Fraser was responsible for the development of the quadruple 14" turret for the 'King George V' class battleships, and the revolutionary dual-purpose 5.25" guns as secondary armament for the 'King George Vs', main armament for the 'Dido' class anti-aircraft cruisers. He had close links with Dudley Pound and with Admiral of the Fleet Lord Chatfield, powerful men to have on his side, though as Chief of Staff to

Pound he found the same problem that Ramsay had faced with another master in that Pound was unable to delegate and took far too much on his own shoulders. On 1 March, 1939, he was made Controller of the Navy and Third Sea Lord, in which post he was responsible for the 'Flower' class corvettes. He was promoted Vice-Admiral on 8 May, 1940, and awarded the KBE in the Birthday Honours of 1941.

As a personality, the feature that comes over time and again is his image as the perfect gentleman: 'Eternally patient, absolutely unflappable, and with it all a perfect naval gentleman.'[27] This is a far cry from Cunningham, Vian, Horton, Somerville and Phillips: only Ramsay can claim to have something of the same style.

In technical, gunnery and ship design matters Fraser was far more influential than any of his contemporaries, at the opposite end of the spectrum from Cunningham who distrusted all 'gadgets'. It is therefore only fair to look at Fraser's record and what he did. He took a large share of the responsibility for the armament of the 'King George V' class battleships and the quadruple 14″ gun turret designed for these vessels still has many question marks over it. Its development was the result of the Royal Navy's scrupulous honesty in adhering to the letter of international naval treaties, but the fact was that the turret was a bad design and never looked like being anything else. Its failure in the almost new *Prince of Wales* can be excused in a ship not fully worked-up and with dockyard engineers still on board. That it failed when *King George V* helped to sink *Bismarck* and was still failing when *Duke of York* sank *Scharnhorst* is far less excusable[28]. The 14″ quadruple turret was a flawed design which never worked properly, a good idea which contemporary British technology was unable to make effective. Fraser made the best out of a bad job. What might have been more useful was someone who spotted that it *was* a bad job and scrapped it in favour of a better one. It was not Fraser's fault that Chatfield (the First Sea Lord) decided to add more armour on to the class, which decision made it impossible to ship three quadruple turrets. Weight factors then demanded that the third turret in these vessels be a twin one, and this in turn meant the designers had to start from scratch because the 14″ gun had originally been conceived of only in terms of the quadruple configuration. Fraser may have been attempting to do the impossible and his turrets put a hole in *Bismarck* and sank *Scharnhorst*. Despite this they cannot be said to be an undiluted success.

The 5.25" gun turrets were a different story. In purely conceptual terms they were excellent, a truly dual-purpose gun that could engage both surface and air targets. In practice they were a failure. They were too heavy for effective tracking and for a sufficiently high rate of fire for aircraft targets. They depended totally on electrical power, highly trained crews and effective directors. On too many occasions this triumvirate was not present. They were too light for surface actions, too heavy for their anti-aircraft role. As with so many so-called advances the dual-purpose concept really needed parallel advances (proximity fusing and advanced radar) before it could come into its own.

Whereas the two guns were at the sharp end of technological advance, the 'Flower' class corvettes were still in the swamps and the caves. They were a dire emergency measure born out of desperation. In one sense they were a disaster. Their speed put them at a disadvantage with a surfaced U-boat, their hulls were too short for Atlantic waves and rolled horribly. Living conditions on board were appalling and depth-charge and gun armament were fairly derisory. Yet in another sense they were a life-saver. They were chosen because, as a variation on an existing commercial design, they could be produced quickly and with relative ease from small dockyards. Their unsophisticated steam propulsion could be serviced and operated by mercantile seamen, reducing the need for specialist training. They may have rolled, but they rarely foundered. They could carry an asdic, a radar, a 4" gun and some depth-charges to where the U-boats were, and without them it would be difficult to see how the war against the U-boat could have been won. Neither credit nor blame can properly go to the Admiralty for them. What they do reveal is what might have been an answer to some of the problems the Royal Navy faced in 1939. The major problem was a lack of escorts. Cunningham pioneered the 'Hunt' class escorts, which were effectively anti-aircraft convoy escorts – a very specialized role. Fraser's contribution was the even more specialist 'Flowers' – slow anti-submarine convoy escorts. Both Admirals went for specialization, simplicity and speed of building. In a Navy that simply could not afford enough vessels of every type, an answer in the inter-war years might have been to

18 *Scharnhorst, Gneisenau* and *Prinz Eugen* proceeding up Channel with accompanying escorts.

19 The loss of the *Prince of Wales*.

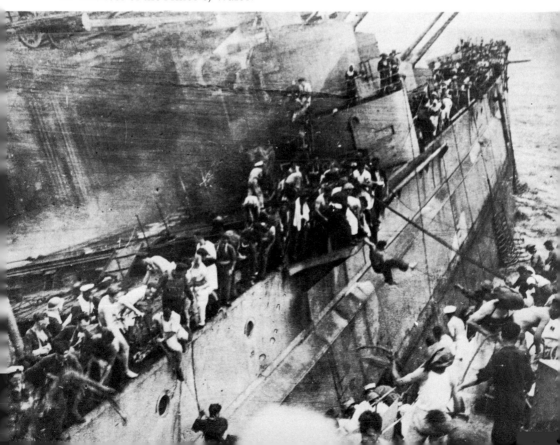

20 'To allow personnel to be sloppily dressed is, in my opinion, the first step to indiscipline.' The naval censor clearly agreed with Cunningham; on this photograph of Fraser wearing untidy uniform on board *Duke of York* was scribbled the message 'Give him a collar and tie and black jacket', duly done for the published version.

21 'A man with a good hold and an excellent way with the men.' Burnett on *Ashanti*.

prepare drawings for highly specialized escort vessels that as stop-gaps could be produced in small shipyards at great speed. More time to think might have produced something a little more warlike than the 'Flowers', and the presence of detailed drawings and a contingency plan for construction, if implemented in 1938, might have produced far more vessels as well as better designs. It would have given the Navy no more ships in 1938, but interfered little with existing building programmes and allowed for a major and early increase in available vessels. It is all hindsight, of course, and so radical a departure from existing practice as to be a retrospective pipe-dream.

Fraser was no coward. He accompanied the 'Pedestal' convoy as a 'guest' on board *Rodney*, and part of his myth was that he shot down a Stuka himself with a bridge machine gun. It was untrue (a Signalman did the shooting) but such stories only attract themselves to those who are well-loved and respected by the men who serve under them. On 8 May, 1943, Fraser took over the Home Fleet from Tovey. Just as Tovey had been haunted by *Tirpitz*, so Fraser from the outset seems to have been obsessed with *Scharnhorst*. Before he could get to grips with her one of the other famous episodes of the war intervened, and he found himself being offered the post of First Sea Lord in October, 1943, in succession to the dead Pound. The story has been well-told elsewhere, and needs little retelling. Churchill is quoted as saying:

In Admiral Fraser, then commanding the Home Fleet, we had an officer of the highest seagoing reputation, who had also long experience of Admiralty administration and staff work. It was to him I first offered the post. The Admiral said that of course he would serve wherever he was sent, but that he thought Andrew Cunningham was the right man. 'I believe I have the confidence of my own fleet,' he said. 'Cunningham has that of the whole Navy.' He asked me to weight the matter longer. I replied that his attitude was most becoming, and after further thought and consultation I took him at his word and decided to face the serious change in the Mediterranean fighting command. Andrew Cunningham was therefore chosen.[29]

In fact there were three men in serious consideration for the post – Cunningham, Tovey and Fraser. Churchill wrote to A.V. Alexander:

> I have most carefully considered the question of filling Pound's vacancy, and I have no doubt whatever that we should offer it to Admiral Fraser. [Cunningham] is an officer of the old school and the pre-air age. This epoch finishes with Pound's four years of splendid service. We must move forward to younger men.[30]

Alexander urged Cunningham. Churchill disliked Cunningham because Cunningham disagreed with him. There was a child-like or childish element to Churchill (commented on by Ramsay) and that simple statement undoubtedly explains a lot of Churchill's animosity to Cunningham. There is some evidence that Churchill wanted to sack Cunningham after the *Bismarck* sinking.[31]

There was an element of truth in Churchill's strictures against Cunningham. There is also a point about what seems to be Fraser's great, if not his greatest, ability, namely his capacity to get on with everyone, regardless. When Fraser took over from Somerville, inter-Staff tension vanished. Australians, Americans and all-comers seem to have warmed to him in equal measure, as if he was a man people found it impossible to argue with or feel anger towards. It even makes his biography sometimes a rather dull and repetitive read, but it points to a remarkable skill. If not a skill that helped him particularly in the fighting part of admiralty, it certainly helped him clear the deck for others to fight.

Unfortunately, relations between Cunningham and Fraser were not good. Cunningham clearly resented holding his appointment by virtue of Fraser's good grace, and the fact that it took a truly remarkable man to stand down in these circumstances, for whatever reason, was not recognized by Cunningham. Possibly Fraser was helped in his decision by his being a bachelor. It left him less concerned by the financial aspects of promotion, and more wedded to his service. It is also true that the selfless standing-aside shown by Fraser is typical of the loyalty to the Royal Navy shown by all the Admirals mentioned in this work, and which was a major feature of the men turned out by *Britannia*. That it is typical makes it no less remarkable. One aspect of Fraser's selflessness is shown by the fact that he, in time-honoured tradition, chose the name of his battle, North Cape, when he received his peerage; Cunningham and Tovey chose the name of their homes.

Relations between Cunningham and Fraser may be seen to start to go seriously wrong when Fraser launched 'Operation Tungsten', the successful air attack whereby *Tirpitz* received fourteen bomb hits on 14 April, 1944. Cunningham wanted an immediate follow-up attack, as he had at Taranto. Fraser refused it, seeing it as suicidal against an alerted and angry defence. When Fraser went to command the Far Eastern fleet in succession to Somerville, Roskill comments:

> Things did not go smoothly between Fraser and
> Cunningham during the build-up of the fleet in Ceylon. . . .
> In mid-November the new C-in-C wrote what
> Cunningham described as 'an unpleasant letter'
> complaining that the Admiralty consistently turned down
> all his proposals', and suggesting he should 'select someone
> whose judgement you would trust and advice you would
> follow.'[32]

It is axiomatic that no letter quoted by Cunningham implies that he is at fault. Cunningham was, by and large, incapable of criticizing himself. Allowing for this, a letter of this type from Fraser of all people was serious business. For that most unflappable of men to be so sharp suggests a tidy degree of interference and a great deal of mistrust. As with Mountbatten and Somerville, personalities had a lot to do with it. Fraser had a massive job when he was sent out to the Far East essentially to team up with the American fleet. For *him* there was little problem:

> There was no pomposity to him at all. With *anyone* who
> shared an existence in the Royal Navy, they were
> partners. . . . Mountbatten's meteoric rise to fame didn't
> worry him at all. Fraser could *never* join a faction . . . the
> factors of age or seniority didn't worry him at all. . . . that
> whole terrible atmosphere of tension and hostility between
> the staffs just melted away.[33]

Comments such as this might seem to be 'puffing' Fraser if we did not have the example of him standing aside for Cunningham to back them up. That very ease was at odds with the fiercely competitive Cunningham, the 'Meat Phaz' of *Britannia*. Things such as promotion *did* matter to Cunningham. He was, as we know, obsessive about dress. It had even been the occasion of a mild reprimand from Pound:

> As you are, no doubt, aware, there is a good deal of mild
> grousing about the orders you have given about the rig for
> officers on shore, the reason being the small number of
> 'whites' in the possession of a good many officers and the
> cost of washing.[34]

Cunningham's reply was 'To allow personnel to be sloppily dressed is, in my opinion, the first stop to indiscipline.'[35]

Fraser, on the other hand, was instrumental in allowing members of his fleet to wear khaki, a *bête noire* of Cunningham's. Fraser cheerfully adopted American signalling procedure, which Cunningham revoked immediately the war was over. Fraser believed that the Americans had proved that endurance at sea could be significantly improved by a proper attention to shipboard amenities, a part of the humanitarian instinct that helped to drive Somerville and Ramsay. Unbeknown to Cunningham, Fraser authorized canned beer to be carried for men in his supply train[36]. In the meantime Cunningham was writing:

> I hope our people will not get too blinded by American
> lavishness. We cannot compete with them in either
> personnel or material, nor do I think we should train our
> men to expect the same waste as is practised in the
> American Navy. I am sure that soda fountains, etc., are
> very good things in the right place, but we have done
> without them for some hundreds of years and I daresay can
> for another year or two.[37]

The above is pure Cunningham. It also ignores the fact that, taken to its logical conclusion, the Far Eastern Fleet should have been fighting the Japanese with wooden-hulled ships carrying smooth-bore cannon. Cunningham's letter shows his parsimony and almost obsessional fear of waste, and also a Calvinistic welcoming of hardship and suffering as being valuable in their own right, something which trains the soul. It is one of the least attractive features of the Scottish cultural inheritance.

Fraser's appointment to the Far Eastern Fleet therefore replaced one conflict (Somerville v Mountbatten) with another, (Cunningham v Fraser), strange in the light of Cunningham's insistence at having his old friend Somerville relieved. However, the conflict never assumed the dangerous proportions that it might have done and most of the rows between the two men fizzled out. A further problem was Fraser's status as The Man Who Sank The *Scharnhorst*. There is no evidence that Cunningham was jealous; it would not have been out of character for him to be so and he could not resist a sideswipe at Fraser in a letter to a friend:

> I agree thoroughly with what you say about the criticism
> of mistakes. I once put my foot down at the Admiralty on
> the subject. A young man brought me a letter to sign
> severely criticising Fraser for the action in which he sank
> the *Scharnhorst*. True enough, he had made one or two
> what might bc called mistakes, but I told the young man to
> go and put the letter, and himself, into the waste paper
> basket, so, regrettably, no lessons were learnt except
> perhaps by him.[38]

This is Cunningham at his worst, playing the false advocate. He manages to state that his client did not commit more than one mistake and offers no defence against that allegation. Once his client has been damned, the advocate then proceeds to set himself up as his defender. In the meantime a junior officer whose only sin has been to tell his commander the truth is sent scurrying away with a flea in his ear, presumably convinced that in the Royal Navy at least it is impossible (or, at the very least, unwise) to criticize one's superiors.

This leads on inevitably to the question of whether or not Fraser did make mistakes. It is a moot point whether the possible errors on his part were mistakes or gambles. As ever, he has one great point in his favour: he won. For Cunningham, used for too many years to being the only British Admiral in that position, this may have been too much to bear.

Fraser had taken one big risk before the battle started, which was to break radio silence if in his opinion this would contribute to the destruction of the German ship. With several forces at sea in appalling weather conditions, he was proved right. The Germans did intercept a number of his signals, but failed to interpret them correctly and failed to report to *Scharnhorst* that a battleship was at sea and threatening her. Breaking radio silence in order to marshall his forces was not a mistake. It was a gamble, similar to Hitler's gamble that the British would not be able to mount a quick response to the Channel Dash, and it worked. Also on his side Fraser had ULTRA which told him of German sightings and certain ship movements almost as quickly as the German themselves received them. If Matapan was won through radar, North Cape was won through ULTRA.

Fraser reversed course twice in the action against *Scharnhorst*, at both times risking losing her. The first time was when Burnett had lost her and Fraser ordered a reversal of course for fear of her breaking out to the west. This was countermanded when *Sheffield's* radar picked up *Scharnhorst*. Initially *Scharnhorst* seemed to want to make a fight of it with Burnett's cruisers and destroyers, hit *Norfolk* twice and damaged her quite seriously in revenge for the hits she had scored earlier. *Scharnhorst* then broke away just as she was coming into range of seven enemy torpedo-carrying vessels. Rear Admiral Bey had 'lost' his destroyers earlier in the action. Burnett shadowed *Scharnhorst*, heading comfortably home and unaware that she was steaming straight towards *Duke of York*. German reconnaissance had spotted the British force, but a combination of circumstances and slow signalling procedures prevented Bey from being informed. Had he been informed he could have turned south-west, pushed his shadowers into heavy seas that would have slowed them down and possibly escaped. As it was, at 1647 on 26 December, 1943, *Scharnhorst* was illuminated by starshell, wholly unaware of a battleship in her range, and with guns trained fore and aft.

Radar played a decisive role at Matapan; it was even more decisive at North Cape. *Duke of York* had one of the best radar fits in the Royal Navy, and it accounted for the accuracy of her fire, and to an extent compensated for the shortcomings of the quadruple turrets. Her *first* salvo straddled *Scharnhorst* and put the forward turret ('Anton') out of action – surely a record in any naval engagement. Fraser ordered his four destroyers just before he opened fire:

Take up most advantageous positions for firing *but do not attack until ordered*. [author's italics][39]

Later in the engagement this order was to prove to be a mistake.

Scharnhorst had been badly hit but still had her speed. She was a faster and better sea boat than *Duke of York*, and Fraser failed to order a destroyer attack when his destroyers were within easy range. When he did order an attack at 1713 the German ship had pulled to over 17,000 yards away and the destroyers were facing very heavy seas. *Duke of York* ceased fire when the range had opened to 21,400 yards. She had fired fifty-two salvoes and made thirteen hits. Fraser had actually started to turn round and break off the action when it was noticed that *Scharnhorst* was slowing. One of *Duke of York's* last hits had penetrated *Scharnhorst's* starboard side and severed a steam pipe as well as doing other damage. It was this hit, at the last gasp, that sealed *Scharnhorst's* fate. The destroyers were able at last to close in, scoring at least four hits with torpedoes, and *Scharnhorst* was sunk by *Duke of York's* gunfire and *Jamaica's* torpedoes.

Fraser's only real 'mistake' was to limit his destroyers' freedom of action and miss the opportunity for an early attack. That mistake did not, in the final count, stop *Scharnhorst* being sunk. Fraser might have shown a little too much public despair: once when he appeared to criticize Burnett by signal for losing contact with *Scharnhorst*, a second time when he plaintively announced he was breaking off the action, but that hardly matters. It should be noted that this mild, friendly man battered into a sinking hulk Germany's remaining fully seaworthy battleship with a single-mindedness that Cunningham would not have been ashamed of.

Fraser had the technical awareness of Somerville, the charm and intelligence of Ramsay, and, when it was needed, the single-minded aggression of Cunningham. In addition he had great personal skills which he was prepared to use on behalf of the service he revered, and a willingness to drop personal ambition for the sake of that same service. Intelligence: power of aggression: Staff Officer skills: personal charm; technical knowledge . . . it is difficult not to see Fraser as a symbol of all that the Royal Navy had been working towards throughout the war. Amidst all this euphoria certain *caveats* have to be sounded. His technical mastery did not lead to major advances in gunnery, but rather to two very flawed designs, neither of which justified the money invested in them. The Royal Navy had a recent tradition of not spotting when it had a good thing. *Ark Royal* was an excellent design of aircraft carrier, rejected after one prototype in favour of the less than outstanding 'Illustrious' class whose armour protection was costly, reduced aircraft capacity and only really came into its own when facing *kamikaze* attack. Fraser was not responsible for that decision, but followed in the tradition of it by supporting the development of the quadruple 14″ turret when it would have been better to devote resources to perfecting the triple 16″ turret or refining the already excellent twin 15″ turret that dated from the First World War. As for the 5.25″ dual-purpose weapon, a far greater need was for a dual-purpose 4″ or 4.5″ gun for destroyers. Financially the Royal Navy was never able to afford all that it wanted or required. It and Fraser chose the 5.25″ gun, and it may be that its development was indirectly responsible for sending many a destroyer, devoid of effective dual-purpose armament, to the bottom of the sea. In exchange it could not even manage to save *Prince of Wales* from the very enemy it had been designed to destroy. Fraser's other 'triumph', the 'Flower' class corvettes, was a desperate measure echoing a similar initiative from the First World War. Fraser's gesture in refusing Churchill's offer and stepping down in favour of Cunningham was noble but also practical. Fraser was shrewd enough to know his time would come and young enough to wait confidently. His decision did not harm his later promotion prospects, relieved him from a job fraught with difficulty and put him in what was arguably the most exciting command position available to any Admiral in the final period of the war. Fraser was a great man who had great luck, great help and who made on occasion great mistakes.

There were other Admirals who did more with less.

9 D-Day and the U-Boat War

Chronology of Events

1944

3 April. Operation 'Tungsten', air attack on *Tirpitz* by Admiral Fraser's Home Fleet.

19 April. Admiral Somerville's Eastern Fleet carries out raid on Sabang, Sumatra.

17 May. Eastern Fleet carries out raid on Surabaya, Java.

6 June. Operation 'Overlord', the invasion of Europe.

June. Admiral Sir Henry Moore appointed C-i-C Home Fleet, in succession to Admiral Fraser who is to command British Pacific Fleet.

3 September. Antwerp captured, but not its approaches.

12 December. *Tirpitz* sunk by RAF bombers using 'Tallboy' bombs.

1945

2 January. Admiral Sir Bertram Home Ramsay killed in air crash.

24/29 January. Admiral Vian launches successful attacks against Palembang, Southern Sumatra.

30 April. Hitler commits suicide.

May. Whole of Mediterranean basin free from German and Italian military threat. In the course of the war the Mediterranean had claimed one RN battleship, two fleet carriers, twenty cruisers, sixty-seven destroyers and forty-five submarines: forty percent of the total Royal Navy warship losses during the whole war.

8 May. Germany signs unconditional surrender.

6 August. First atomic bomb dropped on Hiroshima.

9 August. Atom bomb dropped on Nagasaki.
15 August. Japan surrenders.

The fight against the U-boat and the ability to land troops in France were arguably the two most important naval events of the war – the former to stop Britain losing it, the latter to win it. The major burden for the U-boat war fell on the Commander-in-Chief of the Western Approaches, who for much of the early period of the war was the much-loved Admiral Sir Percy Noble. In November, 1942, he was replaced by Max Horton, one of the most complex and intriguing figures of the war.

Two factors assumed overwhelming importance in the war against the U-boat: the supply of *matériel* (warships, merchant vessels, aircraft and a whole host of other goods), and technological advance. The U-boat war was a race between the German capacity to sink vessels and our capacity to build them. Interestingly, the figures for the first time start to show a slight balance in favour of the Allies in the middle of 1942, when Noble was still Commander-in-Chief of the Western Approaches. This fact is often mentioned in conversation with those who served under him and his successor, and who resented what was seen as the dismissal of Noble. These officers, none of whom have agreed to be quoted, believe that Horton took the credit for Noble's achievements, and that Horton took over as Commander-in-Chief of the Western Approaches at a time when the supply of *matériel* was starting to reach a level at which the Allies had a fighting chance against the U-boat. The Noble v. Horton combat is a difficult one to referee. Noble was a perfect naval gentleman, Horton a rough-rider, and strong personal feelings may well have coloured historical objectivity for those who have taken sides in this debate.

Whatever the truth about the personalities involved, there was little doubt that German capacity to sink our ships and our capacity to resist was to a large extent dictated by technology. At the start of the war the British had asdic, or sonar as it is now known, and for significant periods would have access to the German Naval Enigma code which would allow them to plot German submarine movements. The Germans started the war with only a handful of sea-going submarines. As with so much of the war, a superficially favourable picture for the Royal

Navy reveals itself shot through with holes on closer examination.

Asdic was fixed under the bow of the relevant vessel where it was prone to damage. It could only operate forward and so lost contact in the final crucial moments of an attack when the submarine could jink out of the attacker's path. It did not give a depth reading and German U-boats could dive deeper than British depth-charges could reach. More seriously, asdic was virtually useless when a submarine mounted a surface attack. With a low surface profile and top speed of eighteen knots the U-boat was almost invisible at night, and thus the British technological advantage could be almost wiped out. The Navy had fitted asdic to fleet destroyers and trawlers, many of which were not available for cross-Atlantic escort work. Even if more destroyers had been available they were by no means the perfect answer to a submarine threat, despite popular belief to the contrary. The conventional destroyer had a heavy torpedo and gun armament. This and its high speed made it an excellent vessel for use against surface vessels, but a true anti-submarine vessel needed to exchange some of the destroyer's high speed for long endurance, and some of its weapons for increased anti-submarine weaponry and magazine space for depth-charges. An escort that ran out of depth charges was as useless as an anti-aircraft cruiser that ran out of ammunition. In any event there was an appalling shortage of escorts *and* destroyers at the start of the war, and when more did come on stream they were often the 'Flower' class corvettes whose weaknesses have been noted earlier. In technological and supply terms the answers were clear enough. Gathering vessels for a 'wolf-pack' attack required much signals traffic: good direction-finding equipment could therefore pinpoint a U-boat's position. Good surface radar could again give warning of an attack and stop a surfaced U-boat stalking a convoy *if* that radar was sensitive enough to pick up the small target of a U-boat's conning tower. Radar carried by long-range aircraft was essential if U-boats were to be forced underwater, where their relatively slow speed and low endurance would rob them of the chance of chasing or finding a convoy. Better depth charges, better bombs and forward-throwing launchers for depth charges were needed. Of all these, perhaps more escorts and air cover for convoys were the essential items. This latter area, the provision of air cover, was one of the hottest potatoes of the war. The emphasis on the bombing of Germany caused immense anguish among all naval personnel who could see the shortage of long-range aircraft to cover convoys losing vast number of ships and men, and perhaps losing the war. Tovey added another nail to his coffin by making it quite clear that Coastal Command and the Fleet Air arm had obsolete aircraft; that much more assistance was needed from the RAF and that such assistance could only be forthcoming by a reduction in bombing of Germany; that the bombing of Germany certainly would not win the war, but failure to protect convoys would certainly lose it. Tovey even suggested a mass resignation by the Lords of the Admiralty if more support was not forthcoming in May of 1942[1].

The British devoted far too many resources to the bombing of Germany and far too little far too late to the protection of trade. However, what was needed would come eventually, both air support and everything else, but it took time. In that time a great deal hinged on the courage of British merchant seaman and the training and handling of the few resources that Britain had.

Noble was not a charismatic figure, nor a publicist. He was almost obsessional about cleanliness and personal appearance, but he was above all an efficient, thoughtful and determined commander. He made several major contributions to victory in the Atlantic and he left Horton with rather more than the bare bones of the organization that would defeat the U-boat. There has been a tendency almost to blame Horton for Noble's departure, which is pure nonsense. At the same time Noble has probably never received the recognition he deserves. The victories he won were painstaking, almost wholly without glamour and often not even visible as victories at the time they were won. One wonders if the future will rank Matapan and Taranto in the same league as Noble's battle.

Noble was in many respects a remarkable man. He took the necessary time to get to know his crews, and took the best possible way of learning about conditions at sea by joining escorts himself. His knowledge could have immediate results. He was with one convoy when he found himself on board the only warship within sight, the others having been sent off on fruitless chases after supposed U-boats. This led to a tightening-up of the orders by which escorts could be sent dashing off all over the ocean searching for needles in seaweed[2]. Noble adopted new technology the instant it became available. He set up training schools for escorts and realized the immense importance of Escort Groups. There has been some confusion between these Hunting Groups and Support Groups. Noble's Escort Groups were an attempt to make sure that a body of warships stayed together and got to know each other and their mode of operation in convoy escorts. Hunting Groups were a disastrous idea current at the start of the war whereby warships were sent out all over the Atlantic searching for U-boats: the carrier *Courageous* found one and was sunk by it, as nearly was *Ark Royal*, before the idea was dropped. Support Groups were groups of warships that could be sent to trouble spots or to reinforce a threatened convoy. The latter were a major advance, and Noble was stopped from using them only because in his time the vessels were not available. His influence was shown in other areas. He was instrumental in making sure that merchant vessels with a top speed of fifteen knots were required to sail in convoy (the limit had been dropped to thirteen knots), realizing that the worst losses of merchant ships were those sailing independently. All in all, it is difficult to question his stewardship of the Western Approaches Command.

Admiral Sir Max Kennedy Horton, GCB, DSO, on the other hand, was a man who aroused questions wherever he went.

Horton was born in 1883 into a background that we can now see as being absolutely typical – wealthy (his father was a stockbroker), and from a family committed to military service (his grandfather had been in the Highland Light Infantry). As Horton is the last of so many families whose ancestors had served in the Army, it is worth asking if the existence of *Britannia* created a change in the class of society who normally sent their children to the Army by offering socially respectable officer training at very cheap rates, on the condition that it was the Navy that was chosen. If this is so, it marks a major achievement of *Britannia* and those who created her: a Royal Navy in the Second World War without Horton, Fraser, Phillips, Ramsay and Tovey, all of whom had near relations who served in the Army, would have been a sadly-depleted force. It is outside the scope of this work to know if prior to *Britannia* there had been 'Army' and 'Navy' families; it would make interesting research.

At *Britannia* Horton was a Cadet Captain (the equivalent of a prefect), and showed himself an outstanding sportsman, captaining teams and winning the middleweight boxing prize. Yet at the same time there was a wildness to him that only just stopped short of insubordination, and sometimes went beyond it. His Commanding Officer's report in October, 1907, commented that he was an excellent commander of his submarine, but bad socially. His attacks were excellent, it went on, but he was a 'desperate' motor cyclist, troublesome in the Mess, insubordinate to the First Lieutenant and guilty of using bad language – but also extremely intelligent. The picture outwardly is a simple one – the young hell-raiser chafing at authority and with a fire in his belly that overruled his head.

Horton had taken the unusual step of joining the newly-formed submarine service and may have favoured it for precisely the reasons that made it Cunningham's pet hate. As a young branch of the Navy, it was less stuffy and hidebound. It gave the opportunity of command at a very young age. The proximity of officers and men, and their total reliance for their lives on each other's technical and professional competence, bred a unique atmosphere markedly lacking in 'bull', but in which professional competence was essential. Furthermore, no one was more independent than a submarine commander at sea and under it, and the 'lone wolf' image seems to have fitted Horton all his life. The submarine was also in its own way cocking a snook at authority, the authority symbolized in the vast fleets of battleships, and set fair to destroy that authority.

Horton was an outstanding submarine commander. In September, 1914, he penetrated the Heligoland Bight and sank a German cruiser and a destroyer, for which he received the DSO and a recommendation for early promotion. In December, 1914, he moved to the Baltic, which became known to the Germans as 'Horton's Sea'; certainly he was the only admiral in the Second World War who in the previous war had had a price put on his head by the Germans. He was then relieved in the Baltic (his successor was to die resisting a mob on the steps of the British Embassy at St Petersburg), and spent the time from January, 1916, in the North Sea. Early in 1919 he was given the appalling job of commanding the Baltic Submarine Flotilla, with a desperately complex political situation, war-weary sailors and a permanent question mark over the flotilla about why they were there at all. He won a second bar to his DSO there, and was promoted Captain in June, 1920, at the age of thirty-seven.

This is the success part of the story, the brilliant young submarine commander sweeping all before him. There was a darker side to it all, as there was to be throughout Horton's career. The Second Sea Lord struck a sour note when commenting on a Russian request for Horton to become Senior Naval Officer in the Baltic:

I understand Commander Horton is something of a pirate and not at all fitted for the position of S.N.O. in the Baltic.[3]

Horton had introduced the use of skull-and-crossbones flags to signify sinkings on return to harbour, but the tag 'pirate' meant far more than that. It meant an impatience with authority and orders, a lack of respect for seniority or form, a tendency to raise hell when ashore, to be rude and to live life at fever pitch. He was also an inveterate gambler (to defuse a tense moment his Staff would often suggest a bet on something: Horton might not take it, but it calmed the atmosphere), and, as with many of his contemporaries, there was something frenetic and addictive about his need for sporting activity. He insisted on playing his round of golf every afternoon when in charge of the Western Approaches. This irritated some of his Staff intensely, as Churchill's inability to stick to office hours irritated his, but there was reason behind it in that many submarine battles took place at night. Ramsay was another Admiral who gave his game of golf a very high priority.

The picture emerges of a man frequently at odds with authority, and in that respect at least the picture is not much different from that of Cunningham, despite the fact that there was tension between them; it is perhaps an example both of Cunningham's jealousy and the fact that like repels like. Both men took risks with their vessels, had almost too much aggressive spirit, did not suffer fools gladly and were often on the edge of insubordination in their youth (Cunningham's disciplinary record for his last few months at Dartmouth was not good). There is a further similarity. Both Cunningham and Horton were totally ruthless with their subordinates. The difference was that Horton's ruthlessness alienated senior officers, as well as those under him:

Horton's ruthlessness and blunt manner alienated him from some senior officers who said he was intolerant and obstinate, and that equally good results would have been obtained by less vigorous methods.[4]

Ironically, even Cunningham found cause to comment:

Horton I have a great admiration for, although I do not think his judgement is always sound. His main fault in my opinion is that he sets everyone by the ears and is inclined to bully his immediate juniors. He is, however, full of energy.[5]

His Assistant Secretary in the inter-war period writes:

Most people, including both captains, were frightened of Max who was a bit of a bully. But he was quite amenable if one stood up to him; I was lucky in that in my first few days, he 'tore a strip off me' for something I had not done whereupon I lost my temper and told him a few home truths. I got on very well with him thereafter.[6]

This is very much Cunningham's style of management, but there was a difference:

He loved power and used it mercilessly . . . taking upon himself the mantle of the strong man apart. He was not of the type who could reprimand an officer on the quarterdeck and afterwards enjoy a glass of gin with him in the wardroom. . . . He framed his policy on the survival of the fittest and was sparing with his praise.[7]

Cunningham did have that ability, and also the capacity to mask his essential isolation. Horton's unpopularity was unequalled by any other Admiral except Vian. With the latter, those closest to him either put it down to his being slightly unhinged, or, where a public tribute was called for, took refuge in safe phrases based on an uncompromising ability to attack the enemy or a ruthless pursuit of the defeat of the enemy, very much the phrases to be used with anyone the lower deck would have called 'a right bastard', but who was too famous or

22. 'Noble . . . took the necessary time to get to know his crews.' Noble (holding binoculars) on board *Broke*.

23 Survivors from *Scharnhorst*.

24 'A desperate motor cyclist, troublesome in the Mess, insubordinate to the First Lieutenant and guilty of using bad language'. Horton inspecting depth charges.

25 'A thief to catch a thief'. Horton inspecting a captured German U-boat.

successful to be called it in print. With Horton, his unpopularity came perilously close to being acknowledged even in a newspaper, as this extract shows:

> In past years Horton was universally regarded as a man with a great future should war come, but without one if peace continued. . . . From his earliest days he has been 'unorthodox' in many of his views and ways, and his strong personality, if it has not made him always popular, has earned for him the universal respect of the Navy.[8]

Horton's own attitude seems to be summed up by what his biographer quotes as his favourite lines:

> The ultimate result of shielding men from fools is to fill the world with fools.[9]

It was not that Horton failed to fit into any recognizable category, rather than he fitted into too many, almost overfilling each one and bringing to it and all he did a terrifying intensity. There was no shortage of officers who were well-suited for war, less suited for the peacetime Navy: Captain 'Johnnie' Walker was one such, and there was a strong bond of admiration that tied Horton to Walker. It was a feature of all the officers mentioned in this book that they were wholly intolerant of failure, even the mild-mannered Fraser, and many of them challenged subordinates in order to test their mettle, a technique akin to hitting a wall with a sledgehammer to test its foundations: Cunningham, Somerville and Vian were the leading exponents.

Yet the 'right bastard' image is more than unfair to a very complex personality. Many of his contemporaries would have been amazed to realize the strength and power of the attraction Horton felt for Roman Catholicism, or his deep love of Italy and its civilization. There was a wholly different side to Horton, revealed only to a favoured few. His Second-in-Command in the battleship *Resolution* writes:

> Contrary to all my preconceived notions of Max Horton, he was above all 'approachable'. There was nothing I couldn't discuss freely with him, and it was sometimes

hard to believe that the man who every evening after rounds would discuss the day's happenings with complete candour and a very impish sense of humour was indeed the same man who usually presented such a sphinx-like exterior to the world in general. . . . no one was more ruthless to inefficiency.[10]

His biographer quotes another story in which a submarine captain went to Horton asking to be relieved:

I went down to Northways to see him, anticipating a cold reception and curt dismissal. It was quite otherwise; he asked me what were the causes of my trouble. I haltingly explained that I could not put my finger on any one of them, but that sleeplessness, over-sensibility to noise and smell were among the factors. He at once became sympathetic, remarking that commanding officers suffered the same way in the First War. Instead of dismissal I found myself employed for a time on various staff jobs, and was later given command of a surface ship.[11]

As with Vian, Horton could admit he was wrong; as with Vian, it was not always a public admission. For example, the anti-submarine Tactical Training School at Tobermory became so frightened of his unrelenting enquiries that they became more interested in placating him than in getting on with the training – but when Horton realized this it was put right, and the signal traffic lessened. Dan van der Vat in *The Atlantic Campaign* tells the anecdote of Horton having complained about the reports coming from the Operational Intelligence Centre, being asked to make a report from its available information, being totally unable to do so and thereafter ceasing his recriminations with no apparent aftertaste of malice[12].

Horton's last peacetime command was that of the Reserve Fleet, in the middle of 1937. He must take full credit for the fact that the mobilization of the Fleet when war came was achieved with remarkably little fuss: Horton rarely left a job undone. He was appointed Vice Admiral Submarines on 9 January, 1940, in one respect an obvious choice, in another an inspired one. For all the unpleasantness of which he could be capable, he achieved an excellent relationship with Coastal Command almost from the outset, something essential if every British submarine in sight was not to be attacked by its own forces. The experience in co-operating with other arms was not to be wasted in the Western Approaches. He had great intuitive skill, reading the situation in Norway almost before anyone else in the Admiralty, and making perhaps the only correct dispositions from the outset of that sorry campaign.

There appears to have been a change in Horton's outward personality, the change being more marked with every promotion he received. Whereas the change in Admiral Somerville was a clear one, towards greater dynamism and extrovert playing to the gallery, Horton's change was in the opposite direction. Naval biographers of a more respectful age frequently refer to officers as being 'boyish' or having a 'boyish sense of humour'. This can mean variously a tendency to use foul language, a childish sense of humour, irrepressible high spirits, emotional immaturity or plain silliness: in Horton's case it meant escapades with a motor bike that nowadays would be seen as pure adolescent showing-off. Whichever the feature Horton had, it started to be replaced by a very withdrawn man who hated the use of his Christian name or any sign of familiarity. This was doubly unfortunate in terms of the submarine service, where familiarity was far more the norm than on a large surface vessel. Many of Horton's old messmates received bitter shocks when he turned the full fire of his anger on them for overstepping the mark, and this is one reason why he has received a harsh press. A wise man with a view to history does not turn against his friends and erstwhile colleagues. Some commentators have criticized him for judging people before they had a chance to prove themselves, and for the fact that he appeared to see himself as the greatest submarine 'ace' of the First World War. There were at least two other candidates for this position, and any suggestion of brashness would damn Horton in the senior service of a nation which only values the understatement and the understated. However, it is difficult to know if those who saw Horton as being insufferably arrogant were merely seeking an axe with which to belabour him; given the reserve of the man it is difficult to see that he would ever reveal enough of himself to show how he thought of his own war record. Certainly the reputation for arrogance is hard to square with the fact that he turned down the offer of Command of the Home

Fleet in October, 1940. His reasons for refusing are almost a list of what was wrong with the force at the time. He wrote that it needed its own air forces under its own command (something which mirrored the problems being faced by his German opposite number); that the C-in-C Home Fleet should be shore-based with younger Admirals at sea in command of squadrons; and that the C-in-C 'did not enjoy that degree of independent judgement and action which seemed to me to be essential'.[13] To turn down such a post was a courageous decision. Nor does the image of arrogance square with the man who after the war when he was travelling in France and Euorpe made friends, through his love of drama and opera, who after two years did not even know that he had been in the Royal Navy.

Horton's promotion to the Western Approaches was a master-stroke. Noble had done excellent groundwork and left a smooth-running machine, and with a time of crisis approaching the electrifying effect of Horton (in the sense of both a stimulus and a shock) justified the risk of changing horse in mid-stream. In terms of opposing Dönitz it set a thief to catch a thief. Among Horton's achievement were the rushing through of weapon advances, such as rockets for carrier aircraft, and the very brave decision to reduce all convoy escorts by one vessel, thereby allowing the creation of four Support Groups able to hit back at the U-boats in mid-Atlantic. The Support Groups, favoured by Noble but unavailable because of the lack of resources, were to exert a major effect in the mid-Atlantic gap. Western Approaches was a model of efficiency during Horton's time, and the fierceness of its commander merely matched the fierceness of the war his escorts were fighting.

Horton was suited to his post because he had intelligence, a capacity to make decisions, and a wholesale intolerance of inefficiency. His abrasive personality was no weakness when it came to fighting for scarce resources, his total inability to flatter no weakness when it came to fighting the RAF or Churchill and his technological background (impossible to avoid for a sub-mariner involved in the early development of submarines) a major positive factor in a Command where the side with the best technology was likely to win. Perhaps the most telling comment on him came from his Chief of Staff:

A very great man possessing perhaps a dual personality, having on the one hand charm and kindness of heart not

always realized, and on the other hand hardness which
could at times be terrifying even to the toughest of men.[14]

It was Horton who, when a Staff Officer reported the loss of a
cruiser with his son on board, replied, 'Yes – but what happened
to the ship?'[15]

This same man was instrumental in providing specialist
rescue ships for convoys, to which many thousands of Allied
seaman owe their lives. It was the same man who in the small
hours of the morning, faced with the news of the death of one
of the great escort commanders of the war, felt prompted to
write:

> In the days when the waters had well nigh overwhelmed
> us, our brother here departed apprehended the creative
> power in man, set himself to the task of conquering the
> malice of the enemy. In our hour of need he was our
> doughty protector of them that sailed the seas on our
> behalf. His heart and his mind extended and expanded to
> the utmost tiring of the body, that he might discover and
> operate means for saving our ships from the treacherous
> foes. Truly many, very many, were saved because he was
> not disobedient to his vision. Victory has been won and
> shall be won by such as he. May there never be wanting in
> the realm men of like spirit and discipline, imagination
> and valour, humble and unafraid. . . . His spirit returns to
> God who gave it.[16]

No man without a soul could write that. Perhaps Horton had
too much of one.

Some of the ironies in Horton's own soul may be explained
by his Jewish background. It is the view of his biographer that
Horton received anti-Semitic abuse during his career, and it
would hardly be suprising. Anti-Semitism was certainly a feature of British society before and after the First World War, with
Rupert Brooke, symbol of a nation's loss, being one among many
who found anti-Semitism an easy belief to marry with otherwise
liberal or left-wing views.

Horton may well have been a tortured soul, his passion for
his faith, for music and for drama balms to heal the wounds of
an essentially sensitive man adopting a killing trade. Long-range

psychoanalysis is dangerous at the best of times, but Horton's power may partly be explained by the immensity of the clash within him. He died in 1951, the post-war years filled with a seemingly endless string of operations; perhaps like his beloved Walker he had worn himself out physically as well as mentally.

The sinking of *Scharnhorst* was the last battle to be fought between capital ships in which the Royal Navy was involved. *Tirpitz* was to be battered into submission by aircraft, and the remainder of Germany's surface fleet, with the exception of *Prince Eugen* and a handful of light cruisers, was also to fall prey either to air attack or be scuttled. The Atlantic battle was to be waged right up to the cessation of hostilities, but the major task for the Royal Navy, apart from this, was the D-Day landing. The choice of Allied Naval Commander, Expeditionary Force (ANCXF), was clearly crucial. Pound, when he was First Sea Lord, put forward rather surprisingly the name of Admiral Sir Charles Little. Churchill vetoed this and proposed Admiral Ramsay[17]. Churchill has received much criticism, then and now, for his interference in naval operations, his fondness for expensive sideshows, his inability to get on with people who disagreed with him and all his other shortcomings. It seems to be accepted doctrine that he had a deep-rooted fear of Admirals after his experiences in the First World War. He redeemed many of those failings by his selection of Ramsay, and the steady drip-drip of criticism that has been directed against him since the war might now with hindsight be a little diluted. He appointed Ramsay. He forgave Somerville. He had grace enough to back down when he went for Fraser as his preferred appointment, and grace enough to work with Cunningham. He made something of a mascot of Vian, insisting that he appear in almost every naval operation regardless of his suitability for it. In his own way Churchill adopted the management technique of so many of his admirals, sledge-hammering people to see if they toppled over and then working with them if they stayed upright.

It was not merely that Ramsay's planning was superb, also that, in the words of the official historian:

> I am convinced from his correspondence with the
> Admiralty and others in the High Command that Ramsay
> was a stabilising catalyst in pulling the whole complicated
> matter together.[18]

His triumph was not without its difficulties. The Americans did not like Ramsay's detailed orders:

With us, the Admiral tells us what to do, he doesn't tell us how to do it.[19]

Ramsay's response was:

No argument that has been produced since the operation has led me to change my opinion that full-co-ordination in detail was necessary on the highest naval level.[20]

Ramsay was in a sandwich on several occasions. Cunningham was worried that he was asking for too many resources and ships (yet another example of Cunningham's Calvinistic short-sightedness), while the Americans were worried that Ramsay's plan did not take sufficient account of the threat from E-boats and destroyers. Ramsay was also under pressure from Admiral King (Eisenhower was to write in his diaries that the Allied war effort would have gone rather more smoothly if Admiral King had been shot) to release forces to other theatres, something Ramsay resisted fiercely until he was sure that danger had passed. The Americans were proved wrong and Ramsay right when they insisted on landing an hour ahead of the British and lowering assault craft five miles farther to seaward. It is arguable that had they followed Ramsay's advice Omaha Beach would not have fared so badly. Through all this Ramsay never lost his sense of humour, describing a section of a Mulberry harbour as 'an even more formidable abortion than I had anticipated'.[21]

Ramsay was not afraid of risks. He took the decision to allow landing craft to drive up to the beaches and rest high and dry at low tide, despite the worry that the vessels would not take the strain, and again was proved right.

The invasion of Normandy was one of the most colossal feats of arms ever attempted in the history of mankind. The other, relatively minor, landings which had preceded it provided experience, but nothing on the same scale or near it. The invasion required virtually the major part of the force to be landed and supported by sea. When ashore, the soldiers of the invasion force were on more or less familiar ground for infantry;

getting them there presented the Naval Commander with something for which history had precious little precedent. The whole operation required someone of immense planning skills; a capacity to learn from experience (by no means an automatic feature of top commanders in the Second World War); an ability to work with all comers; a sense of humour; an uncompromising ability to know when to stick to a point and a wholly unflappable approach that commanded the respect of all of those who came within range of its powers. Such a job description would have every head-hunter in the modern age gagging for breath and offering salaries beyond the power of man to conceive. Bertram Home Ramsay happened to be there anyway, and the free world owes him one of its greatest debts for that fact. Churchill said of Admiral Jellicoe that he could have lost the war (an earlier one) in an afternoon which at the best of times is an assertion hardly backed up by the facts. Of all the admirals discussed in this book, it is perhaps fitting that one should finish with the one who could have lost the Second World War most easily, Admiral Sir Max Horton, and the one who did most to ensure it was won, Admiral Sir Bertram Home Ramsay. Ramsay's tragic and senseless death in an air crash was no fit reward for a fine man and an outstanding Admiral.

Epilogue

Cunningham was the most famous and highly-acclaimed fighting Admiral of the Second World War. It is doubtful that he earned this privilege. He was clearly an outstanding leader of men, and an inspirational figure capable of arousing utter devotion among those who served with him. He did much good for the Navy in his pre-war career, was apparently without fear and had more than any man's fair share of the aggression and tenacity of purpose that were *de rigueur* for any successful Admiral of the time. He was also lucky. He won two major victories which could just as easily have been defeats, and he served the Navy well when he became in effect its leader. He fought for his beloved service after the war and was never disloyal to it. Despite all this, there were men who achieved more, and whose final contribution to Allied victory was greater. Cunningham's two victories were the result of pre-war planning in one case and owed much to technology in the other. He took the victories when the opportunity came and thereby won a moral victory over the Italians that was as important as the physical victory. However, his ascendancy was short-lived and by his parsimony and tendency to bully Staff officers he contributed significantly to the sinking of his battle fleet in Alexandria harbour. The loss of two modernized battleships at a crucial stage in the war was in its own way a more damaging blow to the Royal Navy in the Mediterranean than Taranto had been to the Italian Navy. He showed no real understanding or grasp of air power, dismissed technology with the certainty and finality that only true ignorance can bring and in many of his attitudes (clothing, 'luxuries' on board ship, the submarine service) he operated from a deep set of prejudices that his high office allowed him to establish as law. He was bad at using a Staff and bad at planning, at a time when the complexity of naval operations made this a luxury that no navy could afford. He could spot talent, but he could also be jealous and spiteful. There was a puritanical streak in his make-up that made him intolerant, and that intolerance was sometimes inflicted on those whose only sin was to differ from his own views. He did not oppose Crete with sufficient vigour for one who knew it to be madness and at crucial moments his principles and friendships seemed to become stretched, albeit never broken, in the face of political or private advantage. Cunningham was a great Admiral and an awe-inspiring leader. He was by no means the greatest Admiral of the naval war.

The prize for that title could go to a number of men. For all the noise and glamour of the Mediterranean, it was Noble and Horton who between them fought the longest, and the most important, battle. If any Admirals could have lost the war in a day it was them, though it would probably have taken a bad Admiral four to six months to do it. *Bismarck* and *Tirpitz* roaming at will throughout the convoy routes would not have lost the war: the pair of them bombarding Yarmouth would not have done that, and, it can be argued, the loss of Malta would not have lost the war either. Indeed, it is almost blasphemy to ask if the effort expended on preserving Malta was justified and whether its survival was not a running abcess on the Royal Navy's side. The Mediterranean was the only theatre of the British naval war where heavy units were regularly engaged in surface action. It was a dramatic war and a terribly costly one. As a result, its significance may have been overrated. Britain's umbilical cord did not run through the Mediterranean but across the North Atlantic. None of this diminishes Cunningham's achievement but it does point to the fact that the achievement of other Admirals has not been given its due share of credit. The efficiency of Somerville's Force H did almost as much to keep the route to Malta open as did Cunningham's victories, and the effort of that group was sustained over many months, yet the absence of a dramatic victory on their part has stopped Somerville from receiving the credit he deserves. Somerville was popular in his time and received considerable media coverage, but posterity has not consolidated his reputation as much as he deserves, possibly because he has been seen as a media figure and therefore shallow, and certainly because the saga of the feud between him and Mountbatten has been told largely from

Mountbatten's side. In many respects Somerville was a model figure. He was marvellously aggressive, but blessed with real compassion and humanity. He knew how to use and manipulate the media, but was never a playboy or a dilettante, and never lost the respect of fighting sailors, unlike Mountbatten. He had all the virtues of the 'old' Navy – loyalty, tenacity, toughness and a hatred of second-best – but many of the features needed by the new navy, and in particular a respect for technology and air power, and a capacity to work with the Americans.

One judgement of history cries out to be corrected, that which concerns Tom Phillips. He was not an easy man, but he had virtues that the Royal Navy needed in its war, and he has been too convenient and too easy a scapegoat for the fate of Force Z. No one has seen fit to put Cunningham in Phillips' position in the Far East: no one has pointed out that the outcome for Force Z would in all probability have been just the same.

At the time of writing, only Fraser has had a modern biography written about him. It is not difficult to see why. He was one of the few British admirals of the war to win a classic surface engagement, and, as did Somerville, he blended the virtues of the old Navy with the needs of the new. Marvellous man though he was, he somehow lacks the extra dimension and the cutting edge of a Cunningham or a Somerville, and his contribution to the war was arguably less than that of many others. Sinking the *Scharnhorst* was a great victory, but by the time of her sinking *Scharnhorst* was a mere sideshow and a pinprick in terms of her capacity to do real damage. If anyone deserves to be the subject of a novel, it is Horton: only a novelist could do justice to a man so tortured by his own being and the contradictions of his own nature. If anyone deserves to be the subject of a modern biography, it is Ramsay. My admiration for his achievement has been made clear in the preceding pages and in the dedication of this book; it needs no final elaboration, save to say that if one were looking for a symbol of all that was good in the Royal Navy in the Second World War – courage, tenacity, good humour, intelligence, aggression, decency – one could do a great deal worse than look to Ramsay.

Notes

In the following references CA stands for items in the archives of Churchill College, Cambridge; BL for items in the British Library, London; PRO for items in the Public Records Office, London; IWM for the Imperial War Museum, London; NMM for the National Maritime Museum, London. File numbers for these relevant institutions follow the entry where applicable.

Admirals featured in this book are listed by surname only, as are the following whose comments or writings have been quoted: Admiral J.H. Godfrey; Admiral Sir Charles Forbes; Admiral Sir Varyl Begg; Admiral Sir Harold Burroughs; Admiral Sir Walter Cowan; Admiral Sir Algernon Willis; Vice Admiral Sir William Wentworth; Admiral Sir Henry Thursfield; Captain S.E. Norfolk.

Full listings of all published works are given in the Select Bibliography.

Chapter 1. The Making of an Admiral (pp 1–24)

1. Warner, *Cunningham*, p. 152.
2. Cameron, Alan. *Lloyd's List*, 24 September, 1988.
3. CA CUNN 2/1 Cunningham to Godfrey, 25 May, 1963.
4. Hough, *The Rise and Fall of the Royal Navy*, p. 38.
5. *ibid.*
6. CA RMSY Private diary, 20 October, 1914.
7. Cunningham, *A Sailor's Odyssey*, p. 20.
8. Kennedy, *The Rise and Fall of British Naval Supremacy*, p. 217.
9. *ibid*, p. 219.
10. Pack, *Britannia at Dartmouth*. p. 113.
11. Cunningham, *Odyssey*. p. 31.
12. Bonnet, *The Price of Admiralty*. p. 180.
13. Parker, *The Old Lie*, p. 86.
14. *ibid*, p. 87.

15. Pack, *Britannia*, p. 197.
16. *ibid*, p. 117.
17. Gieve, *Life on Board H.M.S. Britannia*, pp. 17–18.
18. *The Old Lie*, p. 86.
19. Pack, *Britannia*, p. 113.
20. Hughes, Thomas. *Tom Brown's Schooldays*, p. 104.
21. I have been unable to trace this signal in the PRO; it is quoted in several published works.
22. Cunningham, *Odyssey*. p. 624.
23. CA DUPO 6/1, Godfrey to Cunningham.
24. Cunningham, *Odyssey*, p. 50.
25. Macintyre, *Fighting Admiral*, p. 185 *passim*.
26. Warner, *Cunningham*, p. 75.
27. Grenfell, *Main Fleet to Singapore*, p. 56.
28. Warner, *Cunningham*, p. 86.
29. *ibid*.

Chapter 2. 1939: The Battle of the River Plate (pp. 25–40)

1. Hough, *The Longest Battle*, p. 3.
2. Roskill, *Churchill and the Admirals*, p. 190.
3. Hough, *The Longest Battle*, p. 6.
4. *ibid*, p. 7.
5. *ibid*.
6. Marder, *From the Dardanelles to Oran*, p. 138.
7. Roskill, *Churchill and the Admirals*, p. 110.
8. Marder, *Oran*, p. 175.
9. CA DUPO 6/1 James to Godfrey, October, 1945.
10. Letter from Sir Stuart Mitchell to Dr Margaret E. Steward, 18 November, 1977.
11. CA DUPO 6/1 Godfrey, unpublished paper.
12. BL ADD 52565 Pound to Forbes, 20 January, 1940.
13. Cunningham, *Sailor's Odyssey*, p. 231.
14. *ibid*., p. 273.
15. Cunningham, *Odyssey*, p. 241.
16. Warner, *Cunningham*, p. 117.
17. *ibid*.
18. Vian, *Action This Day*. p. 63.
19. Macintyre, *Fighting Admiral*, p. 173.

Chapter 3. 1940: Narvik, Dunkirk and Ramsay (pp. 41–61)

1. Macintyre, *Narvik*, p. 40.
2. PRO ADM 199/474.

3. Chalmers, *Full Cycle*. p. 46.
4. *ibid*.
5. Cunningham, *Odyssey*, p. 195.
6. CA RMSY 1/1 letter to mother, 28 October, 1901.
7. ibid.
8. ibid., 7 December, 1901.
9. ibid., 27 May, 1919.
10. ibid., 24 September, 1919.
11. ibid., 14 June, 1919.
12. ibid., 3 July, 1919.
13. ibid., 1 December, 1924.
14. CA RMSY 3/3 Diary 1 January, 1925.
15. ibid., 1 December, 1924.
16. ibid., 6 December, 1924.
17. ibid., 27 January, 1927.
18. CA RMSY 4/1 Diary 12 January, 1928.
19. Chalmers, *Full Cycle*, p. 35.
20. CA RMSY 3/3 Diary 22 November, 1924.
21. CA SMVL 2/1 Diary 20 November, 1943.
22. Cunningham, *Odyssey*, p. 136.
23. Chalmers, *Full Cycle*, p. 21.
24. ibid., p. 163.
25. ibid.
26. see CA RMSY 2/4.
27. ibid.
28. Chalmers, *Full Cycle*, p. 24.
29. CA CUNN 2/1.
30. Chalmers, *Full Cycle*, p. 166.
3i. Canning interview.
32. Chalmers, *Full Cycle*, p. 33.
33. ibid., p. 37.
34. CA RMSY 3/4 Diary 4 July, 1925.
35. CA RMSY Diary 22 August, 1914.
36. CA RMSY 3/4, undated.
37. 'The Influence of the Submarine and Air on the Size of Fighting Ships'. Paper 1933, CA RMSY 5/9.
38. CA RMSY 3/4 4 July, 1925.
39. Chalmers, *Full Cycle*, p. 27.
40. ibid., p. 76.
41. ibid., p. 94.

Chapter 4. Oran and Taranto (pp. 62–87)

1. Macintyre, *Fighting Admiral*, p. 17.
2. ibid., p. 16.

3. Marder, *Oran*, p. 229.
4. Broome, *Make a Signal!* p. 218.
5. Macintyre, *Fighting Admiral*, p. 18.
6. ibid., p. 24.
7. ibid., p. 25.
8. Broome, *Make a Signal*: p. 181.
9. ibid., p. 208.
10. Macintyre, *Fighting Admiral*, p. 32.
11. ibid., p. 84.
12. Letter to the author from Captain W.H.R. Lapper.
13. CA SMVL 2/1 Diary 12 June, 1944.
14. Roskill, *Churchill and the Admirals*, p. 270.
15. Macintyre, *Fighting Admiral*, p. 55.
16. CA MCBE 1/2 Cunningham to Godfrey 17 May (no year).
17. CA WLLS 12/1, Memoirs p. 12.
18. Macintyre, *Fighting Admiral*, p. 69.
19. CA WLLS 12/1, Memoirs p. 12.
20. Macintyre, *Fighting Admiral*, pp. 83–85.
21. Marder, *Oran*, p. 170.
22. BL ADD 52563 Somerville to Cunningham, 8 December, 1940.
23. ibid., 3 January, 1941.
24. Macintyre, *Fighting Admiral*, p. 99.
25. BL ADD 52563 Somerville to Cunningham, 3 January, 1941.
26. Macintyre, *Fighting Admiral*, p. 107.
27. BL ADD 52561 Pound to Cunningham, 1 December, 1940.
28. Roskill, *Churchill and the Admirals*, p. 179.
29. BL ADD 52563 Somerville to Cunningham, 12 June, 1941.
30. Cunningham, *Odyssey*, p. 14.
31. ibid., p. 72.
32. Stanning interview.
33. Pack, *Cunningham the Commander*, p. 3.
34. CA GDFY 1/2.
35. CA WLLS 12/11 Memoirs p. 5.
36. CA WLLS 12/1 Memoirs p. 18.
37. Pack, *Cunningham*, p. 127.
38. CA RMSY 8/26 Diary 15 June, 1944.
39. ibid., 17 June, 1944.
40. Warner, *Cunningham of Hyndhope*, p. 271.
41. Pack, *Cunningham*, p. 199.
42. ibid., pp. 187–88.
43. CA CUNN 2/1 note from E.J. Freestone, DSM.
44. BL ADD 52557.
45. Cunningham, *Odyssey*, p. 231.
46. Pack, *Cunningham*, p. 163.

47. CA CUNN 2/1 Begg.
48. Warner, *Cunningham*, p. 274.
49. Cunningham, *Odyssey*, p. 273.
50. Lamb, *War in a Stringbag*, pp. 112–3.

Chapter 5. Matapan, Crete and *Bismarck* (pp. 88–112)

1. CA SMVL 2/2 15 March, 1944.
2. Stephen, *Sea Battles in Close Up*, pp. 32–3.
3. Cunningham, *Oddysey*. p. 330.
4. Warner, *Cunningham*, p. 131.
5. Macintyre, *Fighting Admiral*, p. 126.
6. CA CUNN 2/2 Letter to Burroughs, 30 June, 1941.
7. Hough, *Longest Battle*, p. 226.
8. Thomas, *Crete 1941*, p. 17.
9. *ibid.*, p. 114.
10. CA CUNN 2/7 Letter to Burroughs, 30 June, 1941.
11. Warner, *Cunningham*, p. 152.
12. Cunningham, *Odyssey*, p. 390.
13. *ibid.*, p. 373.
14. *ibid.*, pp. 369–70.
15. BL ADD 52560 Cunningham to Pound, 18 September, 1941.
16. ibid, 19 August, 1940.
17. Thomas, *Crete*, p. 206.
18. BL ADD 52563 Somerville to Cunningham, 7 September, 1941.
19. BL ADD 52562 Cowan to Cunningham, 2 December 1939.
20. BL ADD 52561 Cunningham to Pound 16 October, 1940.
21. BL ADD 52569 Tovey to Cunningham 17 October, 1940.
22. BL ADD 52561 Pound to Cunningham, 1 December 1940.
23. BL ADD 52569 Tovey to Cunningham, 17 October 1940.
24. Roskill, *Churchill and the Admirals*, p. 130.
25. *ibid.*
26. BL ADD 52570 Tovey to Cunningham, 23 September, 1943.
27. BL ADD 52569 Tovey to Cunningham, 21 March, 1941.
28. Stanning interview.

Chapter 6. *Prince of Wales* and *Repulse* (pp. 113–137)

1. Middlebrook, *Battleship*, p. 305.
2. CA WLLS Cunningham to Willis, 17 January, 1942.
3. BL ADD 52563 Somerville to Cunningham, 20 October, 1941.
4. ibid.
5. IWM Wentworth Papers, Cunningham to Wentworth, 12 October, 1941.

6. Roskill, *Churchill and the Admirals*, p. 119.
7. Middlebrook, *Battleship*, p. 58.
8. Hough, *The Hunting of Force Z*, p. 130.
9. Middlebrook, *Battleship*, p. 59, Stephen, *Sea Battles in Close Up*, p. 114.
10. Bennett, *Loss of 'Prince of Wales'*, p. 33.
11. Hough, *Hunting of Force Z*, p. 124.
12. Marder, *Old Friends*, p. 366.
13. BL ADD 52561 Cunningham to Pound, 5 January, 1941.
14. see Chapter 2, note [9].
15. Marder, *Oran*, p. 167.
16. CA DUPO 6/1 Thursfield to Godfrey, 24 May, 1954.
17. Marder, *Old Friends*, p. 368.
18. PRO PREM 3/163/3.
19. PP Commander M. Goodenough.
20. PP Margery Armitage to Lady Phillips, 20 December, 1941.
21. PP Ralph Edwards, May, 1942.
22. PP Sir Herbert Dowbiggin.
23. PP Rear Admiral Tennant.
24. Grenfell, *Main Fleet*, p. 75.
25. Marder, *Old Friends*, p. 388.
26. PP Stephen King-Hall.
27. PP Admiral Sir Roger Keyes.
28. Lt Cdr R. Dyer to Martin Middlebrook, 27 February, 1976.
29. CA DUPO 5/5 Willis to Lady Phillips 17 December, 1941.
30. Roskill, *Churchill and the Admirals*, 197.
31. PP Norfolk to T.V.G. Phillips, 2 December, 1977.
32. Grenfell, *Main Fleet*, p. 112.
33. *Ibid.*, p. 114.
34. PRO ADMIRAL 199/1149.
35. Middlebrook, *Battleship*, p. 305.
36. Supplement to *The London Gazette*, 26 February, 1948, p. 1238.
37. BL ADD 52561 Pound to Cunningham 29 January, 1942.
38. Norfolk in *The Sunday Telegraph*, November, 1977.
39. Roskill, *The War at Sea*, pp. 13–14.
40. ibid., p. 27.

Chapter 7. The Channel Dash and Sirte (pp. 138–161)

1. see Chapter 4, note 37.
2. Roskill, *The War at Sea*, p. 151.
3. Drury interview.
4. Roskill, *The War at Sea*, p. 135.
5. Stanning interview.

6. PRO ADMIRAL 199 474 (85) 22 April, 1940.
7. Vian, *Action This Day*, pp. 57–8.
8. *ibid.*, p. 77.
9. CA RMSY 8/26 Diary 15 June, 1944.
10. ibid., 17 June, 1944.
11. Cunningham, *Odyssey*, p. 417.
12. Humble, *Fraser of North Cape*, p. 285.
13. BL ADD 52561 Cunningham to Pound, December, 1941.
14. Cunningham, *Odyssey*, p. 425.
15. *ibid.*, p. 434.
16. CA CUNN Cunningham to Willis, 21 June, 1942.
17. Cunningham, *Odyssey*, p. 466.
18. Chalmers, *Full Cycle*, p. 137.
19. ibid., p. 129.
20. Chalmers, *Full Cycle*, p. 141.
21. CA RMSY 6/2 Cunningham to Ramsay, November 21, 1942.
22. CA RMSY 8/26 Diary, 9 February, 1944.
23. Chalmers, *Full Cycle*, p. 143.
24. ibid., p. 149.

Chapter 8. Barents Sea and North Cape (pp. 162–190)

1. Macintyre, *Fighting Admiral*, p. 173.
2. Tomlinson, *Most Dangerous Moment*, p. 57.
3. Macintyre, *Fighting Admiral*, p. 203.
4. CA WLLS 5/5.
5. Conversation with Vice Admiral Sir Kaye Edden K.B.E., C.B.
6. Peter Kemp, quoted in Hough, *Former Naval Person*, p. 207.
7. CA WLLS 5/5 Willis to Cunningham, 10 April, 1942.
8. ibid., Vice Admiral H.R. Moore, 13 April, 1942.
9. Conversation with Commander J. Somerville.
10. Roskill, *Churchill and the Admirals*, p. 249.
11. BL ADD 52563 Somerville to Cunningham, 12 June, 1941.
12. BL ADD 52561 Somerville to Pound, 27 August, 1943.
13. CA SMVL 8/3, 2 September, 1943.
14. BL ADD 52563 Somerville to Cunningham, 4 December, 1943.
15. Roskill, *Churchill and the Admirals*, p. 251.
16. Conversation with Commander J. Somerville.
17. Macintyre, *Fighting Admirals*, p. 193.
18. Hough, *Former Naval Person*, pp. 202–3.
19. Roskill, *Churchill and the Admirals*, p. 257.
20. BL ADD 52563 Somerville to Cunningham, 4 November, 1941.
21. Roskill, *Churchill and the Admirals*, p. 270.
22. Cunningham, *Odyssey*, p. 140.

23. Pack, *Cunningham*, p. 52.
24. Pack, *Cunningham*, p. 24.
25. Letter to the author from G.L.B. Pitt.
26. Stanning interview.
27. Humble, *Fraser*, p. 53.
28. The gunnery log for *Duke of York* is reprinted in *Loss of the Scharnhorst*, by I. Watts.
29. Warner, *Cunningham*, p. 223.
30. PRO M599/3, PM personal minute to A.V. Alexander, 9 September, 1943.
31. see CA DUPO 6/1 correspondence of Admiral J.H. Godfrey.
32. Roskill, *Churchill and the Admirals*, p. 261.
33. Captain Vernon Merry, quoted in Humble, *Fraser*, p. 244.
34. BL ADD 52561 Pound to Cunningham, 23 April, 1943.
35. ibid. Pound to Cunningham, 8 May, 1943.
36. CA WLLS Memoirs, Vol 3.
37. Humble, *Fraser*, p. 259.
38. Warner, *Cunningham*, p. 232.
39. Stephen, *Sea Battles in Close Up*, p. 210.

Chapter 9. D-Day and the U-Boat War (pp. 191–206)

1. Van der Vat, *Atlantic Campaign*, p. 274.
2. Macintyre, *Battle for the Atlantic*, p. 63.
3. Chalmers, *Horton*, p. 19.
4. *ibid.*, p. 34.
5. BL ADD 52561, 19 August, 1940.
6. Letter from Captain G.H. Stanning, DSO
7. Chalmers, *Horton*, pp. 24–5
8. *ibid.*, p. 103.
9. Herbert Spencer, quoted in Chalmers, *Horton*, p. 118.
10. Chalmers, *Horton*, p. 31.
11. *ibid.*, p. 30.
12. Van der Vat, *Atlantic Campaign*, p. 304.
13. Chalmers, *Horton*, p. 101.
14. *ibid.*, p. 241.
15. *ibid.*, p. 242.
16. Funeral elegy on Captain F.J. Walker, CB, DSO, as delivered by Admiral Sir Max Horton: numerous published sources.
17. Roskill, *Churchill and the Admirals*, p. 235.
18. Chalmers, *Ramsay*, p. 195.
19. Woodward, *Ramsay at War*, p. 139.
20. Chalmers, *Ramsay*, p. 205.
21. *ibid.*, pp. 191–2.

Select Bibliography

Ash, Bernard. *Someone Had Blundered: The Story of the 'Repulse'
    and the 'Prince of Wales'.* Michael Joseph, 1960.
Beesly, Patrick. *Very Special Intelligence.* Hamish Hamilton, 1977.
Bekker, Cajus. *Hitler's Naval War.* MacDonald and Jane's, 1974.
Bennett, G. *The Battle of the River Plate.* Ian Allan, 1972.
——, *The Loss of 'Prince of Wales' and 'Repulse'.* Ian Allan, 1972.
——, *Naval Battles of World War II.* Batsford, 1975.
Bonnet, Stanley. *The Price of Admiralty. An Indictment of the Royal
    Navy 1805–1966.* Robert Hale, 1968.
Broome, Captain Jack, DSC. *Make A Signal!* Putnam, nd.
Browne, David. *Carrier Operations in World War 2.* Ian Allan, 1974.
Cameron, Alan. *'Lloyd's List'.* September 24, 1988.
Chalmers, Rear Admiral W.S., CBE, DSC. *Full Cycle. The Biography
    of Admiral Sir Bertram Home Ramsay, KCB, MVO.* Hodder &
    Stoughton, 1959.
——, *Max Horton and the Western Approaches.* Hodder & Stoughton,
    1954.
Churchill, Sir Winston. *The Second World War.* Cassell, 1967.
Costello, John, and Hughes, Terry. *The Battle of the Atlantic.*
    Fontana, 1980.
Cunningham, Adm A.B.. *A Sailor's Odyssey. The Autobiography of
    Admiral of the Fleet Viscount Cunningham of Hyndhope, K.T.,
    G.C.B., O.M., D.S.O.,* Hutchinson, 1951.
Edwards, Commander Kenneth, RN. *Seven Sailors.* Collins, 1945.
Gieve, J & Sons Ltd. *Life on Board HMS Britannia.* Portsmouth, n.d.
Grenfell, Richard. *Main Fleet to Singapore.* Oxford University Press,
    1987.
Hinsley, F.H. *British Intelligence in the Second World War.* HMSO,
    1979.
Hough, Richard. *Former Naval Person. Churchill and the Wars at
    Sea.* Weidenfeld and Nicolson, 1985.
——, *The Hunting of Force Z.* Fontana, 1964.
——, *The Longest Battle: The War at Sea 1939–45.* Weidenfeld &
    Nicolson, 1986.

——, *The Rise and Fall of the Royal Navy*.

Howarth, Stephen. *Morning Glory. The Story of the Imperial Japanese Navy*. Arrow, 1983.

Humble, R. *Fraser of North Cape*. Routledge and Kegan Paul, 1983.

——, *The Rise and Fall of the British Navy*. Queen Anne Press, 1986.

Kemp, P. *Escape of the 'Scharnhorst' and 'Gneisenau'*. Ian Allan, 1975.

Kennedy, Ludovic. *Pursuit: The Sinking of the 'Bismarck'*. Collins, 1974.

Kennedy, M. *The Rise and Fall of British Naval Supremacy*. Macmillan, 1983.

Lamb, Commander Charles, DSO, DSC. *War in a Stringbag*. London, Arrow, 1987.

Law, Derek G. *The Royal Navy in World War Two: An Annotated Bibliography*. Greenhill Books, 1988.

Macintyre, Captain Donald, DSO, DSC. *Fighting Admiral: The Life of Admiral of the Fleet Sir James Somerville, GCB, GBE, DSO*. Evans, 1961.

——, *Narvik*. Evans, 1959.

——, *The Battle for the Pacific*. Pan, 1975.

——, *The Battle of the Atlantic*, Pan, 1961.

Marder, Arthur J. *From the Dardanelles to Oran. Studies of the Royal Navy in War and Peace 1915–1940*. Oxford University Press, 1974.

——, *Old Friends, New Enemies*. Oxford University Press, 1981.

McIntyre, W.D. *The Rise and Fall of the Singapore Naval Base*. Macmillan, 1979.

Middlebrook, Martin, and Mahoney, Patrick. *Battleship: The Loss of 'Prince of Wales' and 'Repulse'*. Allen Lane, 1977.

Morison, Samuel Eliot. *A History of United States Naval Operations in World War 2*. Brown and Co./Oxford University Press, 1947.

Neidpath, J. *The Singapore Naval Base and the Defence of Britain's Eastern Empire 1919–1941*. Oxford University Press, 1941.

Newton, Don, and Hampshire, Cecil. *Taranto*. William Kimber, 1971.

Pack, Captain S.W.C., C.B.E.. *Britannia at Dartmouth. The Story of HMS Britannia and the Britannia Royal Naval College*. Alvin Redman, 1966.

——, *Cunningham the Commander*. Batsford, 1974.

——, *The Battle of Matapan*. Pan, 1968.

Parker, Peter. *The Old Lie. The Great War and the Public School Ethos*. Constable, 1987.

Piekalkiewicz, Janusz. *Sea War 1939–1945*. Blandford Press, 1987.

Rayner, D.A. *Escort*. William Kimber, 1955.

Rhodes, Anthony. *Sword of Bone*. Buchan and Enright, 1986.

Roskill, Captain S.W., *Churchill and the Admirals*. Collins, 1977.

——, *The War at Sea*. Volumes 1–4, HMSO, 1954–61.

Smith, Gordon. *The War at Sea. Royal and Dominion Navy Actions in World War 2*. Ian Allan, 1989.

Stephen, Martin. *Sea Battles in Close Up*. Ian Allan, 1988.

Terraine, John. *Business in Great Waters*, Leo Cooper, 1989.

Tomlinson, Michael. *The Most Dangerous Moment. The Japanese Assault on Ceylon 1942*. William Kimber, 1976.

Vat, Dan van Der, *The Atlantic Campaign. The Great Struggle at Sea 1939–1945*. Hodder & Stoughton, 1988.

Vian, Admiral of the Fleet Sir Philip, GCB, KBE, DSO. *Action This Day. A War Memoir*. Frederick Muller, 1960.

Warner, Oliver. *Cunningham of Hyndhope: Admiral of the Fleet. A Memoir by Oliver Warner*. London, John Murray, 1967.

Watts, I. *The Loss of the 'Scharnhorst'*. Ian Allan, 1970.

Winton, John. *The Death of the 'Scharnhorst'*. Granada, 1980.

——, *The Ultra Secret*. Leo Cooper, 1988.

Woodward, David. *Sunk! How the Great Battleships Were Lost*. Allen and Unwin, 1982.

Index